2/95

DATE DUE

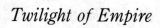

Twilight of Empire

Also by Robert Cullen:

SOVIET SOURCES

Twilight of Empire

INSIDE THE CRUMBLING SOVIET BLOC

Robert Cullen

THE ATLANTIC MONTHLY PRESS
NEW YORK

Published simultaneously in Canada
Printed in the United States of America
FIRST EDITION

Library of Congress Cataloging-in-Publication Data
Cullen, Robert.
Twilight of empire: inside the crumbling Soviet bloc/by Robert
Cullen.—1st ed.
ISBN 0-87113-472-1
1. Europe, Eastern—Description and travel—1981– 2. Cullen,
Robert—Journeys—Europe, Eastern. I. Title.
DJK19.C85   1991   947—dc20   91-13421

The Atlantic Monthly Press
19 Union Square West
New York, NY 10003

FIRST PRINTING

CONTENTS

v

PREFACE

This book recounts my travels and inquiries on the periphery of the Soviet Empire, and in its heart, during the tumultuous years 1989 and 1990. All journalists, I think, wish to witness the great events, the history of their time. Most often, they can only write of the humdrum or, worse, of the events that politicians and other manipulators of public opinion stage for their benefit. Those of us lucky enough to have covered the Soviet Union and Eastern Europe over the past five or six years have had a rare privilege and opportunity.

I wanted to cut a journalist's cross section from this empire, and I believe I did. Some readers may object that Hungary, Czechoslovakia, Poland, the Ukraine, Uzbekistan, Germany, or many other areas were also worth covering. They will be quite correct, but I offer no apology.

A journalist traveling in these parts, like Blanche DuBois, must rely on the kindness of strangers. I certainly did, and I never failed to find people willing to give generously of their time to help me understand them and their countries. If there is cause for optimism about the future of the lands of the Soviet Empire, and I believe there is, it is rooted in the innate kindness and patience I found in the overwhelming majority of the people I met there.

The names of many of them are in the book, cited as sources. I am grateful to all of them. Many others provided invaluable help as translators, drivers, guides, references, or just good company. Some of them, I know, will disagree with what I have written, but I trust they all will realize I have written as honestly and fairly as I could.

In Romania, I am grateful to Artemis Craciuneanu, Vlad Boldea, Eugen Gasnas, Sanda Chiose, Tudor Stoica, Marian Codescu, Dragos Negrescu, to my colleague Mike Meyer, and to Larry Napper of the U.S. embassy.

In Vilnius, I wish to thank Carla Gruodis, Darius Cuplinskas, and Rita Dapkus for their help.

In Armenia, I wish to thank Hasmik Khourshoudian, Ella Vartanyan, Samuel Grigoryan, and David Verkh.

In Azerbaijan, I am indebted to Mehdi Mamedov and to Fahratdin Kurbanov and Nazim Gusseinov at the Azerbaijani Ministry of Foreign Affairs.

In Latvia, I wish to thank Janis Porietis, Janis Jurkans, Vladlen Dozortsev, and Juris Paklans.

In Moscow, I owe particular thanks to my colleagues Bill Keller, Olga Belan, and James Rosen, to my friends Valery Plotnikov and Taya Plotnikova, and to Boris Malakhov of the Soviet Ministry of Foreign Affairs.

In the United States, many people helped me with advice and contacts. I would like particularly to thank Victor Nakas, Jurate Kazickas, Dorin Tudoran, Tom Simons, Ojars Kalnins, Rouben Adalian, Catherine Cosman, John Finnerty, Judy Ingram, Betsy Aaron, Stuart Pape, Dr. Vamik Volkan, Joe Montville, and Greg Guroff.

I am also indebted to Bob Gottlieb, Chip McGrath, and Liesl Schillinger at *The New Yorker,* to William Whitworth and Corby Kummer at *The Atlantic,* to Ann Godoff and Carl Navarre at the

Atlantic Monthly Press, and to Rafe Sagalyn for their support and fine editing.

Last, but by no means least, my wife, Ann, and my children, Peter and Catherine, cheerfully coped with the disruptions caused by my prolonged absences from home. I could not have done without their help.

This book is dedicated to my late father, Gilbert W. Cullen, who, I hope, would have enjoyed reading it.

ROMANIA

August 1989

At the beginning of this century, a young Romanian named Constantin Giurescu moved from his native village of Chiojd, in northeastern Wallachia, to Bucharest. He bought a small, one-story house with a basement at 47 Berzei Street. Romania was a young nation then, just emerging from centuries of domination by the Ottoman Empire. Constantin Giurescu was the first man from Chiojd ever to attain a university education and become a teacher. He became an associate professor at the University of Bucharest and a member of the Romanian Academy before he died in an influenza epidemic that accompanied the end of World War I.

He left to his son, also called Constantin Giurescu, both the family's new tradition of scholarship and the house at 47 Berzei Street. The younger Constantin Giurescu became, in his turn, a professor of history at the University of Bucharest and a member of the Romanian Academy. When he married, in 1926, he took out a loan from the association of Romanian teachers and added a second story to the house. His son Dinu, from whom I heard this history, was born in 1927.

Dinu Giurescu is now a tall, slightly gaunt, courtly man with gray hair brushed straight back from a broad forehead and pale blue eyes. He remembers his boyhood home with great clarity. "The house was made of red brick, whitewashed, with a roof of red terra-cotta tiles. The second floor had a balcony with a carved plaster railing, like many Bucharest homes. It had fourteen rooms. Three of them were libraries, holding my father's and grandfather's books. The ceilings were high, and it was very comfortable. In the back, it had a small garden. We used to raise rabbits in the garden during the war, because there was no meat. The people next door—a former clerk from a tribunal, his wife, their daughter, who was a teacher in the high school, and her husband—had fruit trees and a lot of flowers. Now and then, when the apricots were ripe, they offered us a basket."

From his room on the second floor, Dinu Giurescu could hear the trams rumbling by, heading south down Berzei Street toward the Dimbovita River, a narrow tributary of the Danube that flows through the middle of the city. To the east, a mile or two away, stood the palace of King Carol II. One tram stop to the north, there was a market plaza to which peasants would come from the surrounding countryside and sell their produce. Around the corner, on Stirbei Voda Street, stood one of the city's handsomer Romanian Orthodox churches, an ocher-colored building with bright mosaics of Saints Peter and Paul flanking the front door and characteristic Romanian cupolas shaped like acorn caps. Built around 1760, it was known as the Storks' Nest Church, because of the birds that nested in it when the neighborhood was on the outskirts of the city. Across Berzei Street, an Armenian family ran a small store selling what the neighbors called Oriental wares—principally coffee. Sometime during his boyhood, Giurescu remembers, an Austrian named Meinl opened a competing shop that offered coffee, lemons, and cognac, much to the disgruntlement of the Armenian.

Between the world wars, Romania made a brief and not entirely successful effort to establish a constitutional monarchy. There were many parties, many elections, not all of them honest, and twenty-one different governments. One of the more robust political groups spawned by those years was the Iron Guard, a native fascist organization very similar to the Nazi Party in Germany. Constantin Giurescu belonged to the National Liberal Party, the most successful of the democratic parties, and he served King Carol II in a prewar government as minister of information. But after the war broke out, Carol abdicated in favor of his son Michael, making way for a pro-German, Iron Guard government under General Ion Antonescu. Dinu Giurescu remembers a day in the winter of 1941 when his father and two friends broke out their hunting rifles and stood guard inside the front door at 47 Berzei Street, lest the Iron Guard's thugs come for him and his family. The fascist regime held power until 1944, when the Soviet Army swept through Romania.

The Soviet occupation brought with it a government that Constantin Giurescu's hunting rifles could not keep from intruding. In 1950, the new authorities jailed the elder Giurescu for his connections to the old, bourgeois regime. Dinu Giurescu, who had just received his master's degree in history, could not find a place as a teacher, and he went to work as a laborer, building roads. One morning that year, at about six o'clock, the doorbell rang, loudly and persistently. Dinu awoke slowly.

"All of a sudden, I realized someone was ringing," he recalled. "I went downstairs and, through the frosted glass, I could see the outlines of several people, so I opened a little window and asked what they wanted. I could see two militiamen and two men dressed like civil servants.

"They said, 'Is the family of Professor Giurescu living in this house?'

"I said yes.

" 'Who else?' they asked.

"I said that my grandparents from my mother's side were there, as well as some friends, a doctor and his wife, who had moved in after my father was arrested and were occupying part of the first floor. They handed me a small paper on which it was typed that the family of Professor Giurescu has to move from this address.

"I asked when this was to be done.

"They said, 'Immediately. You have two or three hours to move.'

"My mother had come to the door. She fainted, and I gave her some water and she recovered. There was no other way than to pack rapidly. We were allowed two valises each for our personal belongings. They let us take our mattresses. Everything else—furniture, carpets, books—was taken. We couldn't keep even my father's suits. We were told he didn't need them any longer. In two hours, a truck came up, and they put our mattresses and valises in it. I rode on top. And they moved us to a two-room shanty. One room had a plank floor and the other room had just a bare earth floor. There was no bathroom, no kitchen—just an outhouse out back. In a few hours that morning, we had been left with empty hands."

In those years, Dinu Giurescu and many of his friends still believed that the United States would somehow liberate Romania from its new masters. "It was partly fueled by the radio," he told me, referring to the Voice of America and Radio Free Europe. "Every spring and every fall it was the same story and the same music: They are coming. It is close. The days of these people [the communists] are numbered. Especially when President Eisenhower, in his election speech in the fall of 1952, said that the United States won't rest until Estonia, Latvia, Lithuania, Poland, Czechoslovakia, Romania, and so forth would be liberated. When Eisenhower was elected, I remember being on a train with one of my good friends, and we celebrated his election, very discreetly of course, by drinking some beer in the restaurant compartment and being very happy because they are coming."

But with the passage of a few more years, particularly after the events in Hungary in 1956, it became clear that the Western powers were not coming, despite what the Americans might say in their political campaigns. And, with the death of Stalin, the Romanian regime began to change. In 1955, the government released Constantin Giurescu and those former bourgeois ministers who had survived their imprisonment. Dinu Giurescu sensed that the regime wanted to explore an accommodation with the formerly scorned intelligentsia. In 1956, he found work as a guide in the Romanian Museum of Art and left manual labor behind. "It was rather hard, because my dossier—this is my social dossier—was still in place. The authorities accepted me reluctantly. But then they saw that I was committed to being a hardworking professional, and little by little I got their confidence. Over eight years, I became the curator of old Romanian art."

The Romanian Communist Party at that time had developed a strong streak of nationalism and decided that it needed historians. Its leader, Gheorghe Gheorghiu-Dej, wanted Romania to have the things Stalin had given to Russia: heavy industry, urbanization, independence. Ironically, this required him to resist the role Stalin's heirs wanted Romania to play—that of a breadbasket and forward military outpost. Gheorghiu-Dej made his own industrial development plans. In 1958, he persuaded the Soviets that they could safely withdraw their troops. And he made a place for people like Constantin Giurescu, who could write about the triumphs of ancient kings and princes and give the people a sense of national pride. By the early 1960s, Constantin Giurescu was teaching again at the University of Bucharest. Dinu Giurescu resumed work on his doctorate in history.

Gheorghiu-Dej died in 1965, and an apparatchik named Nicolae Ceausescu took his place as general secretary. Most Romanians believed at the time that the truly powerful men in the Party had put Ceausescu in that position because he was too junior and too weak to threaten them. But in a few years' time, Ceausescu emerged as the Party's unchallenged leader. He also managed to renew the hopes of Dinu Giurescu and his generation of Romanian intellectuals. He started off by exposing some of the Stalinist crimes of the old Party leaders and purging them from the leadership. And in 1968, Ceausescu, alone among Warsaw Pact leaders, supported Czechoslovakia's right to determine its own political course. In 1969, Dinu Giurescu joined the Party.

Four years after that, the family moved back into the house at 47 Berzei Street. "The house had been nationalized, but my father had been trying ever since he got out of prison to get it back. After many attempts, he was successful, in that he got back the first floor as owner. The second floor remained an apartment owned by the state, but I was able to move in as tenant with my wife and two daughters. Four families had been living in it, and it was quite shabby. But I must tell you that I was grateful to the government for giving it back to us." Constantin Giurescu was able to live out his life in his father's house. He died in 1977.

By that time the government, which had become completely subservient to Ceausescu's will, had enacted a law calling for the "systematization" of housing and services in Romania's cities and villages. "On the surface, the law looked really good," Dinu Giurescu told me. "They wanted a judicious organization of the whole territory. They wanted to provide guidelines for construction density and height, for population density. It was flexible enough and vague enough to permit any kind of interpretation, from one which might have allowed historical centers to remain in place up to the total razing of a town. We really read the law as a kind of juridical frame for urban renewal in the good sense." He joined the board of the state commission for the preservation of historic Romanian monuments and threw himself into the work of preserving and protecting the historic centers of Romania's towns.

Gradually, Giurescu realized that systematization would do little to care for historic monuments and nothing at all to preserve the fabric of Romania's older neighborhoods and villages. Ceausescu envisioned, instead, a Stalinist utopia in which every family, urban or rural, had a standard apartment, provided by the state. He intended to tear down much of the nation's old housing to find room to build it. Romania has some thirteen thousand villages. The vast majority of them have fewer than two thousand inhabitants; systematization regarded them as "economically unviable." Carried out to a conclusion, Ceausescu's scheme would have eliminated all of these smaller villages, transferring their population to larger "agro-industrial centers," where people would live in apartment blocs rather than the traditional cottages. In Romania's cities, the systematization program would raze more than 90 percent of existing housing. These figures alarmed Giurescu. "As a historian, I fully understand that with every generation there is change, and that every town and village sees some of its structures torn down and new ones built. But this program tears down houses that are structurally sound and could be improved for much less money than the cost of razing them and building new apartments."

Ceausescu, Giurescu told me, had a purpose for this destruction. He believed "in the Soviet model of the 1930s, in building a new society. If you want to have this type of society, you need a totally new type of human being, a being who will willingly, cheerfully, and diligently implement all the orders given by the leadership. To have such an individual, you need to create a new environment for him or her. If you allow this individual to be on his own, to have personal reactions, then he naturally will oppose this new society, because that's human nature. But if the individual is totally dependent on the collective, from his birth to his exit, then he will react according to the will of the collective."

For a few years, Giurescu managed to publish occasional articles that, while not directly criticizing Ceausescu's plans, at least advocated the preservation of Romania's architectural heritage. But in the mid-1980s, the pace of systematization picked up. Churches, old houses, and whole monasteries began to disappear. The government simply stopped calling meetings of the preservation commission. In September 1986, Giurescu received notice that the city would be razing his house. He was not being singled out. Systematization had simply come to Berzei and Stirbei Voda streets, and 150 other houses were also to be demolished. He would receive eighty thousand lei—the black market equivalent of about eight hundred dollars—for the house. He would have to move by the following July. There was no appeal.

The wreckers came the next summer and worked for about ten days. Giurescu, by then living in a friend's spare room, went back to Berzei Street and watched. "They didn't hurry. They took the roof first, and the window frames." With raw, gaping holes where once there had been light and life, the empty hulk of the house reminded him of a skull. It stayed that way for a few days. "Then, on a Sunday, a steam shovel came and started hitting the walls. The house was stoutly built, and it took several blows, but after a while, it knocked them down, and when the rubble mounted, it took the rubble into its claw and put it into trucks. At first, I wanted to run away. It was my childhood there. I had so many memories. I was remembering my father, my mother, and the good life we had there. Then I told myself, 'No, you are a historian. You have to face these events. You have to know them.' So I stood there for forty-five minutes or an hour as the crane was hitting and hitting these walls. The next day I came back, and the third day and the fourth, and in a couple of days the pile was gone."

Early in 1988, the Giurescu family received permission to emigrate. They moved first to Rome, where the U.S. government processes Europeans seeking refugee admission. "It was the first time in my life I had an opportunity to visit Rome," Giurescu told me, "and it was very exciting. I was so pleased to see that every street in Rome was full of history—not only historical monuments, but the urban fabric of history. This is really important." After sixteen days, the Giurescus moved to the United States, where Dinu Giurescu found a job teaching European history at Texas A & M and published a book, *Razing Romania's Past.*

In the years before World War II, writers fond of Bucharest liked to call it the Paris of the East. When I made my first visit to the city in August 1989, a faint French influence could still be found in the northern sector, where the upper classes once lived. It boasted a triumphal arch and several handsome avenues, lined with leafy trees that shaded blocks of graceful old buildings with mansard roofs and delicate, ornamented lintels and entries. But Bucharest no longer afforded much in the way of a Western, to say nothing of Parisian, ambience. Because of a chronic shortage of electricity, few lights burned at night, giving it the look of a city in a wartime blackout. Urban amenities were crude, when they were available at all. One hot afternoon, walking along the Boulevard of 1848 in the center of the city, I hunted in vain for a café or restaurant that might sell a cold drink. Finally, I found a kind of cafeteria. At a counter, water ran from an open tap. People lined up, grabbed empty soft drink bottles, washed them off as best they could, then filled them up for a drink. When they were done, they left the bottles behind for someone else to wash and use.

There was, at that time, no way for a foreign journalist to probe very deeply into Ceausescu's Romania, to investigate the grisly jails or orphanages. The government barred Western journalists, except for a handful admitted occasionally for special events or interviews with Ceausescu. I went as a tourist, and for a while I confined myself to those things I could observe quietly, beginning with the buildings. Systematization, I found, had transmogrified roughly half of the Giurescus' old neighborhood. On the west side of the cobblestone street stood a mélange of older two-, three-, and four-story buildings. Some were boxy and ordinary, but one stately town house with a tile roof had four ornamented balconies and lovely, intricately carved loggias on the fourth floor. A barbershop, a small grocery, and a pharmacy occupied the ground-floor spaces on that side of the street. In the small alleys and courtyards tucked behind and between the buildings, people grew vegetables. Someone even had a few chickens.

On the east side, where the Giurescu house once stood, building cranes were assembling slabs and pillars of gray concrete into a grid of boxlike rooms that looked a little like an open honeycomb. Next door, at the corner, the builders had already completed the rounded, eggshell-white facade of a ten-story apartment building.

9

Each apartment had a small balcony with a curved parapet of the same eggshell white. On the ground floor, a row of shop windows heralded a bookstore in the making. One window had a display composed entirely of works by and about Nicolae Ceausescu, with titles such as *Socialist Civilization: A Superior Epoch in Social Development.* The next window displayed a new multivolume encyclopedia of chemistry. One volume, opened to the title page, disclosed that the encyclopedia had been prepared under the supervision of his wife, Elena Ceausescu.

Across Stirbei Voda Street, a row of identical apartment buildings stretched for several blocks down a gentle hill toward the Dimbovita. Tenants had begun to move into one or two of them, judging by the flower boxes appearing on the balconies. Behind one of the buildings still under construction, I found the Storks' Nest Church. The builders had moved it perhaps fifteen yards from the street and hidden it away in the back courtyard of the new apartments. Jagged piles of broken construction blocks and other rubble washed up against its portico, and the surrounding, unfinished concrete buildings dwarfed its black cupolas. The church's doors were locked, and there was no sign that anyone had been inside for some time. It was as if a person had moved into a glassy, modern home and, rather than throw away an old armoire that no longer suited him, had stuck it in the garage because someone had told him it might be a valuable antique. Twilight was approaching as I walked away from the church. I saw a man pick up a bundle of two-by-fours from the construction site and walk casually away up Berzei Street. On the other side of the lot, a boy in short pants with a couple of planks under his arm, no doubt less experienced at pilfering, glanced furtively up and down the street before he, too, scuttled away into the evening.

A few blocks to the south, on the other side of the Dimbovita, spotlights played on the massive blue, yellow, and red Romanian flag that flapped atop the centerpiece of systematization, the new House of the People. Despite the electricity shortage, in fact, the whole site was brightly lit, and hard hats were still pounding and clanking away at their work somewhere in the interior of the building. The House of the People is an enormous structure, rising ten stories in three layers, its white facade replete with pediments, columns, and arched windows. Pacing off its perimeter, I estimated it to be 750 feet wide and more than 1,000 feet long; it covered an area roughly three times that of the Capitol in Washington. The new building sits atop a low, sculpted hill that had soft, sparse new grass growing on it. At the bottom of the hill, there is an enormous plaza, fully a quarter of a mile across, where, it seemed safe to predict, great crowds of Romanians would someday be assembled to cheer for their leadership. Despite its name, the House of the People had no staircase by which the people could then actually walk from the plaza up into the building. The only access was via a semicircular drive. The guard posts at its entrances had thick, concrete walls and narrow slits for windows. They looked like pillboxes.

The new Boulevard of the Victory of Socialism began at the House of the People and ended approximately three miles to the east. Ceausescu and his wife signed the decree ordering its construction in 1984. To build it, the state razed nearly everything (except for a few churches, moved and preserved like the Storks' Nest Church) in a straight swath of the central city perhaps a quarter of a mile wide. Roger Kirk, the American ambassador to Bucharest during this period, told me that, by conservative estimates, forty thousand people lost their homes. The boulevard itself is more than a hundred yards wide—a meter wider, the Romanians liked to boast, than the Champs-Élysées. Parallel rows of nearly identical ten-story apartment buildings, ornamented with balconies and columns, flank the boulevard and its median bands of trees and fountains. Flocks of construction cranes hovered over the area like mother birds.

The construction followed a peculiar schedule. When I visited, crews had finished the facades of the buildings that face the boulevard, neatly pointing the masonry and painting them in light, off-white shades. Someone had trimmed the storefront windows on the ground level and stocked them with clothing, crystal, and clocks. There was even an automobile showroom. But behind the windows, the stores were locked and empty. I walked behind the buildings and found that in the rear they were barely half finished. Some were only naked frames that had yet to be walled in. It was a Potemkin village, writ large.

Ceausescu, when a foreign journalist got a chance to ask him about it, generally defended the systematization program as a laudable effort to "raise our people's standard of living and level of civilization in general." And, viewed strictly as housing, the new apartment buildings on the Boulevard of the Victory of Socialism may well have improved the living conditions of those who eventually would move into them. But the real issue raised by his demolition and reconstruction of so much of Bucharest was not, of course, how many square feet of dwelling space the average citizen would have before and after systematization. The real issues involved coercion, scale, and symbolism.

In the Eastern Europe of the old Soviet Empire, urban design meshed with politics. In Warsaw, one of the first acts of the Polish people after World War II was the reconstruction, brick by brick, of the city's venerable central area, the Stare Miasto. In Prague, the Czechs always took pains to preserve the architectural heritage that, to their great good fortune, the war did not destroy. In Budapest, the Hungarians never tried to keep modern buildings out of the historic district along the Danube. One of the Hyatt hotel chain's atrium designs shares the riverbank with the baroque remnants of the Austro-Hungarian Empire, and a Hilton hotel nestles in the ruins of a thirteenth-century Dominican monastery. But the Hungarians preserved a harmony of scale, if not of design. Viewed from the walkways of the Chain Bridge in the middle of the Danube, the Budapest cityscape seems to say that the past is of a piece with the present, which will be of a piece with the future; that empires come and go; and that each generation has its contribution to make to the civilization of the city. It is probably no coincidence that the citizens of Warsaw, Prague, and Budapest, before 1989, put up the staunchest resistance to communist rule of all the people of Eastern Europe.

Bucharest's Boulevard of the Victory of Socialism, by contrast, asserted that the city's past had no value beyond that of prologue to the communist age. Its scale deliberately belittled the contributions of vanished generations, claiming that the Ceausescu era represented a gigantic, irreversible stride forward. Few urban landscapes in the world rival it for size. In fact, perhaps its only true rival may be an avenue that existed solely as an architect's model: the grand avenue that Adolf Hitler planned for Berlin. According to Albert Speer's account of Hitler as builder, the Third Reich's avenue would have been slightly wider than Ceausescu's, but no longer. At one end it was to have a domed Great Hall, roughly the size of Bucharest's House of the People. At the other, Hitler planned a triumphal arch to dwarf the one in Paris. Hitler, Speer recounted, "liked to say that the purpose of his building was to transmit his time and its spirit to posterity." In Bucharest, Ceausescu succeeded where Hitler had failed.

Outside the capital, systematization had yet to transform the landscape so thoroughly. I rented a Romanian-built compact car called a Dacia and drove (despite a flat tire and a muffler that fell off) from Bucharest westward through Pitesti, into Transylvania, and back to the capital via Brasov and Ploiesti. In the cities and larger towns, I could see the beginnings of systematization: raw, empty lots in neighborhoods of older, single-family houses. In general, the bigger the city, the more demolition. Smaller villages seemed to be living in another time. It was harvest season, and I often encountered wagons drawn by horses or oxen plodding along the road, piled high with hay. Women in kerchiefs drove cows and sheep on the highway. And in several of the villages I passed through, farmers were building new single-family houses with tile roofs and tiny loggias, not tearing them down.

I wanted particularly to see the town of Alba Julia, known in Hungarian as Gyulafehervar. It was the capital of Transylvania during the sixteenth and seventeenth centuries, when the principality belonged to Hungary. John Hunyadi, the Hungarian-Romanian prince whose victory over the Turks in 1456 saved Eastern Europe from Ottoman conquest for a hundred years, is buried there. Michael the Brave, the first Romanian king of this millennium to control Transylvania, asserted his claim there in 1599.

I got to the vast, star-shaped citadel that contains most of Alba Julia's historic sites on a Friday afternoon. Inside the gate stands the Romanian Orthodox Cathedral of Reunification, where King Ferdinand and Queen Marie, attempting to emulate Michael the Brave, had themselves crowned monarchs of Transylvania, which was taken from Hungary and given to Romania after World War I. A garden of brightly colored flowers and green lawns surrounded the cathedral, and a priest, dressed in black, was clipping the hedges. An open arcade formed the west wall of the cathedral compound. When I walked through it, I found that on the arcade floor, scattered on beds of straw, lay bits and pieces of broken statuary and stonework—a head or an arm here, a full figure there, a chunk of an inscribed stone tablet propped against a wall.

These pieces, the priest tending the hedge told me, had fallen off the Catholic cathedral, a few yards to the south of the Cathedral of Reunification. There was apparently no money for repairs, so the pieces accumulated in the arcade of the Orthodox compound, where they had, at least, partial shelter from the rain. I walked over to the Catholic cathedral, built, my guidebook told me, in the thirteenth century on the site of a church destroyed in a Tatar raid in 1242, perhaps by one of Jenghiz Khan's sons. This dark and stately church was going to ruin as surely as if the Tatars had once more ridden out of the East and pillaged it. The masonry on the outside walls was crumbling, exposing the worn bricks beneath it. Inside, the arms, faces, or kneecaps of the statues on the sarcophagi of Hunyadi and the other princes interred there had fallen off. More bits of stonework littered the vestibule. Systematization may not have been entirely to blame for this. Romanians, who are mostly Orthodox, associate the Catholic church with Hungary's competing claim to Transylvania, and they tended to neglect the upkeep of Catholic sites long before Nicolae Ceausescu came to power.

Just north of Bucharest, I turned off the highway to have a look at the area around Lake Snagov, a resort favored by the Romanian Communist Party's elite. Ambassador Kirk had told me that this was an area hit by the rural version of systematization. Just off the highway, I noticed whitewashed curbs along the sides of the road. There were no houses behind the curbs, just green fields of corn and grass. I picked up a hitchhiker, a boy who explained that a small village called Vladiceasca, with perhaps one hundred inhabitants, had stood behind the curb until a year or two ago. Then it was razed, and the inhabitants moved down the road to a larger village. It was the only place in Romania where I found that a village had been completely destroyed. The whitewashed curbs were all that remained.

I continued down the road and came to the village of Ciofliceni, which seemed to have several hundred peasant families. The peasant homes in Ciofliceni and the Snagov area fell into three categories. The most substantial had three or four rooms, brick or stone walls, and a tile roof. Some less prosperous families had two rooms, walls of rough, whitewashed adobe, and a tin roof. The poorest families had wooden homes and thatched roofs. Most of the cottages had a little courtyard with a chicken coop, a haymow, a small barn, and perhaps a well with a crank and a tin bucket. The well owners generally left a glass on the rim of the well in case a passerby needed a drink. Some accounts of systematization had listed Ciofliceni as a razed village, but I saw no sign of any destruction there.

Down the road another mile, I came to Ghermanesti, clearly the designated agro-industrial center for the area. About half the land in the village had been cleared, and in the dusty wasteland left behind, construction crews were hard at work on new, systematized dwellings: three- and four-story apartment blocks with balconies, smaller cousins of the ones on Berzei Street. People had moved into some of the new buildings and seemed to be trying their best to make them look as much as possible like the cottages they had lost. Flowers and green plants cascaded over the balcony railings, and corn grew in the small plots of land between the road and the buildings' front doors.

I continued on into the countryside until the signs of systematization disappeared, then turned back. I wanted to ask some of the people in Ghermanesti how they felt about their new homes and life-styles. But in the hour or so since I had first passed through, perhaps a dozen uniformed policemen had arrived in the village and taken up posts on the sides of the road, waiting. It seemed unlikely that people would talk freely about their opinions with a policeman staring over their shoulder, so I continued on. There were more policemen in Ciofliceni, and even a few where Vladiceasca had been. When I reached the highway, still another policeman stopped the car. I could not, he said, turn south and return to Bucharest. I would have to turn north, toward Ploiesti, and wait.

I asked why.

"The Chief is coming," he said.

I drove a couple of hundred yards up the road, turned around, and parked. Behind me, two police cars had formed a barrier; they were holding up all the motor traffic between Ploiesti and Bucharest. Ten minutes later, a convoy of eight small cars came up the highway from Bucharest and turned onto the Lake Snagov road. Ceausescu, I later learned, had a weekend house near the lake. It struck me then that there might be a connection between the completed facades on the Boulevard of the Victory of Socialism and the systematized villages of Vladiceasca and Ghermanesti. Ceausescu frequently passed by all of them.

Nicolae Ceausescu was then seventy-one years old. In bare outline, his life and career closely resembled those of Josef Stalin.

Like Stalin, he was born in poverty, to a peasant family from a village called Scornicesti, about a hundred miles west of Bucharest. He got only a few years of education before he left his family, at the age of eleven, moved to the capital, and found work as a shoemaker's apprentice. Like Stalin, he became a communist and a revolutionary while still in his teens. The Romanian press first noticed him in 1936, when the government tried and convicted him of communist activity; he received an additional six months' sentence for a courtroom outburst. Like Stalin, he got his higher education from fellow revolutionaries in trouble with the law. He spent most of the time between 1936 and 1944 in jail with other Party members. Those senior to him in the Party underestimated him when he became general secretary, but, like Stalin, he used his control over the apparatus gradually to isolate and dispose of them. Then he instituted a job rotation policy that periodically sent Party cadres back to the provinces and prevented any potential rivals from establishing a power base. Ceausescu accumulated power slowly, in increments. He got control over the military in 1969 and became president in 1974. Even in 1989, some professional observers of Romania expressed lingering surprise at what Ceausescu had become. "It happened so gradually," one State Department official told me.

Once he had achieved power, Ceausescu preserved it by means of a nepotism so rife that it assures him a unique place in the annals of communism. His brother Ilie became a vice minister of defense. A second brother, Nicolae Andruta, became a lieutenant general in the security forces. A third brother, Ion, who was a farm laborer when Ceausescu became general secretary, became first vice chairman of the state planning agency. His youngest child and namesake, known as Nicu, became head of the communist youth organization and then party leader in Transylvania. Some feared Ceausescu meant to make him his successor.

Elena Ceausescu's political career took off soon after her husband became general secretary. I spoke about her with Vladimir Tismaneanu, who is now a scholar at Philadelphia's Foreign Policy Research Institute. In the 1950s and 1960s, Tismaneanu, the son of a ranking Romanian official, attended school with Nicu Ceausescu. Mrs. Ceausescu, he remembers, behaved much as any other mother until her husband became the leader. Tismaneanu knew things had changed when an edition of the official Romanian encyclopedia was published, listing the year of her birth as 1917, a year before her husband's. "Suddenly, all those volumes were ordered recalled and destroyed," Tismaneanu recalled, smiling, now, at the memory. "The next edition said she was born in 1919."

Mrs. Ceausescu then decided that she wanted a doctorate in chemistry, although she had never completed grade school. In 1967, she approached one of Romania's most respected chemists, a professor at the University of Bucharest named Costin Nenitescu, and asked him to award her one. He refused. Mrs. Ceausescu then found a more pliant professor at a provincial university in the town of Iasi. She received her doctorate and soon thereafter became the chairman of the National Committee on Science and Technology. Romania's newspapers hailed her as perhaps the most eminent woman scientist since Madame Curie. The unfortunate Professor Nenitescu went into premature retirement.

Mrs. Ceausescu, meanwhile, added political work to her scientific duties. She joined the Romanian Communist Party's Central Committee in 1972 and became a member of its ruling board, the Political Executive Committee, in 1977. By 1989, she ranked second in power only to her husband, controlling virtually all important political patronage and participating in his meetings with foreign leaders.

I contacted two people who had known Ceausescu to ask for their impressions of the man. The first, Ion Mihai Pacepa, served Ceausescu as director of Romania's internal security force until 1979, when he defected to the United States. He later published a scathing book about his former leader, and he lived in hiding, fearful that Ceausescu's agents would find him and take revenge. I wrote to him through his publisher. He declined to meet me, but he did send a long letter. In it, he described Ceausescu as puritanical and ascetic, a man who worked long hours, a man of "native intelligence, phenomenal memory and iron will." Ceausescu had also, according to Pacepa, installed radiation detectors in all his offices and residences to protect against assassination by radioactive weapons, had special bodyguards who tasted all the food prepared for him, and washed his hands with alcohol after physical contact with any stranger.

I also spoke with John Whitehead, who was deputy secretary of state in the second Reagan administration. The Eastern European portfolio went with his job, and Whitehead thus had three extended meetings with Ceausescu. They tended to begin late in the day and go on for several hours. "He's quite formal, and he considers himself the head of a very important country and one of the world's great leaders," Whitehead told me in a conversation just before he left the State Department. "You don't have a meeting with him—he gives you an audience. He has a speech impediment, like a stutter, and sometimes he has trouble getting words out. After he delivers his speech, and it's your turn, he rudely stops listening, talks to his colleagues, and shuffles his papers. He never looks at you—just off into the distance.

"He's in complete control of the country, and he doesn't try to pretend otherwise. He doesn't try to tell you that Romania is a democracy. But he's dreadfully uninformed about what's happening in his country. For instance, at a meeting I had with him in February 1988, he objected to the fact that President Reagan had made a reference to Romania's economic difficulties. He asked whether the president knew that per capita income had been going up steadily for eight years. He claims the country is very prosperous. He also complained about some newspaper article that said he wasn't popular. 'I'm extremely popular. I have evidence of it every day. Every time I make a speech, people rise and applaud,' he said. He's surrounded by a small group of sycophants who make up statistics for him."

A lingering sense of violated privacy colored Whitehead's memories of Romania. Once, visiting a department store, he decided to find out how many plainclothesmen were tailing him. He walked into the women's lingerie department. Within a minute, perhaps a dozen Romanian men followed him into it and stood around, pretending awkwardly to be shopping. His last meeting with Ceausescu, which was of no scheduled duration, broke up at approximately nine o'clock one evening. Ceausescu rose and escorted him out into a hallway. Precisely at that moment, Mrs. Ceausescu emerged from her adjoining office to say good-bye. Ceausescu had pushed no buttons nor otherwise let anyone outside his office know that the meeting was over. Whitehead concluded that Mrs. Ceausescu must have been listening in on her husband's conversation. Whitehead had always struck me as a careful diplomat who, unlike some of his colleagues in the Reagan administration, was not given to harsh or ideological opinions about others. I was a bit surprised, then, to hear his summation of Ceausescu: "I think he's a crazy man."

I arrived in Bucharest a few days before the principal national holiday, the twenty-third of August. Walking around the city in the late afternoon, I often encountered wooden police barricades blocking off a few streets. Beyond the barricades, throngs of people were practicing chants, rehearsing for the big holiday parade. After rehearsals, they would stream past the barricades, with signs and portraits, mounted on poles, resting on their shoulders like tired miners' shovels at the end of a shift in the pits. One common slogan, in white letters on a red banner, read: 1965–1989. THE ERA OF NICOLAE CEAUSESCU. THE GOLDEN ERA. The portraits were all of Elena and Nicolae Ceausescu. Late photographs of Ceausescu showed a man with gray hair, a deeply lined face, and suspicious, hawklike eyes. The ubiquitous official portrait, however, showed him as perhaps he looked years before, with a bushy brown pompadour, smooth cheeks, and a kindly smile playing on full, pink lips.

Few in Bucharest could escape that face as the holiday approached. Romania had one television channel, which broadcast for three hours each evening. I caught most of the program on August 22. The newscast featured a long report on a reception in which the two Ceausescus clinked glasses with the diplomatic corps. A report on counties that had overfulfilled their production plans in honor of the holiday came next and completed the news. Then came a musical hour. A choir, massed under Ceausescu's portrait, sang a long hymn in praise of their leader. A documentary film about the achievements of the Romanian economy followed, consisting principally of clips showing the Ceausescus snipping ribbons, inspecting dams and factories, and greeting happy workers who, of course, were carrying their portraits.

A speech by Ceausescu, outlining the themes for the holiday, had consumed the first three pages of that morning's edition of *Scinteia,* the party newspaper. Western histories of World War II depict the twenty-third of August as a day of opportunism. Romania's pro-Nazi government had let German troops occupy the country. Soon after the German defeat at the Battle of Stalingrad, however, Romanian diplomats opened secret contacts with the United States and Britain, offering to switch sides if the Allies promised to restore Transylvania to Romania. (Hitler had awarded most of it to Hungary in 1940.) The Allies offered the necessary promises. On August 23, 1944, the Soviet Army had already pushed the Germans back into Moldavia and promised quickly to be in Bucharest. King Michael summoned his pro-Nazi premier, General Antonescu, and had him arrested. Late that night, the new government ordered the Romanian Army to stop fighting the Soviets, and two days later Romania declared war on the Third Reich.

Forty-five years later, Ceausescu's speech transformed this palace coup into "the victory of the anti-fascist and -imperialist revolution for social and national liberation . . . an act of will of the whole Romanian nation." He did not mention King Michael or the fact that Soviet troops would soon have reoriented Romania anyway. "Cheers and chants," the newspaper reported, repeatedly interrupted his remarks.

More cheers and chants, along with the sound of marching feet, awakened me shortly after dawn the next morning. From my hotel window, I could see marchers, in phalanxes of several hundred, moving through the streets below, and I went downstairs to watch the parade. Like iron filings drawn by a magnet, the paraders, their icons, and their banners streamed through the sleepy, quiet neighborhoods toward Berzei Street. Middle-aged men in tan suits escorted them. Once in a while, one of the escorts would give a signal, and his group would practice a chant: "Ce-au-se-scu, Er-o-ism! Ro-ma-ni-a, Com-mun-ism!" in a kind of trochaic staccato. As I followed them, I noticed that many groups wore costumes—girls in diaphanous white dresses, dancers in colorfully embroidered peasant clothes with cockaded hats, and wiry young athletes in bright red shirts, red sweatpants, and red caps.

As they neared Berzei Street, the paraders bunched up, stopped, and waited. Some draped their filmy red banners on the curb or the pavement and sat on them, lest they soil their costumes. Some propped themselves against lampposts, smoked, or chewed sunflower seeds, spitting out the hulls. Here and there, a man in a suit walked through a group, pen and paper in hands, writing down names. Parade participation, I heard from several émigrés, was an obligation that rotated among the staff of every factory and office. The leaders of each workplace Party cell appointed the appropriate number of marchers and made sure they attended.

At the head of the line, on Berzei Street, a cordon of policemen stopped me. Behind them, I could see the military segment of the parade. Dark green tanks, mobile antiaircraft guns, and trucks filled with troops waited on the cobblestones, engines idling, filling the air with exhaust fumes. I wanted to walk farther, to get ahead of the parade and watch it go past. But the policemen stopped me. Only people with special passes could stand along the line of march, one of the policemen explained. The parade, it turned out, covered only about three blocks, past a temporary reviewing stand in front of a massive new building on Stirbei Voda Street that was to house a national museum. Only invited diplomats, selected officials, and the

Ceausescus watched it in person. The rest of the nation could see it on television. I turned around and walked back toward my hotel. Along the way, I passed a line of people at a sidewalk table where someone was selling butter. It was the only spontaneous crowd I would see that day.

On television, the parade made an impressive spectacle. A military band, in formation across the avenue from the reviewing stand, provided the music. Legions of chanting workers marched past the cameras, their faces almost obscured by the forest of Ceausescu portraits and banners they carried overhead. The girls in white dresses pirouetted prettily. The young men in the special red costumes, as they passed the reviewing stand, broke ranks and regrouped to spell "C-E-A-U-S-E-S-C-U" in precise block letters. Then they formed the Roman numerals—IX, X, XI, XII, XIII—that designate the Party congresses over which Ceausescu had presided. The cameras panned often to the tribunal where the Ceausescus stood, smiling and waving, she in a white dress, he in a dark suit. In contrast to the custom at Soviet parades, where the Party leadership lined up atop Lenin's mausoleum in political pecking order, the Ceausescus stood in regal isolation. There would be no pictures the next day that analysts might use to spot a potential successor.

When the last marcher had passed, soldiers rolled a red carpet from the reviewing stand to the street. A single black car drove up, and the Ceausescus walked to it, side by side. At the curb, a dozen or so schoolchildren in red neckerchiefs lined up with bouquets of flowers in hand. One by one, they stepped up to one or the other of the Ceausescus and presented their flowers. Ceausescu accepted them with practiced ease, taking each bouquet in his right hand, embracing the child with his left, and kissing a proffered young cheek. As he kissed, the right arm swung out toward an aide, standing just out of the camera's view. The flowers disappeared, the arm swung back, and he was ready to greet another youngster. The ritual consumed but a moment or two. Then, with a final smile and wave, the Ceausescus got into the backseat of the car and were driven away. They looked, I thought, proud and happy.

The embrace of a vast state security system made it difficult to find out what the average Romanian thought of all this. From Dinu Giurescu and other émigrés, I had heard about Decree 408, which required that Romanians report all contacts with foreigners to the authorities. The state had never published this decree. But, four or five years earlier, at every workplace in the country, an official read it aloud and required each person to sign a statement that he was aware of it. Ion Pacepa, in his letter to me, described a security apparatus which had, by the late 1970s, more than 3 million registered informants and collaborators. (Romania had a population of somewhat more than 20 million people.) The security police, he said, maintained a collection of handwriting samples from over 60 percent of the population, and anyone with a typewriter had to register it with the authorities. Therefore, a Romanian tempted to mail an unsigned letter to, say, Amnesty International knew that it might be intercepted and the police might be able to tell, from the handwriting or the typeface, who wrote it. I found, as I traveled around the country, that people with responsible jobs tended to shy away from any kind of substantive conversation. I picked up an agronomist hitchhiking near Alba Julia. He chatted amiably until I asked him why I had never seen corn for sale in a store or market, though I had driven through miles of cornfields. He shrugged. I asked whether the corn was all exported. He shrugged again and seemed to shrink toward the door on his side of the car. "Anything's possible," he muttered, and said no more.

A few people living on the margins of society talked more openly. After the holiday parade, I took the subway to Herastrau Park, on the northern edge of the city. If writers still compared Bucharest to Paris, Herastrau Park would be the Bois de Boulogne. A shaded walk, lined with handsome, leafy hardwood trees led me past gardens and statuary into its interior. Filthy Gypsy children, barefoot and nearly naked, flocked around the holiday strollers, begging for coins. Along the banks of a small lake, people basked in the sun and ate simple picnic meals. I stopped to watch an ancient arcade game in which contestants tossed balls into holes to push their brightly painted racehorses across a green course to a finish line.

A cadaverously thin, sallow man with a concave chest and a drooping mustache walked up behind me and quietly asked, in French, if I wanted to exchange some money. I shook my head. He tried German. I shook my head again. He tried English.

"Sorry," I said.

Having found a common language, he proceeded to bargain. The official, and only legal, exchange rate for the Romanian leu was nine per dollar. The man, whose name was Christin, opened his bidding at fifty and quickly raised his offer to eighty, then ninety, and eventually one hundred lei. I declined, but I offered to buy him a drink. He agreed, and we collected his colleague, Ion, a burly and amiable man in his late thirties who had been sifting the crowd for foreigners in an adjoining section of the park. There was a café, they told me, across the lake. They jumped a queue and hopped into the back of a small blue-and-white boat which ferried people from one side of the lake to the other. I followed them aboard, and we chugged across.

On the other side, we strolled down another leafy, shaded path, past a dozen empty tennis courts, to a restaurant with a large terrace, tucked pleasantly into a grove of trees by the side of the lake. The restaurant was nearly full, and people were walking about looking for vacant tables. Christin and Ion knew one of the waiters, though, and he took us to a corner table, shaded by a bower of spruce boughs. The waiter whipped a RESERVED sign off the table and in short order produced a bottle of white wine and some mineral water. Christin, meanwhile, was chatting about the American films he had seen recently at the home of a black market video entrepreneur. He preferred action films, he said, particularly ones with Chuck Norris.

I asked whether they were uneasy talking about such things in a restaurant.

Ion waved blithely at the surroundings. A table in the open air would be hard to bug, he said. More important, he pointed out that this table had a glass ashtray. The conventional wisdom in Romania was that the security police hid bugs in ceramic ashtrays.

Both Christin and Ion had had some bitter experience with the police. Both of them had applied to emigrate to the United States. Christin said he had spent six months in jail after being arrested outside the American embassy, which he was trying to enter to plead his case for a visa. Ion said that after he applied, the police picked him up and took him to a darkened room in the station, where they beat him for four hours on the hands and the soles of his feet. He could not walk or hold a cigarette for a week.

I might have discounted such stories, considering that they came from black marketeers and would-be emigrants. But even a casual visitor to Romania saw the police as predators. When I arrived at the airport, I stood on the customs inspection line behind a young man who told me he had emigrated to America in 1979. He was returning to visit relatives, and he carried a large vinyl suitcase filled with inexpensive gifts, ranging from plastic toys to a box of Wheaties. The customs inspector pawed through these things suspiciously, until he found a bottle of Scotch. Grinning, he lifted his shirt and stuffed the bottle behind the waistband of his pants. Then he dropped his shirtfront over the bottle and, looking almost pregnant, waddled off to stash his booty.

A few days later, I drove to a Bucharest museum and looked for a place to park. I saw a cluster of half a dozen cars on the sidewalk and parked next to them. A policeman standing nearby blew his whistle and told me I could not park there.

"Where can I park?" I asked.

"Do you have cigarettes?" he replied.

Like any informed traveler in Romania, I went nowhere without a carton of Kents. I nodded.

"Two packs," he said.

We walked over to my car. I got in, and the policeman stuck his hand inside the window. Two packs changed hands. When I left the museum an hour or so later, the policeman's private parking lot had grown by two or three more cars. He smiled pleasantly as I drove away.

Both Christin, who held a job as an electrician, and Ion, nominally an auto mechanic, said they worked the black market to ease the suffering inflicted by the horrendous shortages and inefficiencies of Romania's formal economy. Ion, for instance, lived on the tenth floor of one of Bucharest's new apartment buildings. The elevators rarely worked. Fuses blew if he and his family tried to turn on more than one light per room. The building frequently had no hot water, and sometimes there was not enough water pressure to flush the toilets. In the winter, no heat came from the radiators. "One of the walls of my apartment is black, because we have to turn on the gas oven and open it at night for heat," he said.

Christin had once lived in a ten-room house that his grandfather, a furniture maker, had built in the south end of the city. The city condemned the house under the systematization program, gave Christin's parents twenty thousand lei for it, and tore it down. His parents got a two-room state flat, his sister and niece got a two-room flat, and he received a one-room, cold-water walk-up. Christin worked the black market by buying foreign currency from tourists, then making deals with sailors or other people able to travel abroad. They used the currency to bring back items, from razor blades to videocassettes, that were unavailable for lei. These Christin traded for coffee, sugar, cooking oil, and meat, products that are either rationed or extremely scarce.

A look in Bucharest's grocery stores and peasants' markets corroborated Christin's assessment. The stores offered some peas and pickles in jars, a little flour, and no meat. Though it was late summer, theoretically a time of abundance, people stood in long lines in the peasant markets for tomatoes, grapes, and melons. At the butchers' counters, they could buy pigs' heads and pigs' knuckles. There was no sign of any of the intermediate parts of the animal.

Romania is a fertile land, and only gross mismanagement could bring it to such a state of impoverishment. Ceausescu had duly provided it. In the early years of his reign, he borrowed abroad to build heavy industry, particularly petrochemical factories. World oil prices rose, and the market he anticipated for Romania's industrial production did not materialize. Ceausescu then determined that the nation's top priority must be repayment of the debt he had incurred, lest Romania fall under the influence of its foreign creditors. He squeezed the consumer sector unmercifully, shipping much of the country's food abroad. In April 1989, the government triumphantly announced that the debt had been paid, but no improvement in consumer supplies ensued.

"Things used to be much better," Christin said. "Ten years ago, we had meat. We had Kojak on television. In this park, there were six restaurants. Now there are two. There were discos. Now everything closes at ten o'clock. And all of the money goes to the Chief's pyramids."

I asked why Romania had no political opposition like Hungary and Poland.

"In Hungary, they have blood!" Christin exclaimed. "They say, 'I don't like this, I don't like this' until something changes. Here, no one says anything." And nothing would change, he said, until Ceausescu died.

That, Ion added gloomily, was not likely to happen soon. Ceausescu, he assured me, had a medical staff of twelve Chinese specialists, one to look after his heart, another for his lungs, and so on. And every few months, he said quite solemnly, Ceausescu's doctors drained his blood and replaced it with the fresh, pure blood of healthy Romanian infants.

* * *

Even staunch communists, when they would talk, were fed up with Ceausescu. On a Saturday afternoon, walking near the neoclassical State Opera House, I met an old man named Kiril. He had a barrel chest, thick, wavy gray hair, and an artificial leg. He moved with the help of an aluminum crutch. Slowly, and with great determination, he was exercising by walking around the park that surrounds the opera house. Kiril was eighty-one, long retired from a career as a popular singer, and, because he had no job to protect, less vulnerable to political reprisal for what he might say. He told me he had become a communist in 1924, because he opposed fascism. He formally joined the Romanian Communist Party soon after it became legal, at the end of World War II. From his wallet, he pulled the little red booklet of Party membership and showed it to me. His registration date was November 10, 1945.

Once we had become acquainted, Kiril volubly denounced Ceausescu and the "misery" into which he had thrown the country. Ceausescu, he said, was a "betrayer, a usurper," an uneducated cobbler without qualifications to run the country. How, I asked, had such a man accumulated such power? "We have a Mafia worse than the Mafia in the United States or Italy," the old man said. He paused, mopped his brow, and suggested we make our way toward a beer hall a few blocks to the east. He hobbled on.

He told me that six eminent Romanians, whom he referred to as the "honest diplomats," had recently tried to protest. I had heard of the case. These six, some of whom would return to political prominence in the coming months, had managed to send to the West an open letter to Ceausescu. It condemned the forced eviction of the peasants from their cottages and the unpublished decree forbidding Romanians to speak freely with foreigners. The Boulevard of the Victory of Socialism, they complained, was a multibillion-leu project that "has no public budget and is being built against all existing laws regulating construction and its financing. The cost of that immense building [the House of the People] has tripled because of changes you are ordering every month in the interior and exterior." They charged that factories were forcing their employees to work on

Sundays in an effort to raise production and that the security police routinely opened mail and cut off telephone conversations. The economy was in ruins. They asked Ceausescu to renounce the village systematization plan, respect human rights, and "put an end to food exports which are threatening the biological existence of our nation."

Kiril knew one of the signers, Gheorghe Apostol, through a friend of his wife's. Ceausescu, he told me, had dealt with Apostol and the others with disconcerting ease. He had moved them from their official residences to apartments scattered around the city and placed them under house arrest. Nothing more was heard from them, and no one spoke out publicly in their support. As Christin had said, in Romania, no one says anything.

We came, at last, to the beer hall and walked in. In the middle of the room, beyond a wooden enclosure, a bartender with a black hose was filling mugs of chipped and cracked glass with beer. All the tables were full, and people were standing in the grimy aisles, waiting for a chance to sit down. Kiril scowled, realizing that, unless he wanted to stand around indefinitely on his one good leg, we would get no beer that day. "Civilization!" he grumbled, as we left the room.

I wanted to learn more about the phenomenon Kiril and Christin had both alluded to: the quiet submission of most of the population. Stalin killed or imprisoned millions of Soviet citizens to enforce his will. Amnesty International, in a 1988 report, counted only thirty-five prisoners of conscience in Romania, at a time when Poles, Hungarians, and even East Germans were rising up and demanding change. Why did Romanians allow Ceausescu to flog them mercilessly in a demented effort to catch up to where the Soviet Union had been in 1953?

Centuries of oppression, instilling a strong survivor's instinct into the population, probably accounted for some of this acquiescence. There is a Romanian saying to the effect that the sword does not chop off a head that is bowed. And the government quite cannily used emigration and exile to bleed the country of potential opponents, as had happened with Dinu Giurescu. Those Romanians who most detested Ceausescu's rule could usually manage to escape if they were persistent enough. Hungary then sheltered about eighteen thousand Romanians who had sneaked or bribed their way across the border. Once in a while, there were reports of strikes or unrest. Workers in a truck factory in Brasov rioted in 1987 and set fire to a Party headquarters. But it seemed that a regime such as Ceausescu's would have inspired the birth of a more coherent, organized opposition.

So, on my last evening in Romania, I sought out a man named Gabriel Andreescu, one of Bucharest's few active dissidents. He was a scientist by training, but he had written several essays critical of Ceausescu's regime and sent them out to the West. Late in 1987 the police arrested him and held him for a couple of months of interrogation. A Romanian emigrants' organization had given me his address and assured me that a visit by a foreigner, attesting to the interest of the outside world in his treatment, could only help him. Andreescu lived on the southern fringe of the city, in a neighborhood poised on the brink of systematization. As I walked from the subway station, the dwellings on the right side of the street were all small, dilapidated, one-story cottages of two or three rooms, with walled courtyards, tiny gardens, and, perhaps, a tree or a vine spreading over a trellis. On the left, the land was stripped, brown and dusty, and occupied by ten-story apartment blocs. Andreescu lived in one of the newer buildings.

My arrival seemed to surprise him. Andreescu is a short, slight man in his midthirties, with wavy, receding brown hair and glasses. He led me into a living room, sparsely furnished with a green rug, an orange couch, a desk, and a bookshelf. After I had introduced myself, he told me that he almost never had visitors. Police in plain clothes, he said, followed him wherever he went and watched his apartment. Sometimes, they stood watch right at his door. Not long before, they had warned him that if he continued his dissident activities, they would commit him to a mental institution. In that case, I said, I would understand if he decided not to grant an interview.

No, he said, he would talk. I turned on my tape recorder, and he told me about himself, sitting with his elbows on his knees, hunched over, almost as if he expected to be hit from behind. I told him that I had greetings to pass on from friends abroad. He had me write their names in my notebook, and, next to them, he wrote his reply. After I read it, I scratched out what we had written, on the chance that the notebook might later be inspected or confiscated. I used horizontal strokes. Andreescu smiled indulgently at my naïveté, took the notebook from me, and scratched the names out again, using vertical strokes.

He spoke at length in response to my question about why the Romanian opposition was small and disorganized. For one thing, Romania is an Orthodox country, not Catholic. Each Orthodox nation has its own church, and, in communist countries, the Party had often been able to infiltrate and influence the Orthodox hierarchy. The Catholic church, which is prevalent in Poland and Hungary, is a supranational organization that, as the recent history of Poland showed, could serve as an institutional rival to the Party and an incubator for dissident movements. Moreover, Andreescu said, a regime has to loosen up slightly before there can be organized dissent. The Soviet Union had no Sakharovs while Stalin lived.

But I can give only a paraphrased account of what he said. As soon as I left his building and set out for the street, I heard rapid footsteps falling on the pavement behind me. I picked up my pace, and the footsteps behind me broke into a run. Two young men, dressed in open-necked sport shirts and jeans, caught up with me and grabbed my arms. One of them pulled out a billfold and flashed a badge. An unmarked white car pulled up beside us, and they bundled me into the backseat. We sped off.

The two plainclothesmen, as well as the driver, all began demanding information at once, one in Romanian, one in French, and one in broken English. Who was I? What was I doing? Who had sent me to Andreescu? I showed them my passport and declined to respond. In a few minutes, the car pulled up at a local police station. The trio escorted me through the front door, past a desk sergeant. Behind him, I could see the bars of jail cells. We went upstairs, into what appeared to be a lecture room for the members of the precinct, with rows of students' desks, a long, low counter at the front, and a portrait of Ceausescu, the one with the kind smile, hanging on the wall. The French speaker, who said his name was Edward, offered me a cigarette, and, with a worldly shrug, apologized for the necessity of searching me. He took my wallet, my traveling bag, and all the scraps of paper he could find in my pockets. The other two emptied the wallet and the bag, making neat piles on the counter of my tape cassettes, including the one with Andreescu's interview, and those notes which I had not already sent out of the country. They examined everything quite thoroughly, probing my credit cards for tiny compartments and holding them up to the light to look for secret writing.

Edward informed me that I would have to go with them for more questioning. We got into the white car and drove through the darkened streets into central Bucharest, to a building with no sign over the door. As we arrived, another unmarked car pulled up, and three men in suits got out. The trio in suits took me into a small room off the lobby of the building. In one corner, curiously enough, was a pile of old license plates. Two of the suits sat behind a table, placing my belongings on it. The third, a pudgy man with curly hair, sat beside me on a straight-backed chair. The oldest of the three, a short man with black hair and a bulbous nose, began asking questions in Romanian. The one sitting beside him translated into English. Who was I, really? Whom was I working for? Who had given me Andreescu's address?

I replied that I had received the address in a telephone call from an emigrants' group in Paris. Where, the interrogator wanted to know, had I gotten the photocopy of the Bucharest city map, with Andreescu's street circled in red ink? I replied that I had copied it from a book in the Library of Congress. Already, the interrogator said, I was contradicting myself, saying first that I had gotten the address from some emigrants, and then from the Library of Congress. He looked rather pleased with his deduction.

I said that there was no contradiction, that his translator obviously was not accurately conveying what I said, and that I would prefer to answer no more questions until they produced a professional interpreter. The translator stiffened, glowered, and raised his voice. "You know very good the American police!" he shouted. "You do not want to know the Romanian police!" I said that I took his point.

I was, the interrogator said gravely, guilty of violating Romanian law regarding the activities of tourists. Tourists were supposed to go to museums, or ride buses through the Transylvanian mountains. They were not supposed to interview dissidents. I made a brief argument that the Helsinki Final Act encouraged contacts between people. The interrogator did not seem impressed. I would, he said, come with them.

They put me into the same white car and took me to my hotel. One of them spoke to the desk clerk, who nodded and began preparing my bill. Another went upstairs. After a few minutes, the interrogator and the translator took me upstairs to my room, where they confiscated all the film and tape cassettes they could find. Then they gave me back my belongings, minus the notes, film, and cassettes, and told me to pack. They watched carefully as I obeyed. Down in the lobby, I paid my bill. Then it was back into the white car, this time to Ottopeni Airport, north of the city.

It was ten thirty, and the day's last flight out of the country had already left. The terminal was dim and quiet; a few people slept on chairs in the waiting room. A few janitors were cleaning up. Two plainclothesmen, the pudgy one in the suit and one of the original arresting officers, took me to the diplomatic waiting room, a stuffy place with red chairs and sofas and gold-colored curtains covering the walls. I would, the one in the suit told me, buy a ticket for the first flight out the next morning, which happened to go to Berlin. I agreed.

That done, my guards became quite hospitable. Was I hungry? The man in the suit took me up to the airport cafeteria. It was closed, but he spoke to a woman who was cleaning up. In a few minutes, she put a plate of steak and eggs in front of me and refused my offer to pay.

It was the first steak I had seen in Romania. I told my escort that I hoped he and his colleagues would not hold the evening's events against Gabriel Andreescu, since I had initiated the meeting without Andreescu's knowledge or consent. The man in the suit waved a hand, as if Andreescu's fate was a matter of little or no consequence. Andreescu, after all, was mentally ill.

When I had finished eating, the man in the suit took me back to the diplomatic waiting room. He was going home, he said, and leaving me under the supervision of the remaining plainclothesman. This was a wiry, slender man in his thirties, dressed in a yellow shirt and corduroy pants. I remembered him shouting questions at me in bad English on the ride to the police station, then poking suspiciously through my wallet and credit cards. But when we were alone, he smiled diffidently, and when I asked him his name, he told me: Marcu.

I asked him why, if they were watching Andreescu's apartment, they had waited until I was leaving to arrest me, rather than stopping me on my way in.

"I am sorry," Marcu said. "Those were the orders."

In the waiting room, I took off my shoes, stretched out on a couch, and tried to sleep. But the lights were on, and I could find no switch to turn them off. So I lay on the couch, unable to sleep, listening to the rumbling sounds of engines as maintenance trucks and an occasional airplane moved about on the runway outside. After perhaps half an hour, Marcu stuck his head in the door.

"Do you not want to sleep?" he asked, politely.

Perhaps later, I said.

"You would like to talk?"

Whatever suited him.

So Marcu came into the room and sat on the armrest of a chair opposite my couch. He seemed to be thinking for a moment, perhaps composing words in an unfamiliar language.

"How do you live in America?" he asked.

And he listened intently, a small, wistful smile playing at his lips, while I described my house in the United States and all the rooms in it.

MOSCOW

November 1989

Even two years into the era of *glasnost,* there remained in the Soviet Union a few sensitive questions best raised obliquely; the theater was a place where people could raise them that way. It may be that the cultural bureaucracy treated the theater a little more permissively because few people saw plays, in comparison to the numbers who saw television, films, and newspapers. Perhaps it simply respected a great Russian tradition. At the turn of the century, for instance, Chekhov's *The Cherry Orchard* sounded the death knell for the Russian autocracy without ever saying so directly. In the Brezhnev years, director and playwright Yuri Lyubimov carried the tradition forward at the Taganka Theater in Moscow. A few of his plays, notably *The Master and Margarita* and *House on the Embankment,* provided perhaps the only public forums in the country where people could hear honesty about Stalinism and its legacy—without ever hearing Stalin's name, of course.

The future of the Soviet Empire fell into that category of sensitive questions during the first few years of the Mikhail Gorbachev era. Gorbachev encouraged debate about domestic policies and even permitted criticism of the Soviet misadventure in Afghanistan. But the worth of the empire, and Moscow's ability to maintain it, remained beyond the realm of public discourse until December 17, 1987, when a play called *The Peace of Brest* opened at the Vakhtangov Theater, a beautifully restored old building on Moscow's new pedestrian mall, the Arbat. The premiere represented a triumph for one faction in the ruling elite and a defeat for another. Someone had arranged for the playwright, Mikhail Shatrov, to have access to hitherto secret archival material about the Treaty of Brest-Litovsk, by which Lenin, in 1918, had ended Russian involvement in World War I. According to some of my friends in Moscow, others in the ruling circle managed to keep the play in rehearsal for two years before Shatrov and the Vakhtangov got permission to present it to the public. Once on the boards, it became an instant hit. When I saw it, late in 1989, the Vakhtangov was still adding extra performances to its schedule to accommodate the demand for tickets.

It was easy to see why some members of the leadership would have preferred to suppress it. *The Peace of Brest* depicts a difficult time just after the Russian Revolution. Lenin and his comrades debate an agonizing choice forced on them by the Germans. Do they accept a ruinous peace that would strip away one-third of the population of the old czarist empire, including the Ukraine, Poland, Finland, and the Baltic states? Or do they fight on, relying on the workers in Germany and other capitalist states to join them and ignite the world revolution that, in those days, Russian communists expected to break out at any moment? The play reveals, for the first time, some of the details of the dissension within the Central Committee.

"Are we to give up the Estonians and the Ukrainians?" Nikolai Bukharin demands furiously, his tone suggesting clearly that betraying those proletarians would be tantamount to treason.

Sadly, Lenin insists that for the sake of preserving the revolution, they must indeed give them up. It is, for him, an agonizing dilemma. But at the end of Act One, his mind is made up. Raising his eyes and his arms skyward, he cries out: "We must save the Russian Revolution!" By threatening to resign from the government, he gets his way.

Shatrov's point—and, presumably, that of his Kremlin patrons—was plain. No one in the audience needed reminding that,
some seventy years after the Treaty of Brest-Litovsk, both Russia
and a Russian revolution had again come on difficult times, and
Russians again faced a choice. And again the choice boiled down to
saving a revolution—the democratic one Gorbachev had begun—or
saving Russia's empire.

The Russians are by no means the first people to establish an
empire on the land the Soviet Union now occupies. Over the centuries, since before the existence of people called Russians, many
peoples have established dominion over greater or lesser parts of
the broad plain that straddles Europe and Asia. Cimmerians, Scythians, Sarmatians, Goths, Huns, Bulgars, Avars, and Khazars held
sway over greater or lesser parts of what is now Russia, for periods
of up to four hundred years. Then they fell to new conquerors and
disappeared from history, leaving little except their names, some
shards of armor and pottery, and their genes, subsumed into the
larger pool through enslavement, rape, and assimilation.

Because the land was broad and open, the Russian plain was
a jungle of almost feral competition among the people who inhabited
it. A tribe or group of tribes, perhaps with roots in the West, would
establish a civilization based on agriculture. Sooner or later a hungry
band of nomadic warriors would appear, most often riding out of the
East, from Mongolia and what is now Central Asia. The nomads
would fall upon the town people like hungry wolves preying on
sheep, pillaging and riding on or, in some instances, usurping their
places. If the nomads chose to take up settled life, after a few
generations they would fall to the next band of hungry warriors.

Beginning in the second century before Christ, the nomads of
Mongolia and Central Asia gained a decisive advantage in this semi-
permanent warfare. This was, oddly enough, by means of an invention that today seems rudimentary: the stirrup. Stirrups gave
horsemen the ability to fight and ride simultaneously. With stirrups,

horsemen became cavalry troops, and, for the next fifteen hundred years or so, cavalry troops determined the outcome of most battles on the plain of what is now the Soviet Empire. The nomads rode from childhood; unless they quickly developed the ability to hunt and kill, they starved. They became the world's greatest mounted warriors, and the sedentary peoples of the plain could rarely match them in battle. Under leaders like Jenghiz Khan, they rode to the gates of Western Europe, conquering everything in their path.

But the nomads' genius for warfare did them little good when they had to administer what they had conquered. This meant that periods of loose rule and anarchy generally followed a period of conquest. And in one of those ebb periods between the tides of Mongol conquest, the Russian people appeared.

There is no scholarly consensus about the origins of the Russians. A collection of tribes, referred to by linguists as the East Slavs, appeared in what is now Russia and the Ukraine, perhaps as early as the time of the Scythians. These early Russians fought against the Goths, the Avars, and other invaders; to some they paid tribute. According to the earliest Russian chronicle, whose accuracy is open to question, they numbered twelve tribes, living in 238 towns, by the ninth century after Christ. Finns and Lithuanians occupied some of the same territory, and the Slavs quarreled among themselves.

According to the chronicle, a delegation of these Slavs traveled West in the year 862: "They went overseas to the Varangian Russes. These particular Varangians were known as Russes, just as some are called Swedes and others Normans, Angles, and Goths. [The Slavs] then said to the people of Rus, 'Our whole land is great and rich, but there is no order in it. Come to rule and reign over us.' " If this chronicle is true, the Russian people sprang from Slavic tribes and received their name from a Scandinavian or Northern European prince called Rurik, the Varangian whom they invited to impose order. Over time they became a people of infinitely mixed ancestry, an amalgam of the original Slavs and all the tribes and peoples they encountered in battle.

Some modern Russian historians suggest that the anonymous authors of this chronicle distorted or fabricated the truth to provide their patrons with a politically expedient history. Given the Soviet attitude toward history, their skepticism is understandable. Whatever the case, the first known Russian civilization appeared in the ninth century, at about the time the chronicles offer. It was centered in Kiev, in what is now the Ukraine.

From the outset, the rulers of Kiev engaged, whether they wanted to or not, in the rule-or-be-ruled struggle for existence of the Russian plain. They fought against new waves of nomads from the East: the Magyars, ancestors of the modern Hungarians, and the Pechenegs, a Turkic tribe. They fought against other Slavs, bringing them into the Russian fold. They fought against Bulgars and Khazars and Alans, people living along the Volga River. They fought against the Finns and the Lithuanians. They fought against Constantinople and the Byzantine Empire, into whose ruling family they married, and from whom they took their alphabet and religion. Borders, in this period, were defined by the number of days a Kievan could safely ride from the capital. In the golden age of Kiev, the southern border was about two days' ride away.

Within two centuries, the Russian Empire of Kiev began to decline, weakened both by constant warfare and by struggles within the ruling family for the title of grand prince. The empire degenerated into a loose collection of principalities. And in the thirteenth century, when the next hungry band of invaders from the East appeared, it fell.

Jenghiz Khan, the legendary conqueror, swept into Russia in 1223. He died four years later, but his grandson, Batu Khan, completed the conquest between 1236 and 1242. He destroyed Kiev and pillaged as far west as the Adriatic Sea. This was the campaign that destroyed the original church at Alba Julia, Romania. According to the account of one Western European traveler of the time, at the site where Kiev once stood "we found lying in the field countless heads and bones of dead people . . . barely 200 houses stand there, and those people are held in the harshest slavery." Kievan Russia became a dominion of a Mongol empire established by Batu Khan and called the Golden Horde. While Western Europe prepared for the Renaissance, Russia languished under the Mongol yoke.

Moscow, at this time, was a minor principality on a tributary of the Volga, a Russian outpost in a region populated by Finnic tribes called the Ves, Meria, and Muroma. It controlled perhaps as much territory as the present city of Moscow covers; its princes, of course, paid tribute to the Golden Horde. They did not manage to build a stone-walled *kreml'*, or central fortress, until the fourteenth century. But their Kremlin, on the banks of the Moscow River, like the Tower of London on the Thames, became the kernel from which a great empire grew.

Gradually, beginning in the fourteenth century, the princes of Moscow accumulated land and wealth. They fought and conquered the lands of rival, equally small principalities. One of them married a daughter of the khan of the Golden Horde, gaining useful political favor, and another became the Horde's tax collector, extracting tribute from the other Russian princes. By 1380, the princes of Moscow had become preeminent among the Russian princes, and one of them, Dmitri Donskoi, fought the first successful Russian battle against the troops of the Golden Horde, abetted by the troops of Lithuania.

By the fifteenth century, Moscow had emerged as one of three serious pretenders to dominion over the area that is now the Soviet Union. The first, Lithuania, then controlled an empire that stretched from the Baltic to the Black Sea, covering much of the present Ukraine and Byelorussia, as well as western Russia itself. But the Lithuanians fell under the influence of the Poles, whose political system favored the power of individual nobles over that of the central government. Lithuanian decentralization, for instance, allowed its subject Russian towns and principalities to retain the Russian language and the Russian Orthodox church. Lithuania, as a consequence, grew weaker. The Golden Horde, the second pretender to what is now the Soviet Union, also suffered from disunity. It broke into three khanates between 1430 and 1466.

The princes of Moscow, by contrast, brooked no independence in the fiefs they conquered. Nobles in Russia owed lifelong military service to the center. It was, in the words of British historian Hugh Seton-Watson, a barracks state. And over the next few centuries, Moscow picked off pieces of the weakened Lithuanian and Mongol empires, one after another, and added them to Russia.

At about this period, military technology went through another revolution, and this time the revolution favored the Russians rather than the mounted warriors of Asia. This was a technological revolution; the invention of weapons such as artillery pieces neutralized the superiority of Mongol cavalry. Moscow was hardly a participant in the Western renaissance that fueled these innovations. But it was more open to the West and its ideas than the Mongols were. The first Russian army to conquer a Mongol khanate, at Kazan in 1552, employed a Danish demolitions expert to blow up the town's water supply and fortifications.

At about that time, during the reign of Ivan IV (the Terrible), the character of Muscovite expansion changed. Before Ivan's reign, Moscow had done its share of conquering and assimilating local tribes into the Russian people. But it campaigned principally to gather back the Russian people and land lost to the Mongols in the disastrous thirteenth century. In Ivan's reign, a monk named Sylvester first wrote to the czar that "thou shalt have dominion from sea to sea, and from the rivers unto the ends of the universe, and all temporal czars shall fall down before thee and all nations shall serve thee." Furthermore, Sylvester wrote, Ivan's triumphs would be "won by the people of God against the infidel." Armed with this ideology and tempered by its successful struggle for survival on the Eurasian plain, Moscow began a new phase of expansion, conquering and taking in nations that had never been Russian. Ivan launched campaigns of conquest into the Baltic region, into southern Russia and the Caucasus, and into Siberia.

Ivan's successors in the Romanov dynasty continued what he began. In 1648 the Ukraine asked for Russian protection against the Poles; in 1709 Peter the Great crushed a Ukrainian effort to break free from that protection. Peter also pushed the empire toward Finland, taking Estonia and the present Leningrad region from Sweden. He probed south in search of a warm-water port, reaching Baku, in Azerbaijan, and the Sea of Azov. Catherine the Great added the rest of the Ukraine, Byelorussia, and part of Poland to the empire during the partitions of 1793–1795. She also extended the protection of the empire to Georgia, a Christian kingdom across the Caucasus Mountains surrounded by Turks and Persians. That protection soon became annexation, and the emperors of the nineteenth century completed the conquest of the region, wresting present-day Armenia from Persia in 1828. They first took Bessarabia (the present Moldavia) from Turkey in 1812, at the end of one of no fewer than four wars fought with the Ottoman Empire in the nineteenth century. The campaigns against the Uzbeks, Khirgiz, and other nomads of Central Asia, descendants of the once-proud conquerors, continued almost into the twentieth century.

Many factors contributed to this endless drive to expand. Much has been written about the Russian need for ports that do not freeze in the winter, and the aggressive reflexes bred into the Russian consciousness by the years of Mongol dominion. It was also an age when any self-respecting European power aspired to an empire, when power and prestige were gauged by control of people and resources. Maritime powers like England, Spain, and France expanded overseas into the territories of primitive peoples in the Americas, Africa, and Australia. Russia, nearly landlocked, built its empire where it could. It was blessed with weak neighbors: the declining Ottoman, Hapsburg, and Chinese empires, fractured Poland, an isolationist Japan. The natural order of things seemed to require that an ascendant empire feed on pieces of declining empires. The idea that groups of people, nations, had the right to self-determination was a product of the eighteenth-century Enlightenment that spread slowly and fitfully across Western Europe and even more slowly into Russia.

The Bolsheviks, when they appeared on the scene at the turn

of this century, looked upon the Russian Empire with profound ambivalence. Their ideology told them that capitalism caused imperialism and that empires must disappear along with the economic system that had created them. In 1898 the precursor of the Soviet Communist Party condemned Russian subjugation of the empire's smaller nations and promised them self-determination in the then unlikely event that the communists ever attained power. Lenin looked favorably on some manifestations of national consciousness, notably the referendum by which Norway detached itself from Sweden in 1905.

But that same ideology professed that distinctions between nations are artificial, that the only real distinctions are between classes. Russian workers, it said, had more in common with Estonian workers than with Russian landlords. When the workers took power, national boundaries would become irrelevant. This gave the Bolsheviks ample justification for opposing liberation movements based on nationality rather than class. Besides, Lenin wrote, "big states afford indisputable advantages, both from the standpoint of economic progress and from that of the interests of the masses." He opposed the efforts of Polish workers to separate their homeland from the Russian Empire on those grounds.

When the Bolsheviks came to power in Russia, they inherited a rapidly decaying empire. In the Baltic, the Ukraine, and the Trans-Caucasus, national movements took advantage of the momentary anarchy to press for independence. In several cases, local councils declared independence and established governments. The Bolsheviks, from the beginning, resolved their ideological ambivalence about national rights in favor of central power. They paid lip service to the right of "free self-determination, including secession and the formation of independent states." But they also maintained that under the kind of system they planned to establish, no workers would care to secede. In reality, this ideology and its contradictions were not as important as the reach of the Red Army. In those regions the army was able to conquer, the Bolsheviks found local communist allies prepared to "invite" them in and preserve the notion that worker solidarity, rather than Russian arms, had kept the old czarist provinces tied to Russia. The only real question was whether these old provinces would be absorbed by Russia or transformed into "Soviet republics." The Bolsheviks resolved that decision on the basis of self-preservation. They decided to create a ring of buffer republics around Russia to insulate them from the capitalist counterattack they expected at any moment. Independent governments in the Ukraine, Armenia, Georgia, and other republics were snuffed out before they could establish membership in the League of Nations. In the Baltic region, British and German forces could and did counterbalance the Reds, allowing Latvia, Lithuania, and Estonia to establish governments that the Bolsheviks recognized with treaties in 1920.

When Lenin gave way to Stalin, the balance of Soviet policy tipped completely in the direction of central power. Lenin's policy had favored preserving local languages and recruiting and employing local communists as a way to ensure the loyalty of the various Soviet nationalities. Stalin, though himself a Georgian, imposed Russian as the language of business everywhere in the Soviet realm and relentlessly purged the national Party memberships and intelligentsia to root out the faintest hint of independence sentiment.

During the Second World War, Stalin proved himself a Russian empire builder worthy of Ivan the Terrible and Peter the Great. After concluding a secret agreement with Nazi Germany, he annexed Latvia, Lithuania, and Estonia, the republics that had managed to break away from the old empire after World War I; he also seized Bessarabia back from Romania. At war's end he added new dominions in Eastern Europe: Bulgaria, Romania, Hungary, Czechoslovakia, East Germany, and Poland. A few countries—notably Yugoslavia, China, and Albania—spent a brief period under Russian dominion, then spun out of Moscow's control. But Moscow kept its grip on the contiguous Eastern European countries and on the internal Soviet republics.

In retrospect, from the standpoint of a Russian intent of preserving Moscow's empire, it might be argued that Stalin's policies were not thorough enough. He relied on terror to keep the empire together, and, as long as he lived, and the state was prepared to inflict terror in infinite quantities, the empire seemed solid and immutable. But neither Stalin nor anyone else dared attempt to tear up the roots of national identity within the empire. That would have meant abolishing the republics and the independent Eastern European states and subsuming them into a greater Soviet Union, dispersing their populations, and making Russian the only legal language in the schools. Stalin did in fact do this with some of the smaller Caucasian nations: the Chechens, the Kalmyks, the Crimean Tartars, and others. But even he could not attempt such a thing on the scale that would have been required in nations such as Poland, the Ukraine, or even Estonia. Thus, he flouted the dictum of Machiavelli "He who becomes master of a city accustomed to freedom and does not destroy it can expect to be destroyed by it."

Stalin bequeathed to his successor several times removed, Mikhail Gorbachev, a sprawling empire that, like a radioactive isotope, was inherently unstable and prone to decay. The Eastern European countries had, of course, retained their formal independence even when they lived under Soviet suzerainty. Each of them harbored anti-Soviet feelings and movements of one kind or another. Within the Soviet Union itself the reality of life belied the official line that the Leninist nationalities policy had solved the problem once and for all.

In fact, the nationalities issue in the Soviet Union was a festering boil. The centuries of war, rape, assimilation, intermarriage, and migration had created a mess. It was hard even to define a nation or isolate one on the map. Too many people had a marauding Swede or Mongol somewhere in their ancestry to use a genetic standard. Religion defined nothing; there were Protestant Latvians and Catholic Latvians, Orthodox Ukrainians and Uniate Ukrainians. Language did not always delineate a nation; the mother tongue of many Soviet

Jews was Russian, but that did not make them any less Jewish. Links to a particular piece of land did not define a nation, because Stalin had deprived some nations of their land. Ultimately, there was only one definition acceptable to everyone: a nation would be any group of people that thought of itself as a nation and demanded its national rights.

The untidy, Darwinian history of the land ensured that the game of national assertion in the Soviet Union had an almost unlimited number of players and potential conflicts, and that no rule or set of rules could be applied to the region to produce a settlement that would be satisfactory, or even fair, to everyone. The simple principles of self-determination and secession could not even begin to resolve all the potential difficulties. The U.S. State Department, at one point in the late 1980s, compiled a map showing thirty-one regions where two or more nationalities claimed the same piece of land. Many minority republics had yet smaller minorities living within their borders. And while Azeri nationalists, to take one example, might scream for their right to self-determination and secession, they would shed blood in copious amounts to prevent the Armenian majority in the Nagorno-Karabakh region from exercising the same right.

The history of the land offered no solace to a Soviet leader. It suggested strongly that empires which became loose or federal— Kiev, the Golden Horde, Lithuania—quickly crumbled and became themselves subjects of stronger empires. Moreover, by the time Gorbachev emerged as the Soviet leader, it was slowly becoming clear that the late twentieth century had evolved into one of those rare and important eras when a change in military technology fundamentally altered the balance and nature of power on the Eurasian plain, just as had the invention of the stirrup, which gave the advantage to nomadic warriors from the East, and the invention of artillery and other engines of war, which helped the settled civilizations of the West. The third watershed event in military technology was the invention of nuclear weapons. When the United States dropped an atomic bomb on Hiroshima in 1945, it ended not only World War II but also the era of the Russian Empire.

This is because the nuclear weapon has changed, in a perverse way, the role of military power in world affairs. In ancient times, when a civilization acquired a new and decisive military technology, it almost immediately put that technology to work conquering its neighbors and confiscating their wealth. War paid.

Nuclear technology was different. It soaked up large amounts of money for the construction of missiles and warheads. But its very power made it unusable. More than that, the existence of nuclear weapons made even conventional war between powers with nuclear weapons unthinkable, because of the chance that such a war might escalate into a nuclear conflict. The existence of nuclear weapons and intercontinental ballistic missiles made the old concept of buffer states between great powers obsolete. Nuclear weapons made military might a diminishing factor in the intercourse of nations.

Thus, although the poor Japanese in Nagasaki could not have realized it, they probably witnessed, on August 9, 1945, the last time military power and a technological military advantage played a decisive role in a clash between great powers. The future would belong not to militarily mighty nations but to nations, like those very Japanese, that excelled in putting technology to work for economic purposes. It took Russia and its neighbors almost forty-five years to comprehend this fully. Of course, a power like Russia could use its conventional military strength to subjugate smaller nations on its periphery. But it would gain no wealth from doing so, because in the late twentieth century wealth was increasingly becoming a product of unfettered intellect, not of the accumulation of lands.

And Russia could maintain or expand the empire only at the price of tension with the West that caused an escalation of economically useless military expenditure. Because of nuclear weapons, this tension could never be resolved by military means. Once the Russians and their neighbors realized this, the dissolution of the Soviet Empire became, perhaps, inevitable.

This, of course, could only be a profoundly disturbing prospect for any Russian familiar with his country's history. For once a process of dissolution began, where would it end? Even Russia was a territory patched together by ancient conquest, still harboring many indigenous peoples with national consciousnesses. The Soviet Empire was like a *matryoshka,* a brightly painted wooden doll that is a traditional Russian handicraft. A *matryoshka* has a seam at the waist. Open it up, and nested inside is another doll, slightly smaller. And inside that is another doll, and inside that is another, and so on, until finally you reach a core doll many, many times smaller than the *matryoshka*'s outer shell. Sitting behind the walls of the Kremlin, the kernel from which the Soviet Empire grew, no one could predict how much land would be left outside the walls when any process of disintegration finally ended.

Facing these realities squarely and resolving them would have taxed the wisdom and will of the most confident and optimistic of nations. And, in the fall of 1989, that was not the Soviet Union. Gloom enveloped Moscow, and all of Russia, like a thick fog. Although the supplies in Moscow's stores were, to my subjective eye, not all that much worse than they had been five years before, every Soviet woman with whom I spoke was convinced that the country was nearing a famine—that there was nothing to buy. The mass media for years had drummed into Soviet heads the not entirely credible but still vaguely reassuring notion that their system was gradually catching up to the West and in some respects surpassing it. Now it was gorging on self-criticism, intent on conveying just the opposite impression. I flipped on the television one night and saw, on the first channel, a documentary on farm life in Iowa so idyllic that the Des Moines Chamber of Commerce would have blushed to present it; the contrast with Soviet rural life could not have been greater. On the second channel, Vladimir Posner, moderating a panel discussion, pulled from his pocket a disposable syringe he had bought in the United States and grilled some uncomfortable bureau-crats about why the Soviet medical supply industry still could not turn out a similar product. (In at least one Soviet hospital, patients had contracted AIDS from syringes that were used and reused without proper sterilization.) On another evening, the state gave an hour of prime television time to a man named Anatoly Kashpirovsky, who purported to heal his viewers' ailments through psychic pow-ers. There was a sense that the whole society, depressed, was scavenging in the wreckage of Marxism-Leninism, searching for something to believe in. Even Gorbachev, from atop the Lenin Mausoleum at the November 7 parade celebrating the revolution, refrained from the traditional self-congratulation and talked about how tough times were.

I had dinner one evening during this time with Aleksandr Bovin, the foreign affairs columnist for *Izvestiya*. We ate in a setting that embodied change—a new, ccoperative restaurant called Lazaniya, which offered the first decent Italian cuisine Moscow had known in decades, if not forever. The proprietor, looking sporty in a tweed jacket, greeted us politely at the door and took our coats. He seated us at a candlelit table in a room with dark green walls, and an attentive young woman in a short black skirt, named Tanya, took our order. The chef, I had heard, had worked for years in the Soviet embassy in Rome. Clearly he had learned something there; the spaghetti *alla carbonara* had a smoky, bacony taste, and the veal was tender. Where it had come from, I could only guess. To some-one like me, Lazaniya represented progress, thanks to *perestroika*. Bovin, I suspect, cared more than I that the room we ate in was open only to people able to pay with foreign credit cards, something ordinary Soviets cannot have. In a small way, the place reflected the way that *perestroika* had impressed foreigners more than it had changed the existence of the average Russian.

As we ate, Czech students were filling Wenceslas Square in Prague to demand the resignation of their government. The Berlin Wall had just been breached. Solidarity ruled in Poland, and Hungarians were debating whether to elect a president or a parliament first. In short, the postwar order in which the Soviet Union had invested so much blood and treasure was disappearing like a sand castle under a rising tide. Moscow was responding to all this phlegmatically, with none of the symptoms of previous crises in the socialist camp—no tendentious and ominous newspaper articles, no grim emissaries going from the Politburo to the hinterlands to restore orthodoxy. While there were plenty of people who were anxious over the possibility of German reunification, Bovin was not one of them. He said simply that he hoped the Germans would act cautiously, and peacefully. And when I asked him what principles were guiding Soviet policy through this time of upheaval, he replied by quoting not Marx, or Lenin, but an aphorism that once hung above the sink in my mother's kitchen: "God grant me the courage to change the things I can, the wisdom to accept the things I can't, and the common sense to know the difference."

The sense of fatalism and fatigue that Bovin expressed toward the erstwhile Soviet dominions sprang from several factors. One of the most important, obviously, was the aftershock of the Soviet misadventure in Afghanistan. Although the eventual outcome of the Afghan civil war remains in doubt, there is no question that, despite ten years of struggle, the Soviet Army failed to complete its mission there. With the possible exception of the Winter War against Finland in 1939–40 (a military debacle that nevertheless captured territory), this had never happened to the Soviet Union before. From the Civil War of 1918–1921 to the invasion of Czechoslovakia in 1968, the army had lost some battles, but it had always won its wars.

Lost wars have generally caused Russian society to look inward, to examine itself critically, and to launch reforms. The Crimean War, lost at the end of Nicholas I's reign, led to a series of reforms under his successor, Alexander II, including the emancipation of the Russian serfs. The lost war to Japan in 1905 was followed by a popular uprising and a brief period of reform. And, of course, the Russian debacle in World War I led directly to the Russian

Revolution of 1917. Although comparisons between the American experience in Vietnam and the Soviet experience in Afghanistan are imprecise at best, there is no question that Afghanistan, like Vietnam, shook the Soviets' faith in the use of force. Like the other lost Russian wars, it also shook their faith in the wisdom of their government.

I had a chance to talk about this with a recently retired Soviet general, Ivan Dmitrievich Yershov. In all respects but one, General Yershov had followed the path of an entire generation of senior Soviet officers. He was a cadet in the late 1930s, when ominous black cars periodically came and spirited away the senior officers at his military academy. He stifled his questions about it. He fought through to victory in the Second World War, then stayed in the army. He went into Czechoslovakia, and he served along the Afghan border during the war there. In retirement he was a burly man with thick, white hair and a firm grip who still looked capable of leading men into battle.

His daughter, Tatiana, however, did not follow the path prescribed for the children of general officers. She fell in love with a man, Edward Lozansky, who wanted to emigrate, and did so in the 1970s. Yershov, under pressure from his superiors, refused to allow his daughter to follow him. There were years of painful struggle within the family before the general relented and gave his permission. When I spoke with him, the family had reconciled, and the experience had influenced the general. In retirement he had become willing, albeit reluctantly, to discuss things that most of his comrades, however much they might share his views, would never speak of with a foreign journalist. I asked him about the invasion of Czechoslovakia. He settled back on a sofa and remembered.

"We were told that counterrevolutionary forces were preparing a turn backward, that extremists from West Germany were infiltrating the country, that the republic was in danger, and that the people of the republic were asking our help. We had no basis for protesting our orders," he said. "But when we got there, in the first hours we could see that the situation was quite the opposite, that the people were indignant and rebellious and unhappy with our intervention. Each of us began to think, to one degree or another, 'How can this be? Why are we here?' Because, of course, they weren't waiting for us. They hadn't asked for our help."

The officers and men reacted in a variety of ways, beginning with anger. "We got angry at the fact that we didn't know the true situation. Where were our representatives on the Warsaw Pact general staff? Where was our embassy? Why did they spread disinformation? We weren't prepared for what we found. We didn't have loudspeakers or translators so we could tell the Czechs we hadn't come to occupy them, that we came at their request."

There was also anger at the Czech people. "They weren't friendly. They destroyed bridges, turned road signs around, and when you talked to them they were hostile, especially the young people with their long hair. They tried to provoke us." He smiled tightly. "It's one thing if a girl flips her skirt up and shows her ass to a soldier. The soldier can laugh at that. But when they spit in his face, or throw tomatoes or rocks at him—that causes a reaction. You think, 'These must be the counterrevolutionaries.' "

But the army's anger and surprise in Czechoslovakia did not, of course, lead to much open resistance. Yershov remembered that a few soldiers demanded explanations from their officers. Occasionally, he and his fellow generals might discuss, over a cup of coffee, some of the specific problems in information and preparation. But he could not recall conversations in which anyone suggested that the army's mission in Czechoslovakia was inherently aggressive and unjust. It was too soon for that kind of conversation in a generation that vividly remembered the black cars taking officers away from the military academy to be shot. Moreover, the intervention ended quickly and, superficially at least, successfully. In the Soviet Union, as in nearly all nations, a quick military success is the best safeguard against dissent. "We figured all's well that ends well, that our presence had stabilized things, and that the socialist camp had stabilized the peace. But I personally still had doubts."

Eleven years later, Soviet troops entered Afghanistan and stayed there long enough for the seeds of doubt sown in Czechoslovakia to mature and blossom. "I served along the Afghan border for six years," Yershov recalled. "I know what kind of tough conditions there were. I got sick. Anyone from the North did. And when it was done, I had the same questions. 'Why are we doing this?' And we had the same disinformation and lack of *glasnost.* The same decision making at the top—by Suslov, Brezhnev, Andropov, and Ustinov. We still don't know exactly who decided.

"If the Czech events didn't become fully a lesson for the leadership and the Party, then Afghanistan did. We went there without detailed study. We didn't know why and what for. The decision was taken undemocratically. That's all part of the mistake. We never should have gone into another sovereign country, under any circumstances. It's wrong. It's meddling in the internal affairs of another country, just as you [Americans] did in Vietnam and Grenada. And it cost us very dearly."

As a result, Yershov said, the Soviet people would no longer trust their leadership to make decisions about war and peace on its own, as the Brezhnev generation had done. "It's impossible to trust the men at the top. Now the Supreme Soviet has a permanent committee on defense and security which will have to approve. And the people feel we can't have any more Afghanistans. It's forbidden."

Still, it seemed to me that even if the Soviets democratized their decision-making processes, and even if Afghanistan had left them leery of military intervention, the fundamental interests that had led the czars and Stalin to push the boundaries of empire westward would remain. Russia was still a nation on a plain, exposed to attack. I asked Yershov whether it would not always want a buffer zone in Eastern Europe.

"After World War II, we were frightened, and we wanted to fortify our borders," he replied. "Bitter experience had taught us that. We thought such a zone was justified by military strategy." After forty-plus years, though, the Soviet concept of security had changed, he insisted. If Gorbachev asked him what was required to defend the Motherland against attack, Yershov said, he would reply, "We have to respect the will of people to live as they want. We have to respect democracy, mutual trust, and cooperation. That's the basis for preventing any catastrophe."

Yershov did not want to see the Warsaw Pact dissolve instantly, but he said he would favor the gradual dismantling of both military blocs. If one of the Eastern European countries decided to leave the bloc, he said, "It's their right." He feared a reunified Germany and wanted to see it only "when the common European home is filled with trust and cooperation. Why should the German people be divided? It's not natural. Now, though, there's still too much mistrust."

It felt odd to hear a Soviet officer expressing some of the ideas and ideals of the old American peace movement, and of course Yershov did not represent all officers. His life had exposed him to ideas that most of his comrades had never had to confront. But there has always been a strong romantic streak in the Russian character, a streak that tempers the nation's fear and suspicion of outsiders with a yearning for universal brotherhood. I could hear that streak in what Yershov said. And in conversations with other Russians, I heard some pragmatic ideas that buttressed the new disinclination toward intervention.

I spoke with Andrei Kortunov in his office at the Institute of U.S.A. and Canada Studies on Khlebny Pereulok in central Moscow. I had first met him in the mid-1980s, when he was a junior scholar. A few years later he had been promoted to an administrative role in the institute, and his views were being publicized in books and round-table discussions. He was still boyish and red haired, but he was obviously a rising star in the Soviet foreign policy elite.

As far as Kortunov was concerned, the idea of a deep buffer zone in Eastern Europe became obsolete with the development of nuclear weapons and the delivery vehicles to lob them over the buffer and into the Soviet heartland. It just had taken Soviet political leaders a long time to understand that; in fact, understanding only came with the death of the Brezhnev generation, whose thinking had been formed by the Nazi invasion as surely as the lessons of Munich and Pearl Harbor (don't risk appeasement and beware of sneak attacks) had informed the thinking of its American contemporaries. The long struggle with the West over intermediate-range ballistic missiles drove the point home in the early 1980s. In the absence of détente (in large part because of the invasion of Afghanistan and the deployment of SS-20 missiles aimed at Europe), Moscow could not prevent NATO from deploying a new generation of nuclear missiles in West Germany. Those missiles reduced Soviet warning time against a nuclear attack. To the new generation of Soviet foreign policy experts, including Kortunov, it became clear that the old policy of maintaining and expanding a buffer zone not only had failed to maintain Soviet security but in fact had diminished it. Only a renewed détente, restraining the arms competition with the technologically superior West, was likely to enhance Soviet security. And the Soviets could not expect a renewed détente as long as they insisted on forcing their system on unwilling neighbors in Eastern Europe.

That did not mean, Kortunov said, that Moscow expected the Warsaw Pact to dissolve, or that it saw no military role for the Soviet Union in Eastern Europe. In the future, however, he believed that role would be based on common geopolitical interests. Poland and Czechoslovakia, for instance, occupy lands that at one time or another have belonged to Germany. Even at the time of our conversation, when East Germany still existed, it was clear that sometime in the near future Germany would reunify, and grow richer and more influential. And, given those probabilities, it was at least possible that Germany would start to think again about its old territories to the east. Only the Soviet Union could protect Poland and Czechoslovakia against that possibility. Only the Soviet Union could undertake to protect Hungary against a Romanian government that, at least until the overthrow of Nicolae Ceausescu, seemed capable of gross miscalculation and aggression.

Moreover, Kortunov said, the countries of Eastern Europe had natural economic interests in good relations with the Soviet Union that would survive regardless of their internal political orientation. They depended on Soviet oil and gas. Over the years of enforced cooperation, many of their factories had become dependent on the Soviet market. "We're organically tied," he said. Only an irrational policymaker in Eastern Europe would advocate a rupture of relations with the Soviets. Kortunov believed it possible that as Eastern Europe threw off the Soviet system, irrational policies were possible. "But I believe that possibility has crested."

There was more to the Soviet retrenchment than belated appreciation of the capabilities of nuclear missiles. For some years, Western specialists had been adding up what was known about the Soviet Union's trade with its Eastern European allies (which, along with Cuba, Vietnam, and Mongolia, made up the Council for Mutual Economic Assistance, or CMEA) and scratching their heads. In the classic empire, the metropolitan power enriches itself by buying cheap raw materials in the provinces or colonies and selling back its surplus manufactured goods at high prices. The Soviet Empire, in the years immediately following World War II, indeed enriched the Soviet Union. The Soviets claimed billions of dollars' worth of factory equipment and other property as war reparations from Germany. One scholar, Karen Dawisha of the University of Maryland, estimated that the Soviets extracted $14 billion from Eastern Europe. But, beginning in the late 1950s, the pattern of trade shifted.

To the Soviets' credit, this was partly a result of design. They could have dictated harsher terms of trade. They might, for instance, have required their allies to pay in hard currency for the oil and raw materials they received from the Soviet Union. Instead, they accepted barter goods or currencies that were worthless outside the CMEA. They might have charged the full market price for their products. Instead, they negotiated a price based on the production cost to the Soviet Union, and they locked that price in for each five-year planning period. And, in some instances, they agreed to pay far more than the world price for the goods they bought—Cuban sugar, for example.

To the Soviet leaders of the Brezhnev and Khrushchev eras, this system represented a vast improvement over the exploitative, market-oriented terms of trade dictated by Western countries. It proved the superiority of the socialist system. And because, as Marxists, they defined an empire in economic terms, it proved that the Soviet Union had no empire.

This system also began to drain the Soviet economy, particularly in the 1970s. As world oil prices doubled and redoubled, the Soviets continued almost to give away their oil to Eastern Europe. Every barrel sent to Eastern Europe, of course, represented an increasing number of foregone dollars. In 1983 the Rand Corporation published a study, directed by Charles Wolf, of the costs of the Soviet Empire. The Rand experts calculated that the Soviets' subsidies to the other communist countries, including donated weaponry, rose from 8.6 billion rubles in 1971 to 42.2 billion in 1980. As a percentage of Soviet gross national product, this represented 1.60–1.90 percent in 1971 and 6.10–7.20 percent in 1980. (The figures are approximate because the published data on Soviet trade were so sketchy.) By contrast, the United States spent about 0.37 percent of its GNP on all forms of aid to its allies during the 1970s. In the 1980s, the relative cost diminished somewhat. The CMEA revised its oil-pricing formula, and the price of oil within the empire began to catch up to the world price. Still, Wolf told me in an interview, the Soviets continued to spend 2.00–3.00 percent of their GNP in subsidies to their allies as the decade ended.

Until *glasnost* Western specialists understood this better than the Soviet leaders. I spoke with Aleksandr Shokhin, a sandy-haired, nearsighted young economist from the Ministry of Foreign Affairs whose eyeglass lenses seemed to be about a quarter of an inch thick. I asked whether he was familiar with the Rand study. "We have quite a lot of that kind of research," he replied. "Of course, it's true that we redistribute to these countries through lower prices." But, Shokhin went on, in the Brezhnev period, opportunity cost (the dollars foregone by sending cheap oil, for instance, to socialist countries) did not enter the Politburo's calculations. "It wasn't a problem then," he said. "Our production was rising. The world price was rising [for that portion of Soviet exports which went to the world market]. We had a lot of hard currency, and we didn't have to worry about relations with our allies. We could lose several billion dollars, but it was not considered burdensome. Only specialists spoke about it." To the political leaders of the country, "it was important that our oil price for the socialist camp was lower than the capitalist world's price and that the difference increased year by year. There were some who considered it an advantage of the socialist system that we can have stable prices and not depend on market fluctuations." As far as the Brezhnev leadership was concerned, it was enough that in the 1970s and early 1980s there were dollars in the till at the end of every year. As for the fact that there might have been many more dollars, "We closed our eyes to it," Shokhin said.

The pre-Gorbachev leadership closed its eyes to a great deal. I visited one day with Aleksandr Tsipko, the deputy director of the Institute for International Economic and Political Studies, the Moscow think tank that, among other things, pays special attention to what used to be called the countries of "the socialist camp." Tsipko is a kindly, heavyset man in his late forties. He had worked for twenty years in the institute, in the government, or in Eastern Europe. During the rise of Solidarity in Poland, in the late 1970s and early 1980s, he had lived in Warsaw, writing and observing what went on.

I asked Tsipko if he had ever, during those years, felt that the fall of the Communist Party was inevitable.

"It was clear then that this was an impractical system, planted there by force, and doomed," he said. "But, to be honest, there were nevertheless illusions that the system could be saved through reform into a social democratic system—the old Czech illusions about the possibility of the gradual development of those totalitarian structures into a social democratic state. I had these illusions, and I reported them and the fact that the current system was doomed to Oleg Bogomolov, the director here. I wrote it up at the end of 1980. I still have the text. It was never published. As far as I know, Bogomolov transmitted my report to Brezhnev's aides. And they responded: 'He's right. But hide the report.' I don't think Brezhnev or [Foreign Minister Andrei] Gromyko ever read it."

In the last Brezhnev years, the aging Soviet leadership not only brooked no dissent but also discouraged the expression of views, like Tsipko's, that came from loyal Party members who wanted not to overthrow the system but to reform it, so that it could survive. It was not complete repression, and it was not as brutal as Stalin's. Tsipko actually was invited to speak about Poland, at closed meetings, by both the KGB and the Central Committee staff. "Everyone agreed with me," he recalled, "that this was a long-term crisis of authority, that it was necessary to immediately establish contacts with Solidarity. But I understood that while everyone agreed with me, ideological fear was much stronger. To advocate opening contacts with Solidarity would have involved stepping over the limits. Someone would have said, 'How can we refuse to help our fraternal communist party?' and so on.

"This, I understood later, is the tragedy of all communist leaders. They can't receive advice. They're ready to perish rather than take a decision that exceeds the bounds of their thinking. Any worker at the Ministry of Foreign Affairs, the KGB, or the Central Committee who would have risked taking a stand for such a point of view would have completely risked his career. That was the tragedy of our apparat. Everyone acted only within the limits of revealed truth, and for that he got the opportunity to live for a time abroad, to have a few benefits. And that is how, from the state point of view, we stumbled into all those crises: Hungary in 1956, Czechoslovakia in 1968, Poland in 1980."

Tsipko suffered for expressing his views, even to the limited degree that he did express them. For several years, he could not work on Polish affairs. He could not travel abroad. Worse, his doctorate, which he had earned in Poland, was not recognized in Moscow. He did not get it until several years into the Gorbachev era, and then not until he had written another book.

Of course, the system suffered more from the suppression of people like Aleksandr Tsipko than Tsipko himself did. For all its intelligence agents and diplomats and soldiers stationed in Eastern Europe, the Kremlin actually knew less about the real state of affairs there than any of the Westerners who had dropped in on Poland during the Solidarity crisis. It knew only what its ideology allowed it to know, as Tsipko found out in 1986. With the passing of Brezhnev and his generation, Mikhail Gorbachev began to fill up the apparat with fresh minds. One of those invited to work in the Central Committee was Aleksandr Tsipko, who became part of the staff that prepared policy for Eastern Europe.

"The division I worked in was one of the most intelligent. It was full of people with high intellectual and human qualities," he recalled. They were moralists, dismayed with the Soviet interventions in Czechoslovakia, Afghanistan, and, if they were old enough to remember it clearly, Hungary. For years they had nurtured ties with the men of their generation who were rising through the ranks of the communist parties of Eastern Europe, and, often over drinks, in the privacy of an apartment or a dacha, convinced themselves that they would do better when their turn came. Now their turn had come. But they had a very imprecise understanding of the empire they had been called to administer.

"There was still an illusion that free communist parties would be able to get control of the situation," Tsipko recalled. "Everyone thought that if the Soviet Communist Party would only stop controlling the ruling communist parties of Eastern Europe, then"—he stopped talking, snorting quietly at the memory of their miscalculation—"they would have sufficient prestige and authority to control events. We thought that if you stopped propping up the old, conservative leadership in those ruling parties and moved away from traditional, orthodox communism to a more neutral Marxism, that those ruling parties could in that way win over the intelligentsia and strengthen their position. I believed it. Gorbachev believed it. A lot of people believed it. There was even a thesis, which I remember was discussed in 1987, that as part of this process, it was necessary to recognize a legal opposition. But no one thought that the opposition would win so easily in those countries."

So, Tsipko said, in this atmosphere of moral regeneration, of determination not to repeat the misadventure in Afghanistan, the Soviet leadership in 1988 came to the considered conclusion that it would henceforth not interfere in the affairs of its neighboring countries. At first, when I heard this account of the decision-making process, I was skeptical. It was so much at odds with the kind of decision making that I was accustomed to in Washington. In Washington, if political upheaval threatens a country regarded as an American asset, the policy discussion is almost entirely pragmatic and reactive. What is the situation "on the ground"? What tools does the United States have to influence it? If America intervenes militarily, will the job be done quickly and effectively? The Soviet leaders, I became convinced, did things differently, perhaps because of their heritage as the Party that believed in principles and theories that, properly deduced, could successfully guide the administration of government. They really had, in 1988, arrived at a nonintervention policy as a matter of principle.

This does not mean that there were not pragmatic factors at work. In the mid-1980s Soviet oil production leveled off and even dipped slightly. The country had depleted its cheap, easy oil reserves, and the new oil fields in Siberia would cost much more to exploit. Then the world oil price leveled off and declined. Those two events meant that Moscow could no longer meet its needs for hard currency simply by selling a little more oil for higher prices on the world market.

The problem of Poland also provided some sobering economic data. In 1981, to keep Poland quiet, the Soviets had to agree to major new trade subsidies. "Poland owes us about 6 billion rubles," Aleksandr Shokhin told me. "Since 1981, we've been helping them with subsidized trade that costs us several hundred million rubles per year. We give them oil and fuel at very low prices, and, at the same time, we pay a premium for Polish goods. Direct aid and loans are in addition to that." Maintaining subservient, orthodox communists in power in Eastern Europe was an increasingly costly proposition.

At the same time, the Soviets were growing more and more convinced, after four years of largely unsuccessful attempts to revitalize their economy from within, that their best hope lay in intense trade and cooperation with the West, the only source of the capital and technology they needed. By late 1989 this attitude was widespread. Even Yuri Zhukov, an octogenarian Stalinist who writes commentaries for *Pravda,* shared it. A few years earlier, whenever I had met Zhukov, he was likely to begin a conversation by reminding me that he remembered when the capitalist countries showed their true colors by sending troops to Russia in 1918 in an effort to stifle the Russian Revolution. But when I saw him in 1989, he brought up a different era, the era of rapid Soviet industrialization in the 1930s. That rapid industrialization was possible, he said, partly because the United States was suffering from the Depression and therefore eagerly sold the Soviets any items they wanted to buy. The implication was that, if the Soviets were to launch a new period of industrial progress, they would need the same kind of help from the West. Therefore, Gorbachev launched a concerted effort to persuade the United States and the NATO allies to dismantle the web of export controls and tariffs that had been erected since the

Cold War to inhibit Soviet access to the Western market and its sophisticated technology. And the Soviets realized that they could not expect growing economic cooperation if they were still perceived as an imperial power that kept order and discipline with tanks.

The Gorbachev leadership, in the end, adopted the nonintervention policy because they thought it was the right thing to do. They also thought doing the right thing would promote their economic interests, and morality is always strongest when it serves self-interest. But it was, first of all, a moral decision.

The Soviets could not and did not make a dramatic announcement of this. Since the days of Lenin, the Soviet government had espoused a policy of nonintervention. It would have been awkward, at best, to make an announcement that said, in effect, "This time we mean it." Gorbachev, by that time, had begun to talk of the "common European home." He had clearly established himself as a new kind of Soviet leader. But in Eastern Europe, there was a lot of skepticism. "We feel like we're in a dark room, groping for the walls," a Hungarian foreign policy specialist told me in mid-1989.

Then, in a rapid series of actions and omissions in the summer and autumn of 1989, Gorbachev made clear how broad the Eastern Europeans' room for maneuver had grown. He urged Poland's communists to enter a government led by Solidarity. He tacitly approved Hungary's decision to let East German citizens go to the West, whereupon the East German government fell and the Berlin Wall crumbled.

Throughout this period, I was told by a Politburo member, the consensus against nonintervention held firm. There were no debates about whether to allow one or another development to occur. As the empire bequeathed to them by Stalin began to unravel, the leaders of the Soviet Communist Party reacted by doing, essentially, nothing. In a speech to the Congress of Peoples' Deputies in late

1989, Prime Minister Nikolai Ryzhkov announced that Moscow wanted trade within the CMEA to move to a hard-currency, market-price basis in 1991. This was not an inflexible demand, a senior Foreign Ministry official said. Moscow had no wish to disrupt the economies of its neighbors.

A bit retroactively, the Soviets developed some ideological rationales to dress their new realism as orthodoxy. Largely for foreign consumption, there was Gorbachev's vague and slightly syrupy common European home, in which all the residents would master the "new thinking" and live peacefully together. For internal consumption, Dr. Nodari Simonia, of the Institute of World Economy and International Relations, published an article in the November 1989 issue of the theoretical Party journal *Kommunist* that attempted to explain why the failure of communism in erstwhile Soviet satellites did not discredit Marxist philosophy. Simonia harked back to the original predictions of Marx that communism would be born in the most developed capitalist countries. That prediction had proven inconvenient to Lenin and Stalin, taking power in a backward Russia, and they supplanted it with new theories to explain how the Soviet Union could bypass the stage of highly developed capitalism. But by 1989 the notion that the road to communism leads first to capitalism was convenient again. It suggested that if members of the socialist camp defected to capitalism, there was no cause for alarm. They were simply getting back on Marx's original road to utopia.

Some of the considerations that had led the Soviets to park their tanks during the Eastern European revolution still applied when they turned their attention to the next layer in the *matryoshka,* the restive peripheral republics of the Soviet Union itself. But a new set of concerns weighed in their calculations, concerns about whether the nation could remain a great power if it began to disintegrate. No one I spoke to in Moscow in late 1989 claimed to know how, in the final weighing of all these factors, the balance would be struck.

The post-Afghanistan aversion to military intervention persisted, at least in some quarters, as the leadership turned its attention to the republics. "Times have changed," the novelist and Supreme Soviet member Chingiz Aitmatov told me, concerning military intervention. "The world couldn't accept it calmly. And the world's moral and political condemnation is now of great importance." Aitmatov, a Khirgiz who served briefly on Gorbachev's Presidential Council before leaving Moscow and becoming ambassador to Luxembourg in 1990, was speaking of the Soviet desire to integrate with the world economy and the knowledge that military repression might terminate that process and relegate the Soviet economy to more years of unwanted autarchy.

Moreover, nearly all the Russians I spoke with believed that the same backward model of the center subsidizing the periphery that had characterized Eastern Europe applied to the relationship between Russia and the republics. Academician Pavel Bunich, a leading reform economist and member of the Supreme Soviet, told me that he had seen, and tended to believe, estimates that Russian supplies of cheap oil, gas, fertilizer, and industrial equipment to the peripheral republics amount to a subsidy of 80 to 150 billion rubles per year. That would be well over 10 percent of the Soviet GNP. Because pricing is so arbitrary in the Soviet system, no one knew for sure.

But, as in the formulation of Russian attitudes toward Eastern Europe, economic self-interest was not foremost in the minds of the people I spoke with when they assessed the likelihood that the inner empire, the republics, could spin away just as Eastern Europe was doing. "Economics isn't the only thing here," Bunich said. "It's also a question of prestige and pride."

When they assessed their position in the world, the Soviets in many respects measured themselves against the United States. They saw the United States as a multiethnic federal system not unlike their own, and they tended to believe that a great power therefore should be capable of incorporating a variety of peoples. Comparisons between the American federal system and the Soviet Union are not really apt. Most of the Soviet nationalities were brought into the Russian or Soviet Empire against their will, whereas most Americans, or their forebears, voluntarily chose to come to the United States, knowing and accepting the fact that they would have to adapt to American culture, the English language, and the American political system. (Not coincidentally, the only groups to have been forcibly incorporated into the United States—Hispanics, American Indians, and African-Americans—have in many respects proven to be the ones who faced the most difficulty entering the economic and political mainstream.) Nevertheless, comparisons with America were what the Soviets tended to make.

"In America, you have fifty states; none are trying to leave, because your economy is strong. We have republics thinking about running away only because our economy is in trouble. If America had just one state instead of fifty, it would not be the same great power," Bunich told me.

In his first years in power, Gorbachev had only floundered in the search for an effective policy toward the minority republics. As he told the Central Committee in 1989, he came to office severely underestimating the extent of dissatisfaction on the Soviet periphery. He may well have been a victim of the Soviets' own propaganda, which throughout the Brezhnev years had proclaimed the problem solved. Once *glasnost* allowed the national minorities to vent some of their anger, Gorbachev responded by acknowledging that the republics had legitimate grievances and slowly doling out small compromises. He talked about a new, decentralized federal relationship but wavered in the face of the major concessions that would bring it about. In the fall of 1989, for instance, the Supreme Soviet enacted a bill purporting to give the republics "economic self-sufficiency." At about the same time, Gorbachev introduced a new property law proposal which insisted that land and natural resources belong jointly to the central government and the republics, instead of to the republics alone. In effect, his policies told the republics that their grievances were legitimate but that Moscow was not yet prepared to satisfy them. It was not a formula for stability.

Gorbachev's real strategy, several sources suggested to me, was barely a strategy at all. He wanted to stall as long as possible, avoiding a military confrontation with any of the republics. When the soviets (legislatures) in various republics declared that laws enacted in Moscow did not apply on their territory until they approved them, Gorbachev basically agreed to disagree. Moscow said that the republics' actions were illegal and invalid, but it did nothing to enforce its opinion.

Russian leaders, schooled as Marxists, tended to see economic motives behind most political movements. The republics that were talking about independence, they believed, were rejecting the Soviet standard of living rather than membership in the Soviet Union per se. Their hope was that after ten years or so of *perestroika,* the Soviet economy would be attractive enough that separatist sentiment would wither away. That hope doubtless underestimated the role of nationalism in the separatist movements. And the idea that Russia could somehow stall the separatists for ten or more years was wildly optimistic. But it was the only hope available to Gorbachev and his allies.

For the first few years of the *perestroika* period, Gorbachev got away with this policy, for several reasons. Like the Eastern Europeans, nationalists in the republics had spent some time groping in the dark, trying to find out where the walls were. Only in 1988 and 1989 did they become organized, mass movements.

More important, the conservative forces that would be most intent on preserving the union had been on the defensive since 1985. They were dispersed throughout the military, the industrial complex, the Communist Party, and a few strata of the intelligentsia. They were disorganized. And dissent was not their natural inclination. In the early years of *glasnost,* the visible conservative opposition to Gorbachev had consisted largely of *Pamyat* (Russian for "memory"), an anti-Semitic, quasi-fascist group that never showed itself capable of being any more than a fringe element.

But, by the fall of 1989, a more formidable and, in Soviet terms, respectable conservative opposition was emerging. A group of conservative Russian nationalist writers and intellectuals had taken control of a handful of weekly and monthly journals, including *Nash Sovremennik,* the organ of the Russian branch of the Writers' Union. While the circulation of Establishment organs such as *Pravda* dropped precipitously, *Nash Sovremennik*'s grew from 250,000 to 400,000 between 1989 and 1990.

In their publications, these Russian nationalists carped about a wide variety of Gorbachev's reforms, seeking an issue, or combination of issues, that would attract some mass support. They complained about damage to the Russian environment. They complained about precipitous cuts in military spending. Most often, they railed against Gorbachev's economic program, particularly the appearance of Western-oriented joint ventures and private cooperative businesses, a few of which had begun to accumulate massive profits by dealing in scarce commodities. They advocated instead a return to the supposedly pure collective ownership models of the prerevolutionary Russian village, unsullied by Soviet bureaucratism. "Capitalism in the USSR would lower our living standard to that of Bangladesh," the nationalists' favorite economist, Alexei Sergeyev, warned in a *Nash Sovremennik* interview with conservative writer Anatoly Salutsky.

The Russian nationalists had no particular affection for nationalists in places such as the Baltics, which they tended to see as impossibly small nations fated to live under the sway of either Germany or Russia. But they did not, in 1989 at least, attempt to make much of an issue of Gorbachev's policy toward the republics. In fact, they shared some of the republics' grievances. Just like the separatists in Estonia, for instance, the Russian nationalists wanted to be able to say no the next time a union ministry tried to locate a petrochemical plant along one of their rivers. Just like the separatists, they could flourish only in an atmosphere of pluralism and respect for political rights, and they knew it.

I made an appointment to see one of the leaders of the Russian nationalists, a poet and writer named Stanislav Kunyaev, the editor of *Nash Sovremennik*. His offices were in an old, two-story, yellow building in central Moscow, across a boulevard from the circus and the peasants' market. In a country of spartan furnishings, the journal's quarters were particularly modest, with stained, old linoleum floors and battered tables and chairs. Kunyaev, a pleasant, stocky man with thinning brown hair going gray and silver-rimmed spectacles, was dressed in a wool sport coat and a plaid shirt. He chain-smoked Russian cigarettes instead of the foreign brands favored by most privileged Muscovites, and he indicated that he read absolutely no English when I offered him a copy of a previous article I had written.

"My roots are in the Russian intelligentsia," he began, when I asked him to tell me a little bit about himself. One of his grandfathers, Arkady Nikolaevich Kunyaev, was a provincial doctor who founded, in the town of Nizhny Novgorod (now Gorky), a hospital that still bears his name. His mother and father were a physician and a history teacher, respectively. Kunyaev finished his education at Moscow State University in 1957, a few years after Mikhail Gorbachev. Then he was assigned to work in the coal-mining Verkutsk area of Siberia on a little newspaper called *The Stalinist Way*. He smiled. "After a while, the name was changed to *Maxims of Lenin*." On his own, he began to write poetry, and in the ensuing years he published some twenty volumes. "In the last ten or so years, I began to write more and more criticism and political essays because I wanted to think through the cultural and political process going on," he concluded. He had become editor of *Nash Sovremennik* just a couple of months before I spoke with him. "It's been tough work," he said. "For twenty years, I was a free man, writing my verses. And I won't have that sweet life now."

Kunyaev's philosophy, and that of his journal, was hard to pigeonhole. He was, in the purest sense, a reactionary. He compared Gorbachev's reform process to stomping on the accelerator of a car without brakes. "You can go fast, but there's catastrophe ahead." But he did not automatically line up with conservatives within the Party, such as Yegor Ligachev. He had, for instance, decided to serialize a novel by that implacable foe of the Communist Party Aleksandr Solzhenitsyn, in part because he and his colleagues agreed with much of Solzhenitsyn's critique of postrevolutionary Russia. (The editorial board, he added, had invited Solzhenitsyn to become a member; Solzhenitsyn, from his Vermont exile, politely declined.)

And Kunyaev was hardly the aggressive proponent of suppressing minorities that the stereotype of the conservative Russian nationalist suggested he would be. The national fronts in the peripheral republics, he said, "have a full right to exist. They have a lot of problems in those nations. Their situation is indeed difficult and hard—though no worse than here, of course. The one thing that puts me off about them is that they blame Russia and the Russians for all their tragedies. In fact, it was Russian workers after the war who went in there in tens of thousands to rebuild their terribly damaged economies." When I asked him how he would react to a referendum vote for independence in a Baltic republic, he said he would hope they would want to stay in the Soviet Union. But if the population voted to secede? "Of course, the government would have to respect that."

Kunyaev added a warning that I had heard before in discussions with nationalists. Much would depend, he said, on how the republics propose to treat their Russian minorities. That could be a casus belli for the Russian nationalists. "If the Russians living there are deprived of their democratic rights," Kunyaev said, "there will be a full confrontation." Without that kind of provocation, though, I thought the Russian nationalists might tend, in the end, to be isolationists on the question of secession. What concerned them was Russia. And they had no more idea of how to solve the Soviet Union's ethnic problems than Gorbachev did.

There was no ambivalence, however, in the position of many of the Party apparatchiks, who may not have cared much for Russian tradition but knew a challenge to authority when they saw it. By 1989 they had become increasingly shrill in their demands on Gorbachev. One of them, V. I. Potapov, first secretary of the Irkutsk Party organization in Siberia, stood up at the September 1989 Central Committee plenum and virtually dressed Gorbachev down. He said it was "incomprehensible" that the Politburo had let separatists go as far as they had in the Baltics and called loudly for the restoration of "discipline and order everywhere." Economic progress may require decentralization, one gloomy Moscow scholar told me. But to the Party careerists, he said, "socialism is about power. If the Party has to choose between the economy going to hell and power, it will let the economy go."

The most potent combination for suppression of the secessionists would be an amalgam of the Russian nationalists and the apparat. But in the fall of 1989, such a merger was not inevitable. Russian nationalist values contradicted orthodox Party values in many significant respects. Nationalists, for instance, respected the importance of the Russian Orthodox church in Russian culture. They thought that "left-radicals" in the Party, beginning with Stalin, had brutally and stupidly destroyed much of the Russian heritage. That was why Kunyaev had invited Aleksandr Solzhenitsyn to become a member of *Nash Sovremennik*'s editorial board. If the secessionists played their hands prudently, I thought, the apparat and the Russian nationalists may never get together.

And, of course, by no means all the Party elite would favor repression. Many reform-minded intellectuals in the Party thought that Moscow had at least partly brought the nationalities problem on itself. *Izvestiya*'s Bovin, for instance, told me that, shortly after Brezhnev died, the new general secretary, Yuri Andropov, asked him to write a paper presenting his views on the state of the nationalities issue. This was the time of the sixtieth anniversary of the creation of the Soviet Union, in 1982. The Soviet press was full of self-congratulatory propaganda about the happy family of Soviet nations. Bovin's report, however, was quite different. He said that the predominantly Russian elite that had governed under Brezhnev had grown complacent about the nationalities. It had neglected to make certain that they had reason to feel like equal partners with the Russians. For instance, he said, Moscow had, with great fanfare, taken cosmonauts from each of the socialist countries and sent them into space aboard Soviet rockets. But all the Soviet cosmonauts had been Russians. A myriad of other aspects of Soviet life showed the same pattern, Bovin wrote. Andropov, he said, read his report and said that it might be a trifle harsh for circulation to the rest of the Politburo. Before the matter could go any further, however, Andropov fell terminally ill. During the ensuing two years of drift, while first Andropov and then the equally infirm Konstantin Chernenko served as general secretary, nothing was done to reform the nationalities policy.

For Bovin, as well as for several other members of the Party's progressive wing with whom I spoke, the possibility of secession by one or more republics produced deep gloom. They spoke of the friends they had in the republics and their fear of losing them. They spoke as well of how secession would mark the death of yet another of communism's bright ideals, that in a classless society ethnic and national conflicts would wither as men moved toward a society based on equality and brotherhood among all nations. But each of these progressive Party members agreed that if a republic was determined to invoke its right to secede, Moscow's only choice would be regretfully to let it go. Otherwise there was no point in talking about a government of laws, and the establishment of a government of laws was perhaps the highest priority of the Party's reform wing. "I am a communist," Bovin said. "I take seriously the words in our Constitution that permit secession." The alternative to satisfying national aspirations in the Baltic republics, another Moscow intellectual told me, would be a chronic sore of the type that Israel has in the West Bank, a situation that would be debilitating for the reform movement and for the country in general.

Nobody I spoke to in Moscow claimed to know which side in this Russian debate would win, if and when the time to decide arrived. Much would depend on factors that were not yet clear. How would the secessionists guarantee the rights of the Russians and other minorities within their republics? What would they propose in the way of a property settlement, dividing the factories and railroads built in the years of Soviet power? Would the international situation at the time make the Russians feel secure or threatened? Would the Soviet economy be improving, giving Gorbachev the strength to resist the political backlash that a secession would surely cause?

Most important would be whether the Russians still possessed the capacity for cruelty required of any imperial power. The historian Correlli Barnett traced the disintegration of the British Empire to a religious revival that swept England, and particularly the public schools that educated England's leaders, in the first third of the nineteenth century. It made Britain a kinder, gentler nation but also a nation that, a generation or two later, found it increasingly difficult to countenance the bloodshed required to keep order in the colonies. As a result, the British Empire dissolved.

Religion had yet to revive itself completely in Russia, although it was stirring. But I thought it was at least possible to hope that the impoverishment, fatigue, and enlightenment visited on the Gorbachev generation had had a similar gentling effect and that the Russians were no longer quite capable of the violence that would be required to hold their inner empire together.

ROMANIA

January 1990

The Reformed Church of Timisoara, in western Romania, calls no attention to itself. It shares a grimy, three-story, brick-and-stone building with a key maker's shop, which has the more conspicuous sign on the building's facade. A tramline runs nearby, along Shosse Martie, taking the workers who live in the neighborhood to the motor and chemical factories nearby. From the rumbling tram, the building looks like any other block of flats and shops. It has no crucifix, no spire, no grand entrance. Only the steep pitch of the roof and some large windows visible from Strada Timotei Cipariu suggest the location of the nave, with a dozen or so rows of pews, on the second and third floors. The Reformed Church is Calvinist, and none of the governments that have ruled Timisoara (it was called Temesvar when the Hungarians controlled it) have favored the Calvinist faith.

Until the Reverend Laszlo Tokes became pastor, in 1986, the church's congregation consisted mainly of elderly women. The Reverend Mr. Tokes, who was in his mid-thirties, invigorated the membership of the Reformed Church. "He gathered students and intellectuals; they were attracted by what he said and by his personality," a member of the congregation, Zoltan Balaton, told me. I asked if Tokes preached political sermons, and Balaton shook his head no. "He never was political," he replied, "but every Bible story has its political aspects." Tokes, he went on, had a knack of explaining the biblical injunctions to honesty and fairness in a way that allowed his listeners to draw clear inferences about the lack of those virtues in the Romanian regime. Tokes's sermons, and the kind of congregation he was building, naturally drew the attention of the Securitate, Romania's secret police. But he stayed out of trouble until a service in October 1988 during which three students recited poetry. The rules under which the church operated in Romania prohibited the participation of students in that way.

Six months later, Tokes received notice of his punishment, a suspension from the ministry. It is an article of faith with Tokes's congregation that the bishop who gave the order, Laszlo Papp, worked under the thumb of the Securitate. Laszlo Tokes resisted the order, and his congregation gathered signatures on a petition in his behalf. A month later, the church responded by offering a milder sanction. Tokes could remain a minister, but he would have to accept a new assignment in a remote, tiny village called Mineu—in effect, exile. Tokes and his congregation found that also unacceptable.

At about that time, Tokes crossed an important line. He and his congregation belonged to the large Hungarian minority that Romania, which fought on the winning side in World War I, incorporated when Hungary, which picked the losing side, ceded the province of Transylvania in 1918. The discipline of the Warsaw Pact had for years stifled Hungarian resentment over the loss of Transylvania and the mistreatment of its Hungarians by the Romanian regime. But as *glasnost* expanded the limits of political expression, the fate of Transylvania became a major issue in Hungary. Word of Tokes's plight leaked out to Hungary, and in July 1989 a Hungarian television crew managed to get to Tokes and film an interview. He spoke of his own situation and, more generally, about repression in

Romania. The interview aired on a Hungarian program called "Panorama," that, Balaton said, "everybody who has the right antenna watches on Monday nights at ten." The interview also made its way to Radio Free Europe, the BBC, and other Western radio stations that transmitted to Romania. Foreign broadcasts over Romania's borders, bypassing the state media, played a major role in the revolution, and the Tokes interview was one of the first instances of the phenomenon. His name and situation became known throughout Timisoara.

Many writers have compared communist Romania to Josef Stalin's regime in the Soviet Union, and indeed both countries demonstrated the vulnerability of the Leninist system to absolute dictatorship. But in at least one respect, Romania differed. Stalin's regime tended to deal quickly with any hint of dissent. The police knocked on the door in the middle of the night, and the victim disappeared. In Romania, the authorities preferred a long and visible campaign of intimidation against dissidents. They quickly laid such a siege to Laszlo Tokes. Anonymous callers began to threaten him. Cars filled with idle, watchful men often parked in front of the church. An architect who was working with Tokes on a church restoration project received calls warning him to abandon the project. He refused, and in September his body was found in a Timisoara park; the police ruled him a suicide. On Sundays uniformed policemen, jiggling their handcuffs in front of them, would form a gauntlet that members of the congregation had to walk to go to services. In November four thugs broke into Tokes's residence, beat him, and cut his face with a knife. Finally, a court ordered his eviction on the ground that he no longer had the right to occupy the minister's residence. It set the eviction date for December 15. On Sunday, December 10, Tokes told his congregation what would happen. "If anyone would like to see an illegal eviction," Balaton remembers him saying, "I invite them to come and watch."

* * *

Word of the impending eviction spread quickly, first in Timisoara's Hungarian community and then throughout the city. One of those who heard was Sandor Bicsok, a railroad engineer who lives in Timisoara with his wife and daughter. Bicsok, then forty-eight, is a sturdy man with blue eyes and a wide smile. When I asked him to recount his experiences during the uprising, he invited me to a coffee shop around the corner from the Reformed Church. We stood at Formica tables; in the unheated Romanian building, we could see our exhalations as we talked. As he spoke about the uprising, Bicsok's eyes gleamed with quiet pride and pleasure in his memories.

The Romanian regime had alienated Sandor Bicsok as far back as 1971, when it shut down the city's Hungarian schools. For twenty years he was afraid to express his feelings, and, through much of that time, the conditions of his life had grown steadily worse. His house had no electricity from nine o'clock in the morning until two o'clock in the afternoon. Frequently, the authorities cut off the power from six in the evening until nine, and then again at various hours throughout the night. His family received three kilograms of meat and fifty grams of butter per month. Sugar, oil, and flour were also rationed. In one respect, he was lucky. People in apartment blocks in Timisoara had hot water once a week, and in the winter their flats were rarely warmer than fifty-five degrees. Bicsok owned a small house with a wood-burning stove, and he was able to get wood from the countryside, so he had heat. Wherever I went in Romania, I heard similar stories. City dwellers had survived in recent years by foraging for themselves in the countryside. They might find firewood or a peasant willing to slaughter a hog and sell it to them. The formal economy had almost completely failed.

Bicsok could not, he said, point to anything specific that moved him to go down to the Reformed Church on the morning of Friday, December 15. He is a Catholic, and he did not know Tokes personally. Certainly, the examples set in the rest of Eastern Europe in the past year had influenced Romanians. But there was no plan, no call to revolution. He simply went over to Strada Timotei Cipariu to see what might happen. "It was completely spontaneous."

He found that some fifty or sixty people with similar ideas had arrived before him and were milling about at the entrance to the church. He saw no police, but there seemed to be a few Securitate men in plain clothes standing at the church's threshold. As the hours passed, the crowd swelled to about two hundred. The idea began to spread among them that perhaps if they stayed, the Securitate would think twice about conducting the eviction. Laszlo Tokes, waiting in the church office, opened a window. "He greeted us and said he did not know what might happen, that he was still being required to leave," Bicsok recalled. "Someone shouted, 'We won't leave you, Father! We're with you, Father!'" The crowd continued to swell, and Bicsok noticed that Romanians, Serbs, and other ethnic groups had joined it—"even Gypsies." Several hundred people stood watch through the night.

On Saturday the crowd began to sense both the fragility of the established order and its own power. It was a sunny, unusually warm day, and more and more people took to the streets around the Reformed Church. The mayor of the city, Petre Mot, came and spoke to the Reverend Mr. Tokes, offering a compromise: he could stay on at the church if the crowd dispersed. The pastor even opened his window and announced to those outside that the problem had been solved, and they could go home. But someone shouted back: "We don't trust them, Father!" When the mayor tried to face down the crowd and persuade them to go home, some women spoke up: "We'll stay! You leave!" Later a group of students began singing an old, patriotic song called "Romania Awaken." And as evening fell on Saturday, Sandor Bicsok and Zoltan Balaton both recall, they heard for the first time someone shout: "Down with Ceausescu!"

On Sunday, December 17, after two days of rioting in Timisoara, Ceausescu convened a meeting of the Political Executive

Committee of the Romanian Communist Party. According to the transcript that was published some three weeks later by the newspaper *Romania Libera,* there was a telecommunications hookup from the meeting room in Bucharest to the remote locations where some of his generals and security men were monitoring events. In the transcript, Ceausescu demanded to know why the military had yet to open fire on the Timisoara demonstrators. "Why didn't they shoot?" he asked Defense Minister Vasile Milea. "They should have shot to put them on the ground, to warn them, to shoot them in the legs." Apparently addressing his commanders on the scene, Ceausescu said, "Everybody who doesn't submit to the soldiers . . . I've given the order to shoot. They'll get a warning, and if they don't submit, they'll have to be shot. It was a mistake to turn the other cheek. . . . In an hour, order should be reestablished in Timisoara."

Ceausescu left shortly afterward for a previously planned three-day visit to Iran, apparently unaware of how fragile his situation had become. His support in the Romanian Army had been eroding for years. One of the officers on the scene in Timisoara was Colonel Nicu Pedronescu, the commander of an armored unit stationed nearby. "Even before December 15, the army was very unhappy," he told me. Ceausescu had neglected to provide what the officers considered adequate funds for weapons and equipment. Even more foolishly, he had reneged on payment of some promised bonuses for the officer corps. "For six years, I was one of the officers who did not get a nine-hundred-lei [officially, about one hundred dollars] bonus I was due," Pedronescu said. There had been no meetings or conspiracies among the officers, he said; there did not have to be. He simply knew that neither he nor his colleagues in Timisoara were prepared to shed blood to preserve the regime. When orders came from Bucharest after the December 17 meeting, Colonel Pedronescu determined that the commanding officers at the Ministry of Defense felt the same way. They told him to deploy his troops and to protect the army's men and property. No one told him to shoot demonstrators.

But the regime had other, smaller, armed forces at its disposal—troops of the Ministry of the Interior and Securitate agents trained for combat. On Sunday the seventeenth, thousands of Timisoara demonstrators moved through the city. Many broke into bookstores and tore apart the displays of books by and about the Ceausescus, setting them afire on the pavement. A large group gathered outside the gray granite Communist Party headquarters on the broad Boulevard of August 23. The local Party leader and the prime minister, Constantin Dascalescu, sent from Bucharest to restore order, emerged on a balcony and told the people to go home. The crowd instead booed, and more cries of "Down with Ceausescu!" rang out. The Party leaders withdrew. Emboldened, the demonstrators broke into the building, tore Ceausescu's portraits from the walls, and hurled them out through the windows. They broke into a storeroom and found cases of delicacies such as coffee and salami that the Party had been keeping to itself. These were liberated. A fire truck came to the scene, presumably to disperse the crowd by spraying it with fire hoses. The crowd seized the truck and burned it. At that point, according to Sandor Bicsok, armed men in civilian clothes opened fire; he presumes they were Securitate agents.

The shooting spread to other quarters of the city on Sunday night, the night that Timisoarans came to call "the massacre." Exactly how many people died, and who shot them, will never be known. "There was a lot of confusion," Bicsok recalled. Some witnesses said that Securitate agents in trucks picked up the bodies of the dead and hauled them away, preventing a complete count. The city hospital counted 110 dead, I was told, before its list of victims was confiscated by the Securitate. Nevertheless, reports that thousands of people died in Timisoara, along with tens of thousands in the rest of the country in the ensuing week, were exaggerated, perhaps by people who could not believe that so feared a regime could fall without taking an enormous number of victims with it. A month after the events, the new government announced a revised national count of 689 dead, which seems credible.

The confrontation in Timisoara continued for three more days, with the government either unable or unwilling to kill enough of the city's 350,000 people to end it. Gradually, power began to swing to the demonstrators. Groups of factory workers organized and took to the streets. A revolutionary committee formed in the balcony of the State Opera House, which became the focal point of the protest. On December 20, the rebellion gained control of one of the city's largest factories, a petrochemical plant called Solventul, and threatened to burn it down unless all the prisoners held in the city jail were released. The Securitate let the prisoners go. More important, the rest of Romania began to hear about the Timisoara events. Most people in Bucharest told me they first heard via the BBC or Radio Free Europe on December 18. Timisoarans themselves, fearful they would be isolated and crushed if their revolt failed to spread, began telling friends about it in carefully veiled telephone calls. One woman in Bucharest told me she got a call from a friend in Timisoara who said only "There is a big storm, and the sky is red."

In Bucharest, people began to talk to their most trusted friends about what they might do to help the Timisoarans. Christopher Iosub, an earnest twenty-year-old with a whispy mustache and steel-rimmed glasses, went to Bucharest University and met with two or three fellow students. "We decided we should try to do something, but we thought it had to be secret, because we were scared," he recalled. "We talked about writing flyers to pass out calling for people to go out on the streets and fight like the Timisoarans. We couldn't print them, of course. None of us was allowed to have a typewriter. We thought we might just write them out. Then we thought we might go to the subway station, and just before a train entered, throw them in front of it. The train would blow them around, and people would read them, but we wouldn't be seen handing them out." Despite such timorous plotting, the capital remained outwardly quiet.

*   *   *

Ceausescu returned to Bucharest on December 20 and immediately addressed the nation on television. Anyone who expected him to be conciliatory was disappointed. He called the Timisoara demonstrators "a few groups of hooligan elements" and said that "on the basis of the data available so far, one can say with full conviction that these actions of a terrorist nature were organized and unleashed in close connection with reactionary, imperialist, irredentist chauvinist circles, and foreign espionage services in various foreign countries." Rather confidently, he scheduled a demonstration of support for the regime the following day, in the square in front of the Central Committee building, which is formally known as Piata Gheorghiu-Dej after Ceausescu's predecessor but is generally referred to in Bucharest as either the Palace Square or the Central Committee Square, for the two buildings which dominate it. The Party apparatus got to work organizing the crowd and handing out the usual banners and portraits.

The sight of demonstrators walking obediently toward the square the next morning disgusted Marian Mierla, who saw them from his vantage point in the national art museum, in a wing of the old palace, across the square from the Central Committee; he worked there part-time as a guide. Mierla, twenty-seven, has a gaunt, dark face, a full beard, and intense black eyes. Like many of his contemporaries, he had bent before the Romanian system. In the museum's Party organization for young people, he was the deputy secretary, a job "they suggested very strongly I take." Partly because he wanted to begin graduate studies at Bucharest University, he agreed. Like Christopher Iosub, he had talked, fearfully, with friends about doing something to support the Timisoarans. And when he saw the pro-Ceausescu demonstrators, he recalled, "I couldn't stand it anymore." He left the museum and went out onto the square.

As Ceausescu's rally began, it appeared that the regime would once again be able to demonstrate that the people were, if not loyal, at least docile. Wearing a black fur hat, Ceausescu stepped out onto a shallow, second-story balcony on the building's facade. Mrs. Ceausescu and other members of the Political Executive Committee flanked him. Before them, a crowd of several thousand people had assembled, with their thicket of banners and portraits. "To begin with, I would like to extend to you . . . warm revolutionary greetings," he said, with unintended irony. Cheers and chants of "Ceauses-cu! Ro-ma-ni-a!" answered him.

Dan Desliu, a poet, was standing at the rear of the crowd, near the neoclassical Romanian Athenaeum. Desliu, who was in his midsixties, had left Romania for a few years in the mideighties and lived in Canada before deciding that, in the years left to him, he wanted to oppose the regime in his native country. He returned to Bucharest and got an open letter published abroad in the spring of 1989. He suffered three months of house arrest. Thereafter, the Securitate summoned him periodically for more interrogation and intimidation. At the last of these sessions, on December 12, his interrogator had mocked the temerity of the country's handful of dissidents. "Can't you see that in our country, everything is silent?" the interrogator asked. "Nothing is moving and nothing will ever move."

Desliu had come to the rally not to support Ceausescu but out of faint hope that his interrogator had been wrong. And there was morbid curiosity; he wanted to see what would happen. He saw some jostling and shoving in the crowd in front of him. A lamppost wobbled, and the lamp atop it fell to the ground, shattering with a loud crash. The woman standing nearest to it shrieked in pain, fear, and surprise. Immediately the people around her assumed she had been shot by the Securitate. Someone shouted, "Timisoara! Timisoara!" to suggest that another massacre had begun. Some young people at the edge of the crowd chose that moment to unfurl a homemade banner they had been secretly carrying: DOWN WITH CEAUSESCU. Others began to run away.

The noise and confusion seemed to startle Ceausescu. He stopped speaking and waved his arms. "What? No, no. . . . Hello, hello," he said, apparently thinking that something was wrong with the microphone. He looked, for a moment, old, bewildered, and vulnerable. Mrs. Ceausescu stepped to the microphone and called for silence. The confusion lasted for three minutes, during which Romanian television interrupted the broadcast and played a patriotic song. Then Ceausescu finished his speech, which offered a raise in pensions and the minimum wage. There were even a few obedient cheers and chants from the crowd at the front of the square. But the damage to the regime had been done. The shrieks and confusion, combined with the interruption of the broadcast, had produced a moment of weakness, and that in turn had punctured irreparably the notion that the people of Bucharest would forever submit meekly to the Ceausescus' rule.

The tumult at the rear of the square swept up Marian Mierla and some of his friends from the university. He heard some people singing "Romania Awaken." He and his friends began to shout whatever revolutionary slogans came to mind. "Down with Ceausescu! Yesterday Timisoara, today Bucharest! The army is with us!" The last represented wishful thinking. "We didn't know. We just shouted, hoping they would be with us," he recalled. Soon the streets were full of young people, shouting and singing the same things. Some waved the new banner of the revolution, a red, blue, and yellow Romanian tricolor with the communist seal torn from the middle, leaving a ragged hole.

The epicenter of the turmoil was the university, a few blocks from the Central Committee building. There was ironic justice in this. In 1968 Ceausescu had decided that Romania needed a bigger population to fulfill his plans. He issued a decree banning abortions. For a few years, the birthrate in the country shot up, until women found alternative, albeit often crude and dangerous, forms of birth control. The children born in the late sixties and early seventies were called "decree babies." Because nothing else in the society expanded along with the birthrate that produced their generation, they had always been particularly deprived. There were never enough shoes, or toys, or classroom spaces to go around for them.

Decree babies from the university now filled the crowds in the capital's streets. And decree babies were the army conscripts on which the fate of Ceausescu now depended.

As in Timisoara, different kinds of uniformed soldiers deployed in the streets against the demonstrators. Some apparently were Interior Ministry troops, and some were Securitate men. Most students could not differentiate among their uniforms, and the Securitate agents could well have commandeered other services' uniforms in any case. Marian Mierla judged the soldiers by their eyes. "The soldiers on Bulevardul Magheru [a main street near the university] were different. There was nothing in their eyes," he recalled. He decided that they were Securitate men. When he encountered ordinary soldiers, "I could see it in their faces. They were finished, desperate. They knew they might receive the order to fire. We gave flowers to the soldiers and asked if they would fire at us. They cried."

The regime responded hesitantly and ineffectively to the turmoil in the streets. Around the country, the Securitate rounded up some, but not all, dissidents. Gabriel Andreescu, after our August 1989 interview, had suffered several days of interrogation. Then the Securitate had exiled him to Buzau, a provincial town about sixty miles from Bucharest, where foreigners, he could be sure, would not come knocking at his door. On December 21, agents arrested Andreescu and took him to a cell in Bucharest.

Tanks and armored personnel carriers patrolled in the streets but did not control them. Some soldiers received orders to fire and fired into the air. Others, possibly Securitate agents, wounded and killed demonstrators. Some fired tear gas. Some used fire hoses to try to disperse the crowds. But the regime's ability to intimidate had vanished, due, perhaps, to Ceausescu's display of weakness, to the people's knowledge of what had already happened elsewhere in Eastern Europe, and to an exhilarating sense that Romanians were finally standing up and asserting themselves after decades of humiliation.

Mihaela Serbu, a frail, pretty, bespectacled student of German and English, one of the decree babies, told me how she and some of her friends took the subway to the university after seeing Ceausescu's performance on television. "I couldn't believe the people were shouting 'Down with Ceausescu!' I was so happy. Every five minutes a helicopter would fly over, and we would shout 'Boo!' at it. A fire truck came and started to spray, and I saw people cut the hose. Then soldiers started to shoot in the air and with tear gas. Some people ran, but I couldn't believe that people could be shot in the streets in the middle of Europe in 1989. Then I saw those things that make light, what are they called—tracers? And I heard a pop-pop-pop." She ran, too. But before the night was over, she stopped at a shop window, took out her lipstick, and used it to write DOWN WITH THE TYRANT on the glass.

Ceausescu's downfall came the next morning. He made a final effort to speak to the angry crowds from the balcony of the Central Committee building. That got nowhere. The people booed and, according to one witness, threw things at him, including potatoes and shoes. He retreated inside the building and again ordered the army to fire on the crowds. Instead, the minister of defense, Vasile Milea, was shot. His death was announced as a traitor's suicide, and a later account by the military confirmed that Milea shot himself rather than carry out his orders. Many Romanians believed, instead, that Ceausescu had ordered his summary execution. However it occurred, Milea's death did not bend the army to Ceausescu's will. By that time, many of the soldiers and junior officers had already defected to the crowds in the streets. The crowd surged against the Central Committee building and began to break in. Ceausescu, his wife, and some of his entourage went to a landing pad atop the building, squeezed into a helicopter, and left the city. Mihaela Serbu saw a helicopter flying away, but for a few more minutes she had no idea who was in it.

A little while later, the Dutch ambassador to Bucharest, Kun Storch, went to the home of his friend the dissident poet Mircea Dinescu on Strada Bitolia, in the northern end of the city. Dinescu in early 1989 had met with a correspondent for the French newspaper *L'Humanité* and told him that God had turned his face away from Romania. The Party had expelled him, and he lost his job on the editorial board of a literary magazine. Securitate agents showed up on the street in front of his house and stood guard, putting him under the same kind of house arrest other dissidents suffered. They were still there on the morning of December 22, and they restrained the ambassador before he could go inside. But Storch stood at the entrance anyway, and shouted the news: "Mircea! Mircea! Ceausescu ran away!" Dinescu recalls that he did nothing for a while, afraid that the Securitate might shoot him in revenge. But half an hour after that, Dinescu's neighbors came and gave him even better news. The Securitate agents had run away as well. Dinescu is a burly man with close-cropped, unkempt, dark hair. When I met him, he was wearing jeans and boots, which added to his tough appearance. But on that day, when he left his home freely for the first time in months, he was crying.

Dinescu walked to the nearest main street, Calea Dorobantilor, where a welcome afforded to few poets awaited him. A crowd was coming up the boulevard from the center of the city, heading toward the television station to take it over. An army tank, flying the Romanian tricolor with the hole in the middle, rumbled slowly along with it. A colleague in the crowd recognized the tearful man walking in the opposite direction. "It's Mircea Dinescu!" he shouted, and the crowd, which had heard nothing of Dinescu since his *L'Humanité* interview, began to shout, "Mircea Dinescu is alive! Dinescu is alive!" Someone handed him a revolutionary flag, and someone else gave him a boost atop the tank. Holding the flag, he led the crowd to the television station. They entered without opposition and made their way to the broadcast studio. Sympathetic technicians patched them into the national radio and television network, and the first news most Romanians had of the events of that morning came from the tearstained, stubbly face of Mircea Dinescu, who told them, "God has turned his face toward Romania again."

On Calea Rahovei, at the Securitate jail, a guard came to the cell where Gabriel Andreescu was staying. He took him to a front office. "They said, 'You can go.' They were very irritated," Andreescu recalled. "I didn't know Ceausescu had fled. I walked out of that building looking over my shoulder, because I was afraid they wanted to shoot me and claim I had been trying to escape." When he got to the street, he saw a column of people, both workers and students, gleefully shouting the new revolution's poetic couplet, *"Ole! Ole! Ole! Ceausescu nu mai e!"* which means, "Hurrah! Hurrah! Hurrah! Ceausescu is no more!" Andreescu, recalling the moment two weeks later, spread his hands and shook his head, searching for words to describe how much it had moved him. "I still didn't believe Ceausescu was gone. But for me, the most important thing was that these people were no longer humiliated, that they had found the strength to fight the dictatorship."

At the Central Committee building, meanwhile, power seemingly lay for a moment on the littered floor, available to whoever had the wit and determination to grab it. I spoke with a witness to the events in the building, a tall, sturdy, seventy-year-old man with thick glasses named Valentin Gabrielescu. He had been an officer in the Romanian Army during the Second World War. Afterward he joined the National Peasant Party. As the communists solidified their power, he was arrested and served ten years in prison. In the thirty ensuing years, he had worked as a lathe operator. Gabrielescu was in the square when Ceausescu's helicopter took off, and he went into the building a few minutes later through a window. He made his way to Room 229, a large hall with access to the second-floor balcony that overlooked the square. In the confusion, Gabrielescu recalled, no one seemed to be in charge. Prime Minister Dascalescu came out onto the balcony and announced that Ceausescu's government had been dismissed. There was, according to a later newspaper account, a short-lived effort by a member of Ceausescu's Political Executive Board, Ilie Verdets, to form a successor government. That ended after less than an hour when Ion Iliescu arrived in the room.

Iliescu is a stocky, broad-faced man with thinning hair and a wandering forelock that frequently falls down over his face, giving him a sincere but harried look. He was part of a group of once-prominent Party officials who had run afoul of the Ceausescus and had been, as the Romanians say, "marginalized." He belongs to the generation that followed Ceausescu's into the Party, coming of age after the war. His father had been a worker, killed during a strike in 1933. In 1949, according to a contemporary, Vasile Negrescu, Iliescu became one of thousands of Romanian students who went to Moscow for their higher education. He studied engineering at the Institute of Hydroelectric Power and was elected leader of the Romanian students' organization. Another student in Moscow at the time was Mikhail Gorbachev, who was studying law at Moscow State University. It was widely reported that Iliescu and Gorbachev were friends. Iliescu, however, disclaimed any relationship with Gorbachev, and Negrescu, who spent the same five years in Moscow, agreed that it was highly improbable that the two students, studying at different institutions, could have known each other well, if at all.

For fifteen years after his return from Moscow, Iliescu rose steadily through the ranks of the Romanian Communist Party. He led the Party organizations in Timisoara and Iasi, became a secretary of the Central Committee, and finally a deputy member of the Political Executive Committee. In 1971 Ceausescu sacked him; the cause, according to several accounts I heard in Bucharest, was a dispute over economic policy. He was demoted to director of the state's water resources program. Although he apparently did a creditable job, he was demoted again, to a position in a state publishing house.

Ceausescu did not leave Iliescu without friends or contacts. He remained a member of the Romanian Academy of Social and Political Sciences, which, at the time, harbored a group of marginalized intellectuals. Mihnea Gheorgiu, a Shakespearean scholar, was president of the academy in those years. In 1988, Mrs. Ceausescu ordered his removal. He was restored to his post after the revolution. He recalled that in the seventies and early eighties, a group that included Iliescu, Ilie Roman, Corneliu Manescu, Silviu Brucan, and several senior military officers would gather at the academy's baroque mansion, not far from the Central Committee building, for "seminars" on issues such as the systematization program or the agricultural system. "The discussions were not openly or strikingly critical, but they were critical," Gheorgiu told me. On the street, afterward, they would whisper to one another of their feelings toward Ceausescu. But there was, Gheorgiu said, no organized conspiracy.

Valentin Gabrielescu remembered Iliescu arriving at the Central Committee building along with another marginalized official, Dumitru Maziliu, and almost immediately taking charge. From his account, it would appear that Iliescu had some trouble shedding the ideas and habits formed in a lifetime of service to the Party. "He went out on the balcony to address the crowd in front of the building," Gabrielescu said. "I followed him. He began to speak by saying, 'Comrades!' Some of the crowd hooted. I suggested he say, 'Ladies and gentlemen.' He changed it to 'Citizens.'" Iliescu announced that he would like to appoint a Ceausescu holdover, Verdets, as prime minister. The crowd booed. Iliescu went back inside, Gabrielescu recalled, got on the telephone, and summoned Brucan and other people he knew from the Academy of Social and Political Sciences, asking them to come to the Central Committee building. These men became the core of the ruling group that emerged in the next hours, calling itself the National Salvation Front.

In the weeks after the revolution, there were reports that a cabal of ex-Party officials led by Iliescu and Brucan had plotted a coup, perhaps with covert Soviet support, and either fomented or took advantage of the events in Timisoara to stage it. Some fragmentary evidence supported that idea. In the summer of 1989, a letter from the "National Salvation Front" arrived at Radio Free Europe, urging the Romanian Communist Party to reject Ceausescu as leader at the congress held in November 1989. The ruling group that emerged after the revolution used the same name. Marian Mierla, the student, told me that the night before Ceausescu's December 20 speech, he met with a young man named Adrian who purported to be part of a large, organized group planning an action against Ceausescu on January 5. But in the weeks after the revolution, no one came forward to claim credit for that group or for the summer letter from the "National Salvation Front."

Brucan, then seventy-two, a silver-haired communist who had once edited the Party newspaper, had composed the letter criticizing nearly every aspect of Ceausescu's rule that I had heard about in August 1989. Operating quietly and secretly, he got five other aging former members of the elite to agree to its contents and managed to get a copy out of the country; it was published abroad early in 1989. After interrogating him, the Securitate forced him to move to a two-room cottage with an outhouse in the village of Damaraoia, outside Bucharest. Police erected a spotlight to illuminate his doorway day and night, and prevented him from receiving visitors or leaving the village. Brucan told me it was entirely coincidental that the name "National Salvation Front" was used twice. And, he pointed out, being under house arrest he could hardly have participated in a conspiracy during the months before the revolution. His neighbors in Damaraoia, when I visited them, agreed that he had been completely isolated during his time there.

Valentin Gabrielescu's account suggests a spontaneous transfer of power that did not smack of a plan; as a member of what had become an opposition party, he would have had a good motive to paint Iliescu and the others as conspirators whose goal was the preservation of communist power through the ouster of the hated Ceausescu. According to Gabrielescu, as well as several other participants, the army commanders essentially conferred power on Iliescu, whom they knew and respected. "What alternative did they have?" he asked me. "The others there were only students or workers."

Iliescu and Gen. Stefan Gusa soon appeared before the crowd to announce that the army had gone over to the side of the revolution. "We will go inside now to set up the Council of National Salvation," Iliescu said. He, Gusa, Maziliu, and several others began to do precisely that, Gabrielescu recalls. Iliescu also, according to two witnesses with whom I spoke, called the Soviet embassy and asked for military help to defend the revolution against an expected counterattack by forces loyal to Ceausescu. Gabrielescu recalls hearing General Gusa arguing with Iliescu about it, telling him that the army could handle the situation without Soviet help. Bucharest radio made a brief announcement the next day about the request for assistance. But, according to a Front official, General Gusa's argument prevailed before any Soviet military assistance could arrive, and the revolution proceeded without outside intervention.

Some six hours after the departure of Ceausescu, Iliescu and his cohorts decided that the place to solidify their authority was the television station, occupied by Mircea Dinescu and the group of rebels who had arrived there in the early afternoon. The situation that night was still one of spontaneity bordering on chaos. Marian Mierla had gone to the television station, along with hundreds of others, to protect it against a counterattack. "I was standing in an entrance. Someone came downstairs and said the council needed a student. Someone pointed to me and said I was a student. That's how I became a member of the council." He went to a conference room on the eleventh floor. The windows had been broken, and it was cold. Iliescu, Brucan, Dinescu, and a couple of dozen others were completing a communiqué to the people. Mierla did not remember voting on it, but a few moments later the statement was issued on behalf of the Council of National Salvation.

Beginning that night, the Securitate struck back. Its men used helicopters and an abundance of assault weapons stashed in a secret network of tunnels under the Palace Square and other key points in the city. The fighting was vicious. It reduced the buildings around the television station to blackened hulks, their facades peppered with bullet holes. Across the square from the palace and the Central Committee building, the baroque Central University Library looked, two weeks after the fighting, like a bomb had scored a direct hit on its rounded cupola. I found its director, Dr. Ion Stoica, sifting through what was left, supervising crews who were trying to salvage books from the rubble and, at the same time, rebuild the roof enough to enclose the building. "On the twenty-second, Securitate men fired incendiary bombs into the library and set it on fire," Dr. Stoica said. "They wanted to distract attention from the Central Committee building across the street, which they were trying to take. We managed to put the fire out that night. But the next night, a couple of dozen of them got into the upper floors and started sniping at the soldiers in the square. The soldiers shot back at the library, and it caught fire again. That fire we couldn't put out. It burned itself out. We lost 500,000 books." We walked up a staircase, past marble walls trimmed in gilt and soot, into the stacks. On shelf after steel shelf, the remains of the books sat in neat rows, charred a pale gray. A cold wind blew through the hole in the roof and rustled along the stacks, lifting a fine ash into the air.

At the height of the fighting, Iliescu and his colleagues in the Front decided to dispose of the Ceausescus. According to an account given by the deputy chief of the national police a week afterward, the Ceausescus' helicopter had landed near Tirgoviste, northwest of Bucharest. They commandeered a car and drove to Cimpulung, where they hid in a seed distribution center. The local police, however, handed them over to the army. On Christmas Day, a military tribunal tried the Ceausescus for, in the words of the unidentified prosecutor, "serious crimes against the people, which are incompatible with human dignity." They looked, on the videotape that was later released, wan and a trifle dazed. To the end, Ceausescu admitted nothing. "I am not an accused person," he said, just before sentence was pronounced. "I will only answer to the Romanian people. Have you not seen how the people cheered when I went into the factories?" A firing squad shot both of them, and it was reported that there was an abundance of volunteers to serve on it.

Late the next night, Romanian television showed Ceausescu's

corpse, lying in a pool of blood. After that, the Securitate resistance wilted, although sporadic sniping continued for a week or so. It turned out that not all the Securitate fighters were Romanian. A ranking member of the National Salvation Front told me that about one hundred of them, among those who fought the longest, were from Syria, Iraq, Libya, and other countries with histories of involvement in terrorism. They had come to Romania ostensibly as exchange students but in fact received commando training. In return, they served the Securitate for several years before going back to their own countries. As these foreigners were captured and accurate rumors about their origins began to spread, the Front publicly denied that any Arabs had been involved with the Securitate. But it did so, this source told me, because it wished to avoid any trouble in relations with the Arab world. What, I asked, would become of the captured Arab commandos? The Front official responded by silently drawing his index finger across his throat.

Ceausescu's demise completed the extraordinary cycle of revolution in Eastern Europe in 1989. In some ways it was the most significant of those transforming events. Of the Eastern European communist leaders, only Ceausescu tried to crush the popular forces that rose against him. His failure invalidated the first principle of political life in the communist world, the belief that, in the end, the Party has the means to force the people to submit. It suggested instead that the communists still in power might well face a choice between yielding power gracefully or yielding it as Ceausescu did. It was no coincidence that, a month or so after Ceausescu's demise, Mikhail Gorbachev decided that the time had come for the Soviet Communist Party to seek legitimacy through some kind of multi-party system and that even the conservatives in his Party went along with him.

In Romania, the Front quickly began to reverse some of the worst excesses of the Ceausescu regime. The communiqué issued from the television station on the first night promised democracy, pluralism, an end to the destruction of villages, and free elections in April. In the ensuing days, the Front merged the Securitate with the army. It annulled the decrees forbidding abortion and requiring people to report conversations with foreigners, register their type-writers, and address one another as "comrade." One early decree forbade any further exports of food. Red meat appeared in the grocery stores of Bucharest, although there were still long lines in many of them.

Some, but not all, of the old regime's servants retired or were fired, their places taken by people whom they had lately been op-pressing. At the Union of Writers, the old president was deposed, and the members elected Mircea Dinescu president and Dan Desliu vice president. At other institutions, the problem was a delicate one, because the vast majority of people with responsible positions had been required to join the Communist Party to get them. I attended a faculty meeting at the Polytechnic Institute in Bucharest where the professors tacitly agreed that there should be no personnel changes; all but one of them were Party members. They spoke instead of a plan to loosen up a curriculum that had required students to attend labs and lectures for as long as twelve hours a day, giving them no choice of courses or time for independent study. At the University of Bucharest, however, students insisted that they would no longer tolerate those teachers whom they judged to have gotten their jobs solely for political reasons or to have parroted the regime's line too zealously.

At Bucharest's City Hall, a pleasant, mustachioed physician, Dan Predescu, became the acting mayor and confronted the task of heating people's apartments and deciding what to do with the nearly completed buildings along the Boulevard of the Victory of Socialism. There was no choice, he told me, but to complete them and offer them to people who had been evicted from the neighborhood. He had heard various suggestions for using the House of the People, ranging from university classrooms to a museum depicting the world's worst dictatorships; no one seemed to know what would happen to it. Heating and electricity, he judged, were more important problems. "There was practically no investment in these areas under Ceausescu," he said. "We're just hoping to stabilize the situation until the elections." After the elections, Dr. Predescu said, he wanted badly to return to his research in cell biology. He had won a fellowship from Yale in 1980, but the regime had refused to permit him to go abroad. He hoped Yale would invite him again.

The new regime threw open some of the Chief's pyramids and let people have a look. Inside the House of the People, it turned out, there were about fifteen hundred rooms, many of them the size of respectable college gymnasiums. The interior decor leaned heavily on white marble, massive columns, and gilt. According to an army officer named Lt. Col. Mihai Evores, who showed reporters around the nearly completed building in January, Ceausescu dropped by two or three times a week to supervise the twenty thousand construction workers. Almost every time, he would order some design changes. He changed the scale or materials of the staircase in the south foyer twelve times.

On a journalists' tour of Ceausescu's residence in early January, I found evidence of greed and paranoia. The walls were covered with art from Romanian museums, and an occasional knickknack cabinet might have rare coins that he had appropriated. Among some papers strewn on a coffee table in the entrance hall, I saw a document from a hospital laboratory certifying that a case of cooking oil sent to the residence's kitchen had been tested and found free from contaminants. A Bucharest physician with whom I spoke told me that all of the children who presented the Ceausescus with flowers were selected in advance, sent to hospitals, checked, and certified free from infection before they were permitted to proffer their cheeks for his kiss.

Others poked into the Securitate's chambers, a little like children exploring a house they have just learned is not haunted. A physician in the provincial city of Medias told me about the contents found in the Securitate headquarters there. On the ground floor, there was a bank of electronic equipment that could tap and record conversations from any telephone in the city. In the basement, there was a chamber with an operating table, a device for electroshock, and various instruments of pain, including needles and a vise. In a bag secreted in a wall, the Securitate's files were found to contain a list of several dozen women, with notations about their sexual specialities, who were being blackmailed and forced to ensnare others.

Some of the people I met were eager to tell me how they had suffered under the Ceausescus, now that they finally could speak without fear of retribution. Vasile Negrescu, Iliescu's old classmate, had been director of the state's metals trading company in the 1970s. After an earthquake demolished the company's headquarters in 1977, Negrescu told me, he had solicited relief donations from foreign companies with whom he did business. He collected $2 million for the construction of a new headquarters building and deposited it with the state bank. One day, ready to begin the project, he called the bank's director about drawing the funds. The money was no longer there, the banker said, because "She took it." Negrescu had known precisely whom his friend meant, and he had known that there was nothing either of them could do about it. Now he was hoping to regain some kind of position in the new order.

The Front's first communiqué promised that Romania would remain in the Warsaw Pact. The Soviets, in turn, seized the chance to demonstrate both support for the Front and their intention to continue to play a role of influence in Eastern Europe. Foreign Minister Eduard Shevardnadze arrived for talks on January 6. Afterward he announced that the Soviets would maintain their oil and gas shipments, even though Romania would not, for the time being, be shipping any food to the Soviet Union. He also reported that the Front leadership had "promised to respect existing borders" between the two countries. This was a polite reference to the territory the Soviets call the Moldavian Soviet Socialist Republic. Until the

Molotov-Ribbentrop Pact of 1939, it was a Romanian province called Bessarabia, and its Romanian-speaking population is now quite restive. By agreeing not to seek the return of the territory, the Front spared Moscow an exacerbation of its multitude of ethnic problems.

The Front abolished the Communist Party's monopoly on power, and within a few days veterans of some of the pre-1947 parties emerged from obscurity and hiding. Valentin Gabrielescu and some of his old colleagues reestablished the National Peasant Party, declaring it the Romanian representative of Europe's Christian Democratic tradition. They dusted off their forty-year-old platform, calling for a revival of Romania's religious tradition, giving of land to the peasants, and, eventually, the restoration of Bessarabia. The new party got the keys to one of the Romanian Communist Party's old buildings, on Piata Rosetti, not far from the university. "The building was called a study center by the communists," Gabrielescu said sarcastically on the day I visited. "We found a lot of cases of Kent cigarettes and whiskey in the attic. They must have been serious students of Marxism."

Dozens of people were milling about in the entry hall, talking and filling out membership forms. Most of them seemed, however, to be about as old as Valentin Gabrielescu. And, apart from the cigarettes and the liquor, the party had almost none of the tools needed to mount a campaign. "We have one typewriter," Gabrielescu said. "A Norwegian newspaper correspondent came by and felt sorry for us, and she gave it to us."

The Front, once the Securitate resistance had died down, selected an executive board and about a dozen commission chairmen to serve as a provisional government. This inner circle moved into the Foreign Ministry building on Piata Victoriei, under guard by a detachment of bored-looking soldiers and a couple of tanks. What it stood for was not immediately clear. Silviu Brucan, who had moved into the well-heated office that once served the foreign minister, published his concept of an ideological manifesto in a newspaper article on the last day of the year. History had so stunted Romania, he wrote, that "at least for some time, we shall have to give up such concepts as socialism, communism, capitalism, fascism, etc." What was important was that the Front had "unquestionable legitimacy," forged in the revolution. A few days later he told a press conference that the Front would itself run candidates in the promised elections. The old Communist Party was a spent force, Brucan said, and unless the Front stepped forward, Romania would suffer from a dangerous political vacuum.

In many respects, the Front indeed slid quickly into the vacuum left by the abrupt dissolution of the old order. By the middle of January, it had developed local and regional branches that replicated the old Communist Party structure, right down to the election of representatives from each workplace collective. While one newspaper, *Romania Libera,* did publish harsh critiques of some Front leaders, most of the rest of the media, including the television station, seemed simply to shift their allegiance from the old master to the new ones. The erstwhile Party newspaper, *Scinteia* (Spark), changed its name to *Adevarul* (Truth) and published the full text of Iliescu's speeches on the front page, just as it had done with Ceausescu's. In Timisoara, as in many other towns, the Front leadership moved into the old Party headquarters and began using the same chauffeured cars and fulfilling much the same role. When I asked the man who at that time headed the Timisoara branch of the Front, Ioan Lorin Fortuna, about the similarities between the communists' administration and the Front's, he seemed puzzled. "What do you think—that there was another way to seize power?" he asked.

Some of the Front's leaders plainly reveled in the abrupt reversal of their fortunes. Brucan, in his office at the Foreign Ministry, recounted to me in great detail the story of his struggles with Ceausescu, whom he called a "cultural illiterate," and how he had managed to overcome the dictator's efforts to silence and discredit him. "I was like a bone in his throat," he said. And he laughed, slowly and with evident relish: "Heh. Heh. Heh." Another Front leader, whom I met at a dinner party, had been an unhappy engineer desperately looking for a country that would allow him to immigrate, until the revolution. He arrived for dinner an hour late, accompanied by an army major who was serving as his bodyguard. His chauffeur waited outside in the car.

I went to see Mircea Dinescu one morning in January in his new office at the headquarters of the Writers' Union, a palatial old merchant's home a few blocks north of the Palace Square. After telling me the story of his triumphal ride to the television station, he excused himself, saying he had another meeting, and invited me to resume the conversation that afternoon at lunch. Lunch, it turned out, was a five-course meal featuring steak and French fried potatoes, served to fourteen of Dinescu's friends in an immense, red-walled dining room, complete with a grand piano, adjacent to his office. Two waiters in white jackets kept everyone's glass filled with his choice of a cold Riesling, a dry red, or Romanian cognac. One of the guests played something light and gay on the piano. I asked Dinescu whether he had given any thought to abolishing the Writers' Union and letting writers work on their own. He had not, he replied. In fact, he said, a properly run union would be a great benefit to the country's writers, and he intended to expand its activities by establishing a new magazine and a new publishing house.

After Ceausescu's death, the weather grew cold. Snow fell, no one shoveled it, and the sidewalks turned to ice. The university postponed the resumption of classes. Students placed flowers and thin, amber candles where their friends had fallen, creating little islands of warmth and light amid the blackening snow. They watched the Front closely, and many of them grew anxious over its stewardship of a revolution they felt belonged to them. Marian Mierla, the student who had been plucked from the barricades and made a member of the Front's council, told me that after issuing him an identity card, the Front leadership had stopped notifying him of its meetings, and he had largely lost contact with it. "I don't trust them anymore," he said.

But neither Mierla nor his fellow students had a detailed concept of how politics might be organized in a democratic system. "All I want is liberty and democracy," Mihaela Serbu, the language student from the University of Bucharest, told me. "I'm not interested in the name of the system." She did not plan to join a political party or vote in the elections, which she expected the Front to win. And if the Front turned out to be only a scant improvement over the old regime? "Then the people will go out into the streets again," she said.

A few days later, on January 12, politics did return to the streets. A crowd of about five thousand people marched to Piata Victoriei and laid siege to the Foreign Ministry, screaming for the blood of communists and Ceausescu loyalists they perceived in the Front. Iliescu and Petre Roman, the new prime minister, tried to calm them, and promised to outlaw the Communist Party. A day later, they reversed the decision. In the following week, there was another large anti-Front demonstration and an even larger pro-Front demonstration that bore the signs of being manufactured in the Ceausescu tradition. Dumitru Maziliu and Silviu Brucan were purged from the Front leadership, and the council was enlarged to include opposition parties. The Front agreed to postpone elections from April to May so that the new parties would have more time to organize. But the country seemed to be teetering on the edge of chaos.

Gabriel Andreescu met me one evening at the Inter-Continental Hotel, which overlooks one of the largest of the students' shrines. He told me what had happened to him after our meeting the previous summer and then began to talk about the present situation. The fact that we could meet and talk at all was evidence of the progress his country had made, of course, but Andreescu had no illusions about the future. The problem, he said, was that Ceausescu had obliterated nearly all Romanian institutions that were not under his complete control, leaving the country to grope along with none of the political structures a democracy requires. In such conditions, the Front, or whatever government succeeded it, would almost inevitably resemble Ceausescu's regime. "The most important thing at this moment is to create a civil society," Andreescu said. "We need free trade unions, a free mass media, lots of different structures." He himself had embarked on an effort to establish an independent Romanian human rights organization. Until Romania had such a civil society, he said, "elections are of no significance. The parties are only names. If we are lucky, a good government could emerge and give us freedom and liberty. But only a civil society can assure it."

LATVIA

March 1990

Some seaports have a touch of raffish elegance about them, inherited from the days when boys dreamed of going to sea and important people embarked on important trips from their piers. Other seaports handle the dregs and the poisons of industrial societies, the scrap metal and the automobiles, and there is nothing raffish about them. In New York, Manhattan is a seaport of the first type and Elizabeth, New Jersey, typifies the second. In Latvia, the old Hanseatic port of Riga retains a little down-at-the-heels charm. On its cobblestone riverside streets you can still find a guild hall with Gothic arches and stained-glass windows and buildings with rooftop sculptures of black cats and sturdy braumeisters: reminders of more prosperous days. Ventspils, on the Baltic coast a hundred miles to the west, has brown, sickly meadows, acres of railroad tracks, pipelines and oil storage tanks, and a pervasive odor, the product of animal renderings and petrochemicals. It is a town where the schools recently issued gas masks to all the children, and taught them how to use them.

The city gets its name from the Venta River, which flows through it to the Baltic Sea, and the word *pils,* which means fortress.

The remains of an old stone tower with battlements still stand near the mouth of the Venta. In the days when Germans, Swedes, Danes, and Russians waged their struggle for control of the Baltic, the site was worth defending, because it almost never froze over. That feature made it attractive as well to Soviet economic planners in Moscow, and, beginning in the 1960s, they remade Ventspils. When I visited in March 1990, I could see the results of their work from the potholed roads on either side of the Venta. On the river itself, freighters lined up next to the blue steel girders of a loading facility that fills their holds with potassium chloride from the interior of the country; they take it to Western Europe and Latin America for use in fertilizers. Just to the north, hundreds of cylindrical railroad cars lined up to disgorge their contents: oil, ammonia, methanol, acrilnitrilacid. Many of the cars had POISON GAS painted on their grimy walls. At the exit from the tank farm stood a red-and-yellow billboard, from which a picture of a stern, fatherly man peered down over his eyeglasses at the departing workers. HOW DID YOU WORK TODAY? he wanted to know. His words were in Russian, because most of the laborers in the complex are Russians who have moved to Latvia over the last thirty years. The city's population was about evenly divided between Latvians and non-Latvians.

I met Laimdota Sele, a blonde, slightly stout, and very pleasant woman in her forties, near the banks of the Venta, across from the potassium chloride loading facility. We sat in an old house that had recently become the office of a city agency charged with preservation of historic buildings and monuments, among them the remains of the town fortress. A wood stove and chimney, encased in white tiles, provided all the heat the room had. A cold wind blowing in from the Baltic chilled us, and Sele moved her chair up against the chimney tiles to stay warm as she told me about some of the things that had happened recently in Ventspils.

Sele, a fourth-generation Ventspilsan, worked for the local newspaper, *Voice of the Venta*. When she became a journalist in 1985, the name of the paper was *Soviet Venta,* and the editor told her that one thing she was not to write about was the pollution emanating from the port complex. In knocking around in various jobs, and in writing her own poetry, she had gotten accustomed to the idea that there were certain things in Latvia that were beyond the realm of public discussion. Neither the selection of Mikhail Gorbachev as general secretary of the Soviet Communist Party in Moscow nor his proclamation of *glasnost* changed that—at least not immediately.

Change came slowly. There was no day when someone announced a new order; rather, there was a sporadic, cautious exploration of the new limits. The editor who told Sele that she could not write about pollution fell down drunk one night on the streets of the city and the police picked him up. In the Brezhnev years nothing might have happened. But in this case he lost his job, and a woman named Edite Melngalve, who taught the history of philosophy at the Ventspils branch of the Polytechnic Institute, became editor. Then, in the spring of 1988, a physician named Andrejs Eizans, the deputy director of the city's Department of Health, published two startling articles in *Soviet Venta*. Environmental catastrophe threatened the city, Eizans wrote. Poisons were leaking from sloppily constructed tanks and pipelines; the bottom of the harbor was a layer of oil and glycerin as much as two feet deep. The clouds of potassium chloride that billowed from the docks and spread over the city were killing its trees and causing asthma and bronchitis in Ventspils's children. After she read the articles, Sele waited for the authorities to react— not against the polluters, of course, but against the doctor and the newspaper. But neither the KGB nor the local Party committee did anything, at least not publicly.

Alarmed by the articles and emboldened by the lack of reaction from the authorities, Sele invited some dozen friends, including Eizans, to her apartment. A Latvian environmental movement, along the lines of West Germany's Greens, had recently been established in Riga. The dozen people in Ventspils agreed to form a local chapter and decided to stage a demonstration. They applied to the Ventspils city council for a permit.

The local branch of the Communist Party ran the council then, as it did every other organ of government in Latvia. The council was accustomed to seeing two demonstrations per year in Ventspils, one to celebrate May Day and the other to celebrate the 1917 Russian Revolution. For a while it dithered over the environmentalists' request. "Some of them thought, 'Why should we allow such stupidity?' " Sele recalled. Others thought that, in the spirit of *glasnost*, they should permit the demonstration, relying on the assumption that very few people would participate. People in Ventspils were thought not to care, and there were ways to make sure their lethargy was undisturbed. The latter faction prevailed. The environmentalists got their permit, but the Party refused to allow the local news media to print so much as a classified ad to publicize the demonstration. The environmentalists made leaflets and tried to post them around the city; someone tore the leaflets down. "We expected to get maybe two or three hundred people," Sele recalled.

Ten thousand people, one-fifth of the city's population, turned out. It was as if everyone in town had been silently, anxiously, waiting for the chance to express himself, hoping that his silent neighbors felt the same way. Eighteen months later, Sele shook her head, still marveling at the sight of all those people and the way she and her friends had reacted. "We were terrified," she said. "We couldn't believe our eyes. We had no experience with crowds of that size. We thought it might be uncontrollable." It was not, of course. Eizans made a speech, Sele read some of her poetry about Ventspils, someone from the movement in Riga read a message of solidarity, and everyone went home.

The demonstration began the destruction of the old political order in Ventspils. Before that day, the Communist Party could claim to have the allegiance of the population. Even though almost everyone suspected this was a fiction, there had been no countervailing facts to place against the drumbeat of support for the Party from the media, from the carefully staged parades on May 1 and November 7, and from the old-fashioned, one-party elections. Now there was such a fact. Once exposed, the old order crumbled quickly.

The first secretary of the local Party organization, a Russian, was the man who had forbidden publicity about the demonstration. He was replaced. The chairman of the city council, a Latvian, was fired and given a job as a teacher in the local Party committee organization. His deputy, a Russian, was a man who had once derided the complaints of the local environmentalists by saying he would gladly bathe in potassium chloride. Seeing that local office was no longer a sinecure, he tried to leave his official post and establish himself as director of a new, private enterprise that would have the contract for the city's public works. "We picketed and blocked that," Sele recalled with satisfaction.

In December 1988, the city council elected an economist, Aivars Lembergs, as chairman. "He had worked for the Party, so people didn't trust him, but he turned out to be all right," Sele recalled. "He's a businessman at heart." She gave Lembergs credit for going to Moscow and knocking on doors at the Council of Ministers until, for the first time, the city government was allocated a portion of the hard currency revenues generated by the port. Using that money, the city could begin to address some of its problems without getting the support of Moscow. Lembergs and the environmentalists found they could work together.

That type of coalition was not uncommon in the Baltic area after the summer of 1988. The insurgents had taken advantage of *glasnost* to demonstrate that they, and not the Party apparatus, had the support of the population. And that summer Gorbachev convened an extraordinary Party conference in Moscow. The conference decreed that henceforth power should shift from the Party organizations to the elected councils (in Russian, *soviets*), at the republic and local levels. Local Party leaders would normally also serve as chairmen of the corresponding local soviets, just as Gorbachev was leader of the Party and chairman of the presidium of the Supreme Soviet. But to retain their Party posts and their power, they would have to be elected to their soviets by the people, and, for the first time in the history of the Soviet Union, those elections could be competitive. Around the country, this reform did not always work as it was intended to. But in the Baltic republics, in 1988, 1989, and 1990, it precipitated the effective overthrow of the Communist Party. Throughout the three republics the ruling communists tended to splinter. A progressive faction, which included most of the ethnic Latvians, Lithuanians, and Estonians, joined forces with the insurgents in popular fronts. The rest of the Party apparatus began to wither away as a political force. In the spring of 1990, the Party as such did not even put up candidates in most of the Latvian electoral districts.

Meanwhile, around Latvia more explicitly nationalist emotions surfaced and fused with progressive political currents such as the Ventspils environmental movement. Sele recalled a series of national epiphanies. In June 1988, at a meeting in Riga that was televised live throughout the republic, a journalist named Mavriks Vulfsons stated that what had occurred in Latvia in 1940 was "not a revolution, but an occupation." Of course, Sele said, "we knew it was an occupation, but to hear it stated out loud, on television, no less . . . I dropped my cigarette." Vulfsons, from that day on, became for Latvians the man who first uttered the word *occupation* on television.

That same month, at a televised demonstration in Riga, Sele saw the flag of independent Latvia, a crimson banner with a single white stripe, for the first time in her life. "I said, 'Lord, it's our flag,'" she recalled. "I knew what it was because my grandparents had described it to me." The sight of the flag galvanized her emotions. "For the first time in my life, I knew what a flag was. I had seen movies, you know, in which Soviet soldiers talked about dying for the flag, and I couldn't understand why anyone would feel anything for that red rag. But when I saw our flag, I knew what that feeling was, and I cried." Later that summer, on August 23, at a rally commemorating the signing of the Molotov-Ribbentrop Pact, the Latvian flag made its first appearance in Ventspils since 1940. "People knelt down and kissed it."

Sele felt that there was something almost mystical about the process of national awakening that year. In October, at another big demonstration in Riga, she and thousands of other people sang a long-banned hymn, "God Bless Latvia." She had heard the words once from her grandmother but never memorized them. As far as she knew, her son, who was eleven at the time, had never heard them. Nor, she was sure, had most of the rest of the crowd. Yet they sang them. "I don't know where it came from," she said. "It was inside us, I think."

Such songs were the one thing that no other nation had ever been able to take from the Latvians, so songs were very precious to them. The Latvians were a pagan, pastoral people with no central government when, late in the twelfth century, knights from Prussia pushed northward along the Baltic coast to baptize and colonize them. The arrival of the Germans inaugurated more than seven centuries in which foreign aristocracies dominated the Latvians and their land. In the middle of the sixteenth century, Ivan the Terrible launched a persistent and eventually successful Russian effort to conquer the territory of what is now Lithuania, Latvia, and Estonia and gain access to the ports along the Baltic, including Ventspils. The army of Peter the Great captured Riga in 1710, and the Russian Empire completed the annexation of the Baltic area in 1795, although it left the German landlords in control of their Latvian peasants.

The various conquerors imposed their religions, their taxes, their languages, and their leaders on the Latvians. The Latvians clung to their national form of folk song, called the *daina*. A *daina*, usually no longer than a few couplets, can be about anything, from the beauty of the forest to the taking of a bride, and there are hundreds of thousands of them, though not all have a unique melody. Latvians joke that each of them has his own *daina*. Mothers taught the various *dainas* to their daughters until, in the middle of the nineteenth century, a Latvian scholar named Kristian Baronis began to collect them in written form. Baronis's work played an important role in the development of Latvian national consciousness, and music and politics became inextricably intertwined. In the summer of 1873, when the Russian Empire was embarking on a policy of Russification in its Baltic provinces, the Latvians held their first song festival, a gathering in Riga to celebrate and perform the *daina.* It was, a historian named R. O. G. Urch wrote some seventy years later, "the most important representative gathering of this period." Singing helped bind the Latvians together as a nation.

That in itself was not enough to give them independence, but it enabled them to take advantage of the unique opportunity provided by the exhaustion of both Russia and Germany at the end of World War I. On November 18, 1918, the Latvians declared their independence, shaky though it was. The fledgling Latvian government would have fallen to either German colonialists or Bolshevik revolutionaries, or both, had it not been for the British navy and the Polish army, which offered shelter and military support at times when the enemy controlled most of the country. Finally, in 1920 the Russian government recognized Latvia.

Independence lasted for a little less than twenty years. Latvians today recall this era as the Golden Age, but contemporary sources suggest a baser reality. Several Latvians told me that during the independence period their national economy operated at the Scandinavian level. In fact, according to *The Statesman's Year-Book* for 1939, Latvian per capita exports were only half the per capita exports of Finland, the closest Scandinavian country. Despite being farther north, Finnish farmers got substantially better yields for staple crops such as rye and potatoes. Latvia made its way in the world by exporting food, primarily butter and dairy products, to the wealthier, industrialized nations of Western Europe.

The years of German and Russian rule had left Latvia with a cosmopolitan population. In 1937, of the nearly 2 million inhabitants, only 77 percent were Latvians; Russians accounted for 12 percent,

Jews for about 5 percent, and a hodgepodge for the rest. The Latvian constitution assured the rights of all nationalities, and Latvians now insist that ethnic harmony reigned throughout the independence period. Again, contemporary sources differ with that burnished recollection. George F. Kennan, the American diplomat and historian, spent several years in Riga in the early 1930s and recalled the state of interethnic relations this way in his memoirs: "Riga had the advantage of a variegated and highly cosmopolitan cultural life: newspapers and theaters in the Lettish [Latvian], German, Russian and Yiddish tongues, and vigorous Lutheran, Roman Catholic, Russian Orthodox and Jewish religious communities. . . . The politically dominant Letts [Latvians], becoming increasingly chauvinistic as the years of their independence transpired, were concerned to put an end to all this cosmopolitanism and eventually did succeed, by 1939, in depriving the city of much of its charm."

The new government had to cope with all the tensions that plagued Europe in those years: between nationalities, between economic classes, between ideologies. Like most of its neighbors in central and eastern Europe, Latvia could not maintain a democracy. In 1934 Prime Minister Karlis Ulmanis staged a coup d'état with the help of the military, jailed his political opponents, and declared himself the *Vadonis,* which means in Latvian what *Führer* means in German and *Duce* in Italian. Latvia's brand of authoritarian rule was mild in comparison with those of its larger neighbors, but pictures from the period show that when Ulmanis appeared in public, little girls dressed in white scattered flower petals in his path.

None of which, of course, earned Latvia the fate that Stalin and Hitler decreed for it and the other Baltic states on August 23, 1939, in the secret protocol to the Molotov-Ribbentrop Pact, wherein Hitler ceded Latvia to the Soviet sphere of influence. Stalin immediately demanded and received the right to station 25,000 Soviet troops on Latvian soil and to use the port at Ventspils. The following summer, with Soviet troops occupying the country, Stalin completed the annexation. The Ulmanis government resigned, and, under the eyes and rifle barrels of Soviet troops, the Latvians adopted a new election law that only one party, the communists, could manage to satisfy. People were required to vote in this snap, one-party election, upon pain of losing their jobs. The communists, not surprisingly, won about 98 percent of the vote and immediately formed a government that petitioned, on July 21, for admittance to the Soviet Union as a republic. The petition was granted.

Latvia in fact had an indigenous communist movement. Latvian riflemen had formed Lenin's Praetorian guard. Many of the early leaders of the *Cheka,* forerunner of the KGB, were Latvian. The threat of agitation and revolt by socialists and Bolshevik sympathizers helped prompt Karlis Ulmanis's right-wing coup d'état. And there was no shortage of Latvian communists willing to work in the postannexation Soviet government. But there has never been any credible evidence that the communists constituted more than a minority of the population, or that the elections that led to the annexation of the Baltic states represented a fair test of public opinion.

The Latvians had only two choices: to submit or to be crushed. They chose submission. Perhaps they would have done better to emulate the Finns and fight. But the Finns had no Soviet troops in their territory when their Winter War with the Soviets began late in 1939. Latvia and the other Baltic states, by acceding to the 1939 ultimatum and permitting a Soviet occupation, had in effect given up the ability to resist.

Even before the ensuing years of deportations, war, famine, and collectivization were over, the Latvian song tradition reemerged. Just as the czars had thought singing a harmless expression of local culture, so did the communists. At the university in Riga in 1946, a mixed choir was reestablished, and in 1948 a men's choir resumed singing. The quadrennial song festivals started up again, in a beautiful, pine-ringed amphitheater in a seaside park a few miles from the center of the capital. Laimdota Sele, who loved to sing and did so in a pure, high voice, was sometimes one of the participants, although she chafed a little at some of the rules the communists imposed: there could be no songs that referred to Latvia as an independent country, and there must always be some Russian songs on the program.

That, of course, was before the little revolution that arrived in Ventspils in 1989. With the money that began to come in from the share of the port revenues that Aivars Lembergs had wrung from the Moscow bureaucracy, the town started to clean itself up. The gas masks were just a palliative that satisfied no one, a feeble effort to protect against explosion at the tank farm. The town also bought new loading equipment for the docks that cut the amount of potassium chloride dust by a factor of 30. It bought new medical diagnostic equipment for the hospital and West German street-paving machinery. It bought new, Western paints that began to replace the faded, peeling colors of the old section of the city with bright pastels. "We did in one summer work that used to take five or six years," said Girts Kristovskis, the twenty-eight-year-old chairman of the local branches of both the environmental club and the Latvian People's Front, who dropped in briefly on my conversation with Sele.

In the fall of 1989, the insurgents began to organize for the municipal elections, forging a coalition among members of the environmental groups, the Latvian People's Front, and the more radical nationalists in the National Independence Movement of Latvia. Their platform, in essence, was simple. "We are for an independent Latvia; we can improve Ventspils when we are free from Moscow," Sele summarized. The insurgents nominated half a dozen Russians and almost eighty Latvians for the eighty-five seats they were able to contest (five represented military bases). Aivars Lembergs was one of their candidates; so was Sele. They won about two-thirds of the seats. Early in 1990, almost fifty years after Stalin's referendum, communist control of the local government in Ventspils came to an end.

The insurgents' victory and similar victories in other parts of Latvia led to some dramatic changes in city life. Meetings of the city council were held in Latvian, not Russian. The local police force, which was about 70 percent non-Latvian, began a language-training program. Sele one day had the great pleasure of receiving a visit from the police chief, a Ukrainian, who gave her a report written in Russian, and then, in halting Latvian, apologized for the fact that it was not in her language. The newspaper declared that it was no longer the organ of either the local Communist Party or the city council, or anyone else, and nearly all the writers and editors who were Party members publicly resigned. They changed the name of the paper from *Soviet Venta* to the one the old local paper had borne in independence days, *Voice of the Venta*.

Changing the name of the newspaper proved, of course, much easier than changing some of the city's more profound problems, particularly those that stemmed from the port. The Latvian's in Ventspils felt, with justification, that the Russians in control of the Soviet economy had used their town as a colony. They had burdened Ventspils with dirty, dangerous industry, managed by transplanted Russians. These Russians had no commitment to the town and would probably leave it for better jobs in Moscow if they consistently met the quotas set for them by GOSPLAN, the planning ministry. Local government had no authority to close down a polluting factory, or even to require that it install pollution control equipment. But the new establishment in Ventspils could begin to monitor pollution levels and start serious research about the consequences of environmental degradation. It could loudly call attention to pollution problems.

Sele, therefore, was happy to arrange for me to meet with Inguna Sokolovska and Dr. Valdis Kupelis. Sokolovska, a twenty-eight-year-old biochemist, was a member of the Green Party who had recently been elected to the city council and was running against a Russian general for a seat in the republic legislature. We met her in the council members' chamber at City Hall. It seemed incongruous to meet someone not male, or middle-aged, or communist, someone who spoke openly about the city's problems, in such a citadel of the Soviet apparatchik.

Ventspils was just beginning, Sokolovska said, to understand the sources of its pollution. The environmentalists knew that some of the city's factories belched unfiltered smoke into the air; they did not know exactly what was in that smoke. They knew there were unhealthy levels of phenols in the waters of the Venta; they did not know where they came from. They could not always trust those monitoring sources that existed. They knew, she said, that radioactive cargoes sometimes came through the port. The dockworkers saw them. Once they had measured a cargo that carried a radioactive warning sign and found that it exceeded Soviet safety standards. On another occasion, when a dockworker reported a radioactive cargo, they had asked the port authorities to test it. The authorities reported back that it emitted only two hundredths of a milliroentgen per hour, which was within safety limits. But, Sokolovska said, "I know that their equipment isn't sophisticated enough to make that kind of calibration. It can't measure anything smaller than five hundredths. So they were lying to us."

Sokolovska suspected that radioactivity was at least one of the causes for the most dramatic manifestation of the city's pollution problems, its rate of birth defects. We drove to the regional maternity hospital, near a park on the outskirts of town. Sele and Sokolovska discussed, as we drove, what would happen to the various Soviet monuments we passed. Yuri Gagarin would probably go, Sokolovska said. But she did not agree with those who wanted to tear down the statue of Lenin and sell it for scrap metal. She thought it should be preserved in a museum somewhere, as a reminder of part of the city's heritage.

The maternity hospital was a white building on a patch of bare earth at the edge of a cluster of apartment blocks. Inside, it was dim and quiet. A few new mothers walked slowly through the corridors, but there was none of the cheerful bustle I recalled from maternity wings in hospitals in the United States. In an effort to protect newborns from infection, Soviet maternity hospitals do not generally allow visitors.

Dr. Kupelis, director of the Obstetrics Department, met us in a vestibule, wearing a limp, wrinkled set of white coveralls. He is an agreeable, slightly brusque man with bushy, graying hair and thick spectacles. He took us to his office, sat down, and began pawing through the files and papers on his cluttered desk. From one file, he pulled a sheaf of charts on which he had recorded, by hand, the incidence of birth defects in the hospital since 1977.

The Ventspils region, with a population of about 68,000, has about 1,000 live births every year. In 1977, 0.8 percent of those children had been born with what he called "deformities." A little more than 3.0 percent had infant illnesses that required hospitalization. Those percentages had risen very slowly, through 1988, when the percentage of deformed children was 1.3 and the percentage of ill children was 7.3. Then, in 1989, there had been an alarming jump. The percentage of deformed children more than tripled, to 4.3. The percentage of ill children rose to 13.8.

Only about 27 percent of the mothers in Ventspils carried their children for a full term and delivered babies with no defects. That was about half the percentage for Latvia as a whole. When I returned to the United States, I checked with the March of Dimes and learned that about 90 percent of all pregnancies in the United States go to term and produce normal babies. So a pregnant woman in Ventspils is twice as likely as another Latvian woman to have problems, and more than three times as likely as the average American.

Medicine has yet to determine the causes of most birth defects. Infectious diseases, such as rubella and syphilis, account for some; some drugs, such as thalidomide, are proven causes. There have been a few documented cases, in Japan and the Middle East, in which mercury got into the food chain and was proven to cause birth defects. But no one has shown a definite correlation between general environmental pollution and birth defects. Nevertheless, when

I asked Dr. Kupelis what he thought had caused the rise in birth defects in Ventspils, he replied without hesitation. "I think it comes from dirty air, dirty water, dirty land and food," he said. "That's how we live. Maybe, when the occupation ends, we'll be able to do something about it."

Dr. Kupelis pointed out what was, to him, a particularly alarming aspect of the birth defect problem in Ventspils. Latvian women, who tended to have better educations and white-collar jobs, had heard about the environmental dangers in childbirth and reacted, in many cases, by avoiding pregnancy or getting abortions. Non-Latvian women, principally Russians, tended to have less education and to work in blue-collar jobs. Like less educated women everywhere, he said, they paid less attention to health and science. "The immigrants don't care," he said. "As a result, we have more Russian births and fewer Latvian births."

Conversations with Latvians that began on subjects ranging from birth defects to politics often ended on just that point, the demographics of the republic. The Latvian share of the population had fallen from 77 percent during the independence period to 62 percent in 1959, and to 57 percent in 1970. By 1990 the widely quoted figure was 52 percent, but some people suspected that the actual Latvian population was lower than that, perhaps not even a majority any longer. In some cities, particularly Riga, the Latvian population had become a distinct minority.

It was not that all Latvians viscerally hated the Russians and wanted nothing to do with them. Latvian society was partially and informally segregated. Latvian children generally went to Latvian schools and Russian children to schools where the language of instruction was Russian. (The Latvian schools had to take care that their pupils learned Russian well, but the Russian schools taught Latvian haphazardly at best. I never met a Latvian who could not speak Russian, but I met many Russians, including some who had been born and educated in Latvia, who could speak little or no Latvian.) Even at the university level, the segregation continued. Courses were offered in both Russian and Latvian, and each group tended to choose its own language. There was no segregation in housing, although Latvian families tended to live in older neighborhoods in the center of Riga, and Russians, who were frequently newcomers, tended to cluster in the large public housing tracts on the outskirts of the city. Latvians tended to have intellectual jobs, if they lived in the city, or to be collective farm peasants. Most of the blue-collar workers were Russians or members of other Soviet nationalities.

But there was a fair amount of social interaction between the groups. I asked a young Latvian named Einars Repse, who was running for the republic's legislature as a strong advocate of independence, whether he had dated Russian girls before his marriage. "If they were beautiful," he said, grinning. Intermarriage between Latvians and Russians was not uncommon, and people in mixed marriages were not shunned. Latvians had, after all, generations of experience in adapting to the presence of non-Latvians on their land.

But the Latvians tended to blame the Russians, particularly the newcomers, for many of the ills that plagued their society. As in most of the Soviet Union, housing was terribly scarce, and young married couples generally had to live with one or the other set of parents. Recent Russian arrivals, particularly military officers and industrial managers, often got housing faster than native Latvians. Latvians saw Russians behind their environmental problems. Most of all, they felt the Russians were threatening to make them a minority in their own homeland, thereby putting independence forever out of their reach.

For many Latvians, the face of the Russian population was an organization called Inter-Front, which emerged in January 1989 and became the major opposition to the Latvian People's Front in the elections of March 1990. In contrast to the LTF (the Latvian People's Front's initials in Latvian), whose offices were at once shabby, lively, and crowded, Inter-Front occupied a quiet suite in what was once a merchant's building in the old section of Riga. A secretary took my coat and ushered me into the office of its leader, Igor Valentinovich Lopatin. Lopatin is a short, sturdy man, with a florid face, who was dressed in black trousers and a black turtleneck. His manner reminded me of the more capable Soviet officials of the Brezhnev era: stolid, blunt, and tough. I asked him to tell me about himself.

"Well, I'm a Russian," he said, putting first things first. "I'm fifty-six years old. I'm a communist [by which he meant a member of the Party]. I have been one for most of my life, thirty-three years. I was a career military officer. I served thirty-seven years in military aviation. First I was a flyer, then I had staff jobs." This was the life he had been raised to lead. His father, also a military man, and his mother and his sister were all Party members. Throughout his childhood and adolescence the cult of Stalin had permeated Soviet life, and he had grown accustomed to it. When Stalin died, he recalled, "I had a feeling that the world would end." I asked him how he had reacted to the revelations, beginning in 1956, of Stalin's crimes. "I didn't want to believe it," he said. Even after all of *glasnost*'s revelations, he said, he felt that communism was still valid but that it had been ill served by Soviet leaders.

In 1988 he completed his military service in Riga with the rank of colonel. Theoretically, as a retired officer, he could have settled nearly anywhere in the Soviet Union he wanted. In reality, however, the housing shortage gave him few choices. There was no chance to get a decent apartment in Moscow or Leningrad, Russia's most sophisticated cities. He opted to keep his apartment in Riga and settle there. He had lived in Latvia for a total of eight years—three during a tour in the 1950s, three more during his final military assignment, and two since his retirement.

I asked him whether he spoke any Latvian.

"No, I don't," he said.

I asked whether he was trying to learn.

He sighed, as if the question exasperated him. "I would like to, but, first of all, there's nowhere to do it, because of a terrible shortage of instructors, and second, I'm working twelve to fourteen hours a day, and I don't have the energy."

The importance of speaking Latvian was one of the emotional issues that separated Inter-Front from the Latvian People's Front. Earlier in 1989, the Latvian legislature, under pressure from the insurgent forces of the People's Front, had enacted a law promoting the use of Latvian. It required people in jobs that dealt with other people—from doctors to hairdressers—to learn enough Latvian to conduct their business, or, after a grace period of several years, lose their jobs. The idea was that no one in Latvia should have trouble obtaining essential services because they spoke only Latvian. (Latvian and Russian are not closely related.)

Lopatin maintained that this law violated the Russian population's human rights. "No doubt there are some jobs where two languages are needed, such as a doctor, or a salesperson in a store. But why should an engineer, who works in a factory where 90 percent of the staff speaks Russian, be required to learn Latvian?" To Lopatin the language law was "just an effort to chase out a large part of the non-Latvian population."

Lopatin couched many of his arguments in the language of human rights, as if he and Inter-Front were trying to pick up the banner of the late Andrei Sakharov. Inter-Front opposed, for example, Latvian efforts to prevent more non-Latvians from moving into the republic and tipping the demographic balance still further against the indigenous nationality. "We think that the Soviet Union needs to introduce the situation envisioned in the Helsinki Accords, that you should not have to have government permission to live somewhere," he said. Lopatin was being disingenuous. The Helsinki agreement was about letting people out of countries they wanted to leave, not about forcing countries to accept unwanted immigrants. Obviously, however, the language of human rights sounded a lot better than the language of occupation in the midst of a political campaign.

Lopatin's understanding of Latvian realities differed profoundly from that of the Latvians with whom I spoke. He told me that, as far as he was concerned, Latvia's leaders had freely signed the October 1939 agreement which invited Soviet troops into their country. I asked whether he knew that Stalin's government had dictated that agreement to Latvia under an ultimatum. That was true, he said, but just because the Soviets had given Latvia an ultimatum did not mean Latvia had to capitulate. "The Finns fought," he pointed out.

Many Latvian workers and peasants had welcomed the Soviets' arrival, he insisted. When I asked how he knew that, he said that old propaganda films proved it. Why, then, I asked, did so much of the Latvian population now want independence? For that Lopatin blamed the Latvian media, which he considered to be under the control of nationalist intellectuals. He said they had brainwashed the population to regard the Soviets as an army of occupation.

Predictably, Inter-Front opposed independence for Latvia. "We don't think it's sensible," he said. "First, it's economically not profitable. Practically all the republic's industry would be paralyzed. Now the republic gets its raw materials at prices substantially lower than the world levels. If it became independent, it would have to get them at the world price, and that would mean a sharp drop in the standard of living." The notion that Latvia could reorient its economy toward the West was wishful thinking, he said. "It would require that we get an absolutely different level of technology. And the West hardly needs another competitor."

But Lopatin's real argument against independence was the threat of violence by the republic's Russian minority and intervention from Moscow. "Independence would exacerbate intercommunal relations," he said. "About 1.1 to 1.2 million people here are not Latvians, and many of them don't want to live in another state."

Inter-Front did not have a membership list per se, he said, but he told me that public opinion polls showed that about 600,000 Latvians agreed with its positions. Inter-Front had supported thirty-three strikes by Russian workers in Latvian factories to protest the language law in 1989. More civil disobedience was likely if the independence forces pushed their program further. Inter-Front, he added, did not advocate tight control of Latvia from Moscow. But there were certain rights that the Soviet constitution guaranteed to Russians in Latvia, and "we think that Moscow should stop" the attempts of Latvian nationalists to take them away. It reminded me of what Stanislav Kunyaev, the editor of the Russian nationalist magazine *Nash Sovremennik,* had told me a few months earlier, about the possible grounds for armed Soviet intervention in the Baltics.

Many Latvians, of course, saw Inter-Front as a stalking horse for just such an intervention by Moscow. Lopatin insisted that it was not. The leaders of the Soviet Communist Party in Moscow neither supported nor opposed Inter-Front, he said; the Party leaders in Latvia opposed it. Inter-Front had money, judging by its offices. Lopatin said all its money came from voluntary contributions and the sale of its newspaper, which was called, with no evident irony, *Yedinstvo,* or "Unity."

Lopatin embodied the stereotype most Latvians had of the Russian immigrants: a retired military officer who chose Latvia as a residence because of its relatively high standard of living, much the way a British officer might have chosen, generations ago, to retire in Jamaica or Gibraltar because his pension would stretch further there. But there are hundreds of thousands of Russians in Latvia, with thousands of reasons for being there.

I met Ludmila Timoshevskaya one afternoon while waiting for a meeting at a branch of the Latvian Academy of Sciences, where she was an administrative assistant. She is a plump, pretty woman, then in her midforties, with close-cropped red hair, doing the best she could to be chic with what was available in Riga's stores. I waited as she phoned around, trying to find the man I wanted to see without success. Between calls we chatted, and she apologized for not speaking English. She had studied it, she said, but she was afraid her accent would embarrass her if she tried to speak it. That thought sparked some reflections in her.

Silence, born of fear, was a characteristic of her generation and of the Russian generations who had preceded it, she said. Her daughter, who was fourteen, studied English; she would not have hesitated to practice with a foreigner. Her daughter also rebuked her for being silent so long about the injustices and errors of life in the Brezhnev years. Her daughter's generation, she hoped, would be different.

I asked how long she had lived in Latvia.

More than twenty years, she replied. She was a Muscovite, the daughter of a Party member. She had studied chemistry at Moscow State University, the Soviet Union's most prestigious. While an undergraduate, she had worked as an assistant in research on nucleic acids. Two of her colleagues eventually wrote their doctoral dissertations on the project, and she, too, had "an unlimited future."

But she fell in love with a Latvian and moved to Riga in 1968, ending her education. She knew then only what she had been taught in school about the history of Latvia and Russia. She believed that Latvia had voluntarily asked to join the Soviet Union. Then, shortly after she moved to Riga, Soviet troops rolled into Czechoslovakia to snuff out the Prague Spring. The Soviet press said the troops were extending brotherly assistance to the Czechs against capitalist aggression, and Timoshevskaya believed that, too. But her brother-in-law, watching the news with her, commented bitterly, "You're occupying them like you occupied us."

The words shocked her, and she started to read whatever she could find about the history of 1940. At that time, all the available books gave, in more or less elaborate versions, the story she had always heard. She saw the same documentary films Igor Lopatin had seen, showing the cheering crowds as the Soviet troops arrived. Only in recent years, she said, had she heard the full story. By the time I spoke to her, she understood that most Latvians hated the

Soviet occupation, although she thought there were some, in the lower classes, who had welcomed it. She believed that the Red Army had indeed liberated Latvia from the Nazis, as she had been taught. But she felt that, a few years after World War II, the army should have withdrawn from Latvia instead of trying to force the Soviet system on it.

Timoshevskaya's personal life had fallen apart after ten years in Riga. As a hobby her husband judged judo competitions. He did this well enough that he often received permission to travel to international competitions. Without warning, he failed to return from a competition in London in 1978; a short time later, he married an Englishwoman.

That marriage mitigated the disaster his defection meant for Timoshevskaya. Had her husband defected for political reasons, she might have lost her job. As it was, her boss felt sorry for her and protected her, and the police did not harass her. Still, she felt things could hardly have been worse. She was left with a four-year-old daughter and a few rooms in an old cottage that barely had running water. Had her ex-husband's parents not taken pity on her and their granddaughter, she might not have survived.

She decided to move back to Moscow. But that was not easy. The housing shortage confronted her, as it had Igor Lopatin. She could not simply rent an apartment in Moscow. She would have to trade. And the only thing she could get in a trade for her old, cold-water cottage in Riga was a room in a communal apartment in Moscow, with "who knew what kind of neighbors." She felt she was too old to move back in with her parents. So she stayed in Riga and for several years tried to work out some way to return to Moscow. She failed. And by then her daughter was older and considered herself a Latvian. She had no intention of moving to Russia. So Timoshevskaya stayed. Talking to her, I had the sense she felt her life was slipping tragically, wastefully, away. "I've been here such a long time," she said, sighing.

She thought the Latvians probably deserved their independence, but she yearned for a moderate course, between the nationalism of the independence movement and the reaction of Inter-Front. If independence came, she expected she would feel rather isolated. She knew precisely how some Latvians felt about the Russians in their midst. Every once in a while, they reminded her. The year before, she said, someone had walked up to her on the street and, in Latvian, asked directions. Timoshevskaya spoke Latvian, but she was more comfortable in Russian, so she answered in Russian. "Russian pig," the Latvian snapped. "Go back where you came from." In 1990 such verbal assaults dwindled, but she had no illusions about why. The Latvians, she realized, needed at least some Russian votes for the Latvian People's Front in the March elections to the republic's supreme soviet, or legislature, if they wanted the legislature to declare independence. They would hardly get them if Latvians on the streets were calling Russians pigs.

The campaign trail in Latvia started from a wooden house in the old section of Riga, on a narrow, cobblestone street near the Daugava River—the headquarters of the Latvian People's Front. The building's sagging, winding staircases connected a warren of little rooms and offices, including the newsroom of *Atmoda,* the LTF newspaper, which was published in Latvian, Russian, and English. I saw one of the once ubiquitous portraits of Leonid Brezhnev tucked away in a dark corner of a stairwell. Someone had sanded most of his face away and drawn fangs where the mouth used to be; Brezhnev was still identifiable, though, because of the wavy black hair, the heavy jowls, and the medals on his chest. People were scurrying about, and it was hard to have a conversation not interrupted by a ringing telephone. The bustle in the main office had gotten so bad that the Front had recently rented another suite of offices, over a bread store in a building about a mile away, where its leaders were supposed to be insulated from the parade of visitors to the LTF headquarters. But the phones rang almost as often at the new building.

Einars Repse, the LTF's candidate in a rural district some sixty miles from Riga, was about to hit the road. Along with Dainis Ivans, the president of the LTF, we clambered into a green van and set off, into the setting sun, on the road toward Ventspils. For the first ten miles or so from the capital, the road had four or six lanes, divided. After that it narrowed to two lanes of asphalt, running past the brown, muddy fields of collective farms and, occasionally, past an old manor house with three or four chimneys and some outbuildings, slowly falling to ruin.

Repse, like most of the LTF leaders I met, was quite young, twenty-nine years old. He was so thin that every bone in his head was apparent, and his face was all sharp planes and angles, with a jutting jaw and forehead. He wore suspenders under his gray suit— not to be fashionable but to hold his pants around his spindly waist. He had a thick head of blond hair that fell toward his blue eyes, and almost no cheekbones. He was a physicist by education, and he lived with his wife and two babies in one room of her parents' Riga house. An ex-wife and a third child lived nearby. Ivans had four children, and I was told that Latvian independence leaders felt that large families set a good example for their compatriots, who until recently had tended, like most urban families in the European part of the Soviet Union, to have one, or at most two, children.

Repse could not remember when his support for Latvian independence had crystallized. He remembered, as a boy, gradually becoming aware that the picture of life the Soviet media were trying to sell him did not correspond with reality. He picked up bits and pieces of Latvian history from his parents, although he recalled that they had tried not to teach him anything that might prompt him to stand up in school and contradict his teachers. And he listened to the BBC and the Voice of America, in part to help himself learn English, which he spoke reasonably well. As soon as *glasnost* allowed the formation of a Latvian separatist movement, he joined it.

At first he belonged to the National Independence Movement of Latvia (LNNK in its Latvian initials), a group that from its foundation had advocated independence. But after the Latvian People's

Front came out for independence in 1989, he gravitated toward it. The two groups maintained separate offices and had separate platforms. The LNNK program included a drive to register what it considered to be legitimate Latvians, those who had lived in the republic before 1940 and their descendants; Russians, such as Igor Lopatin and Ludmila Timoshevskaya, who had immigrated during the past fifty years would be disenfranchised. The LNNK's voter list would then elect a congress that would have the right to declare itself the legitimate Latvian legislature and proclaim independence.

The LTF, by contrast, was not prepared to disenfranchise the immigrant population. It endorsed some Russian-speaking candidates, as long as they supported the goal of independence. Both groups recognized that it would be far easier to attain independence if a significant part of the Russian population supported it. For the March 1990 elections, they ignored their differences and presented a single slate under the banner of the LTF. Repse told me he could have been elected easily in a Riga district. But he agreed to stand in a rural district "because I am popular, and I can win there, too." Apparently Latvian politics had not yet evolved to the stage where candidates felt obliged to present a facade of modesty.

I asked Repse what he thought about the Russians' ability to hold their empire together. He replied that he did not think they had the strength to do it much longer, thanks to the debilitating effects of seventy-odd years of communism. His own experience had not instilled any fear of the central authorities. When he first became a pro-independence activist, in 1988, he had gotten a couple of calls from the local KGB. "They sent messages to my office and called me at home. I had no choice but to meet with them," he recalled. They met on neutral turf, in a restaurant. But the KGB's message was surprisingly mild. "They said that what I was doing was legal and should be done. They said they hoped our political fights wouldn't get violent." Repse got the impression the KGB agents were interested in finding out as much as they could about his views and his character, not in intimidating him. He felt certain that they continued to monitor his telephones and activities and report back to Moscow. But they were not interfering with the independence campaign. That being the case, he expected that by the time the process of disintegration in the Soviet Union ran its course, the empire would have lost the three Baltic republics, the three Caucasian republics, and the Ukraine.

He showed me a graph, printed by one of the Apple computers donated to the LTF by foreign supporters. It broke down the candidates in the election by occupation. The LTF's candidates came primarily from intellectual pursuits: writers, academics, doctors, lawyers. The opposition candidates were disproportionately drawn from the ranks of collective farm and factory managers, military men, and Party apparatchiks. Neither group bothered to nominate many workers or peasants. "Why should we?" Repse asked when I mentioned this. "Can a worker write a law?"

This was a clash of rival elites. The Latvian intellectuals stood to gain the most from independence. It would assure the survival and enhance the role of the Latvian language, Latvian newspapers and books, Latvian music, the Latvian university. Their opponents stood to lose the most from independence. An independent Latvia would no longer have collective farms, its factory managers would not be appointed by Moscow, and it would doubtless offer few employment opportunities to Communist Party apparatchiks.

The Communist Party as such did not have a slate. Some of its leaders, declaring themselves for independence, received LTF endorsement. Others got endorsement from Inter-Front or ran independently. Some did not run at all. In most districts, Repse said, the Party had chosen not to nominate anyone openly but to work behind the scenes for local candidates perceived to be more comfortable with the old ways of doing things. That, at least, was how Repse perceived his opponent.

Darkness was falling when we reached the site of his debate with that opponent, in a village called Pastende, at a collective farm called Friendship. We drove past a couple of four-story apartment buildings and a school to a two-story brick building, the farm's cultural center. Inside, in a second-story room, a brass band was rehearsing, blowing earnestly and sourly into its horns. On the walls hung black-and-white photographs of recent fests at midsummer and at New Year's. There were not many children in the pictures, and the one hundred or so voters who gathered in the main hall on the first floor seemed old, with wrinkles like plow furrows etched into their stolid faces. The hall smelled strongly of fresh varnish, and it looked a bit like a high school gymnasium in a small town in Kansas that served as a site for all the town's major gatherings. At one end there was a small stage, with a piano to one side and a vase of fresh red tulips atop it.

Repse's opponent was the deputy chairman of the collective farm, Valdis Girgensons, a potbellied, bald, middle-aged man wearing a brown sweater and muddy boots. His towheaded granddaughter climbed into his lap during the speeches.

Dainis Ivans introduced Repse, arguing that even though Girgensons was a local man, Latvia's next legislature would need representatives with a national point of view. Repse then delivered a speech on agricultural policy that could have been written for Margaret Thatcher. He called for breaking up the collective farms and returning the land to the individuals from whom it had been taken, including those who had left Latvia fifty years ago, should they want to return and claim it. He advocated cutting subsidies and letting the market set prices. The elderly people in the audience listened impassively, and I wondered how often in their lives they had listened to speeches by confident young men from the cities who came to tell them of the reforms that would dramatically improve their lives. When Repse finished, he received polite applause.

Girgensons spoke very briefly, without bothering to have someone introduce him. Everyone knew him and knew where he stood, he said. He got a smattering of applause, too.

When the time came for questions, the farmers expressed some concern about the possible consequences of independence.

Where did Repse expect to find the money to fund pensions, never mind the increases he was advocating? (When we stop sending money to Moscow, it will be available.) Where will we get medicine and drugs? (We'll need humanitarian help from abroad at first, and then we'll increase our own production.) They asked about the shortage of teachers for the local schools, about the redistribution of collective farm property, and about the pornography that, under *glasnost,* had made its appearance in Riga in the form of salons that showed X-rated videos, bootlegged in from the West. Repse somewhat uneasily made the liberal argument that the previous suppression had created an interest in pornography, which would fade away if left alone. Girgensons stood up and said he was ready to suppress it again.

But neither he nor anyone else in the hall wanted to debate the central tenet of the LTF platform, the desire to break free from the Soviet Union and restore the independent statehood Latvia had lost in 1940. Nor did anyone debate the issue at the other campaign events I attended. No one seemed to see any point in it. People who favored independence did so for reasons that, as Laimdota Sele had suggested, sprang from so deep within them that they seemed genetic. Most people who opposed independence were equally impervious to persuasion.

I saw Repse once more, on the speaker's platform at the LTF's final rally on the eve of the election. Although winter still had a few days to run, the sun shone brilliantly and warmly over the crowd, and a mild breeze lifted the dozens of crimson-and-white Latvian flags they carried. Others waved homemade banners. ONE LANGUAGE, ONE SPIRIT, ONE LAND, said one. DOWN WITH THE OCCUPATION! said a second. ETERNAL GLORY TO THE COMMUNIST PARTY OF THE SOVIET UNION, FALLEN IN THE FIGHT FOR COMMUNISM, said another, mocking both the style and substance of the Party's slogans. The LTF, consciously or not, had followed the oldest rule in the manual of American politics and located its rally in a sliver of parkland between the old section of the city and the Daugava River, a place a bit too small for the crowd it expected. People packed the riverside esplanade as far as I could see. An LTF official estimated the crowd at 200,000, and, although I had earlier guessed 40,000, it was impossible to argue with him.

The rally seemed more like a concert than a political event. A brass band of about fifty pieces assembled in front of the platform half an hour before the speechmaking began. On the platform, among the politicians and journalists, stood the now elderly men of the university choir that had gotten started again in 1948 and sung together ever since; they all wore a uniform brown cap with a short bill and a crimson stripe around the crown. The band struck up a song about the mother of Latvian rivers, the Gauja, which ended with the words "I was, I am, and I will remain a Latvian." Then came a song about the Baltic Sea, in which a boy meets a girl and says to her, "You're a Latvian girl, and therefore I love you." The crowd sang along, and the people closest to the platform locked arms and swayed to the slow, stolid rhythm of the music.

Dainis Ivans, wearing a sweater and slacks, opened the speeches with his four-year-old son clinging to his leg. "God and the sun are smiling on us," he said. There were more speeches, evenly interspersed with more songs. The Roman Catholic bishop of Riga told the crowd that just as the Lord had led the Chosen People out of Egypt with a strong hand, he was calling on the people of Latvia now to believe in the LTF. "Irrespective of the election results, we shall be firm in our belief that God has led us to this place and given us this land, and we will not give it over to strangers," he declared.

Einars Repse, squinting into the bright sun, read a speech that called on Latvia to stop sending its young men into the Soviet Army. He raised the slogan of the French Revolution, *Liberté, Égalité, Fraternité!* and the crowd cheered.

A beautiful young woman in a maroon dress, an American of Latvian origin named Laurie Wood, stepped to the microphone, accompanied by a young man with a guitar and another with a bassoon. They were part of a group of Latvian Americans called the Chicago Quintet, and in the years before *glasnost* their recordings of patriotic Latvian songs, smuggled into the republic on cassettes and played surreptitiously, had helped keep the embers of nationalism glowing. Now they were in Riga to express the support of the communities of Latvian emigrants around the world. In a sweet, soprano voice, Wood sang a lament about a hydroelectric project on a Daugava tributary that had destroyed a piece of Latvia's natural patrimony, a waterfall. People in the crowd wiped away tears, and, when she was done, they carried their children to the edge of the platform and held them up so they could give her flowers.

The next day, Einars Repse won election to the Latvian Supreme Soviet, although Inguna Sokolovska lost in her contest with the Russian general. The LTF won almost exactly two-thirds of the seats, enough to amend the republic's constitution and, should it so choose, declare independence. And that put it at the beginning of the path that Lithuania, which had elected its new Supreme Soviet three weeks earlier, had already begun to explore.

LITHUANIA

March 1990

When I first met him, during his visit to Washington in 1989, Bronius Kuzmickas was fifty-four years old and bore the lengthy title of Chairman of the History of Lithuanian Philosophy Department at the Institute of Philosophy of the Lithuanian Academy of Sciences. He is a shy, soft-spoken man, with wavy gray hair brushed straight back off his forehead and a gray mustache. His clothing stamped him as a Soviet citizen: muddy gray polyester slacks, scuffed brown shoes with Velcro tabs, eyeglasses with wide plastic frames. He said he preferred to speak English rather than Russian; his English was not, of course, as good as his Russian, but it sufficed for most of what he wanted to say. Occasionally he would make a mistake, referring, for instance, to "convicted communists" when he wanted to say "convinced communists." Whenever I asked a question to clarify what he meant, he blushed bright red.

Kuzmickas was not quite five years old in 1940, when the Russian soldiers seized Lithuania, but he remembered the event vividly. "One summer day, we saw Russian soldiers, cars, and trucks," he said. "I remember that the other people of the village were surprised by how the Soviet soldiers looked: very tired, pas-

135

sive, without enthusiasm. Lithuanian soldiers carried themselves more proudly."

Kuzmickas lived then in a village near the town of Marjampole, which means "Mary's fields." (During the Soviet years, the government changed the name to Kapsukas, after a communist leader.) His father, Juozas Kuzmickas, had emigrated to the United States in 1911, when he was twenty-one and Lithuania still belonged to the Russian Empire. Juozas Kuzmickas lived in various places, including Chicago, and worked at various jobs, including mining. After the Depression broke out, he returned to Lithuania, which by then had become an independent state. With the money he had saved in America, the elder Kuzmickas bought a farm and took a young bride. "He had eleven hectares [about twenty-seven acres]; he built a house in the American style," his son recalled. He was a peasant of the middle rank—not as rich as those who would later be deemed *kulaki* [farmers wealthy enough to employ labor] by the communists, not as poor as many. As the threat of war grew, Juozas Kuzmickas thought about trying to return to America, but he did not act quickly enough. When the Soviet troops arrived, that option vanished. Lithuania, exactly as Latvia and Estonia, had become part of the Soviet Union.

"During the first year of Soviet power, I remember my father was very afraid of being deported to Russia. We heard that in a neighboring village families were captured and deported. As the family of an American, we were in danger," Kuzmickas recalled. At the time, there were some empty houses in the area. The remnants of the Baltic German aristocrats had been warned that the Soviet occupation was coming, and they had left for Germany. Their houses did not stay empty for long. "Families from Russia or Byelorussia started coming there to live. I didn't know their nationality exactly, but they had long beards and were barefoot, and they looked strange." After the vacated German houses were filled, some of the incoming Russian peasants, themselves the survivors of Stalin's brutal collectivization, began gathering outside the Kuzmickas house. It was an almost feral scene. "They were waiting for us to be deported," he said.

Before that could happen, in June 1941, Hitler turned on Stalin, and German troops entered Lithuania. Once again Bronius Kuzmickas witnessed an armed invasion and, like any boy, noticed the machinery involved. "One afternoon, the German troops burst in on motorcycles. Then, a big contingent of the German Army passed through. The German soldiers were very proud, very impatient, but very correct, I might say. I remember, for example, they came into our house and asked for eggs, milk, and bacon. And they paid for it, very exactly, with a German scrip. We didn't know the value of this money, and my parents gave it to me to play with. To me, as a child, they were very good. They gave me sugar and candy. At first, people were very content being liberated from Soviet control and the danger of deportation."

The Germans soon spoiled this favorable impression with the cruelty of their administration. They executed friendly Lithuanians in reprisal for the deaths of German soldiers that, in all probability, were the work of Russian partisans. And they began to round up Jews. "This left an awful impression," Kuzmickas told me. "There were none in my village, but in the towns there were a lot of them." Not all Lithuanians thought this was awful. Many helped the Germans extend the Holocaust to the Baltic. Kuzmickas remembered them as *"lumpen* elements," and he remembered as well that "there were many cases where Lithuanians in the towns and villages helped the Jews, even after the Germans declared that it was forbidden to harbor Jewish children." In any event, there were not nearly enough such cases; of the quarter of a million Jews in Lithuania in 1940, some eight thousand survived the war.

Bronius Kuzmickas's father thought that America would save Lithuania from both the Germans and the Russians. "In the evenings, he talked about politics with the neighbors. They were waiting for American help. Because in Lithuania most of the people were convinced that the only way out was for America and Britain to open the second front [invade German-occupied Western Europe] and to do something with the Soviet Union. They were all waiting for America to start. They hoped one day to see Americans liberate Lithuania."

Lithuania, like its neighbors Latvia and Estonia, had always suffered from its size and location: a small nation squeezed between Germany, Poland, and Russia. Its fate, since medieval times, had depended on the benevolence of one or another of those greater powers. Even its modern independence, after World War I, had been declared during a German occupation; for a time, the legal currency in independent Lithuania was the German mark. After less than a decade of democracy, a right-wing politician named Antanas Smetona, who favored wing collars and a Vandyke beard, led a coup d'état that forced the president to resign and dismissed the legislature. He ruled until the incoming Soviets forced him to flee, first to Germany and then to the United States. America was simply the latest of the great powers in whom the Lithuanians invested their hopes.

The Kuzmickases hoped in vain. The Soviet Army pushed the Nazis out of Lithuania in 1944, on its way to Berlin. In the army's wake, the agents of communist power returned. "Those were difficult times," Bronius Kuzmickas recalled. "There were forced, hard requisitions. The Germans had had requisitions, but the Germans were interested in maintaining and not ruining the peasantry." The Soviets, of course, had no interest in maintaining the peasantry. They were merely waiting for the war to end before taking the peasants' lands and putting them to work on collective farms. "Under Soviet power, there were requisitions after requisitions after requisitions. And then there were deportations. Many neighbors from other villages were deported with just a few hours to take what they could. Some people panicked and lost their minds. Our family remained, maybe because my father was a middle peasant and not a *kulak*." According to one study, the Soviet police arrested and shipped 220,000 Lithuanian farmers to Siberia or Central Asia in the last years of the 1940s.

Once people had seen what happened to *kulaki*, it was easier to persuade them to turn their land and animals over to collective farms. "The first victims of collectivization were the horses," Kuzmickas recalled. He could even smile a little at the arrogant stupidity of the collectivizers. "They took all the families' land and horses along with the tools and wagons. We had two or three horses, in very good condition. But they saved no fodder. Comes the winter, and the collective farm gets cold and there is no fodder, and in one winter all the horses died. Good peasants loved their horses, and they even would try to sneak into the collective farm barn at night to feed them something, but they would be punished as bourgeois ideologists for doing that."

Most of the peasants, Kuzmickas recalled, stoically accepted their fate, and at night, after their day shifts on the collective farm, worked the small private plots they were permitted to keep in order to grow enough food to maintain their families. But some rebelled. From the time the Soviet Army returned to Lithuania, there were bands of guerrillas, called Forest Brethren, operating in the woods. They received some covert aid from British and American intelligence services, delivered by Lithuanians who had escaped into Europe when the Germans retreated and were willing to sneak back in by sea. But the KGB proved adept at spotting British and American operatives and infiltrating their networks. By the early 1950s, the Soviets had managed to isolate and then defeat the guerrillas. "The Soviet rules were that when they killed some partisans, the corpses were brought to the nearest town and dumped there. I remember there was a little village called Silapotas with a church that we went to, and they would dump them next to the church, so that people would see them on Sundays. They wanted to frighten people, and they also wanted to find out who the guerrillas' friends or family were. So the families were afraid to claim the bodies and bury them."

Some Lithuanians collaborated. Kuzmickas remembers that his teachers were so frightened that they parroted the Party line of the moment, condemning those who resisted Soviet rule as "bourgeois nationalists." Some have-nots saw the new regime as a means to get even with the former haves. "Their ideology was expressed in one sentence: take from the rich and give to the poor," Kuzmickas recalled. "Get from, give to me. I remember a neighbor of ours was talking with my father, and my father asked him why he wasn't sowing his field that year, and he said, 'Why should I? I know some *kulak* will be deported and there will be more for me.' "

Some people simply sold out. A woman named Ina Navazelskis told me a story from those days. A Lithuanian poet who had written popular, patriotic verses in the precommunist days received a summons from the KGB. His verses, they told him, were too bourgeois, and his career as a writer was over—unless he could show his loyalty by performing a service for the new regime. The writer agreed. They told him to go to another city and organize a cell of Lithuanian patriots, potential resisters. He did so. Then, again under orders, he gave their names to the KGB. All of them disappeared. The KGB kept its bargain. The poet was published again, and his verses, particularly for children, became quite popular once more. Lithuanian parents read them to their children at bedtime. The poet drank more and more, and, toward the end of his life, visitors sometimes found him alone in his apartment, an empty bottle of vodka on the kitchen table. He would be scrabbling about on his hands and knees. He was looking, he would tell them, for his conscience.

Sometime in the mid-1950s, many Lithuanians began to feel both an end to their former hopes of liberation and the beginning of a new kind of optimism. Stalin's death and Khrushchev's denunciation of him at the Twentieth Party Congress in 1956 raised the possibility that the Communist Party might reform itself. Those deportees who had managed to survive their Siberian exile returned to Lithuania, suggesting that the worst of the repression was over. And the American decision not to aid Hungary's 1956 revolt laid to rest any hopes that intervention from abroad might yet liberate Lithuania. "It seemed that something like progress or social justice

was taking place, and there was some optimism," Bronius Kuzmickas recalled, although when I asked him what he had believed
of all the pro-communist propaganda he heard, he replied, "Nothing.
I am from peasant views." But he, too, shared in the belief that at
least things might get a little better.

"I graduated from secondary school in Kaunas at the age of
twenty. We saw that Soviet power was strong, and there was no
other way. So we accepted the rules of the game." He belonged to
the Communist Party youth organization, the Komsomol. He attended Vilnius University and then graduate school in philosophy.
He spent one year on a special fellowship, working on a critique of
Catholic philosophy, at the Academy of Sciences. It was a schizo-
phrenic existence. On the one hand, he had to observe certain
conventions, quoting Marx and Lenin in the preface to his paper and
adopting a critical posture toward the Church. On the other hand,
when he got married in 1965, he and his bride chose to have an
unofficial church ceremony in addition to the Soviet registration
procedure. He mixed with the Russians and other Soviet nationalities at the Academy of Sciences and appeared to be becoming a good
example of *Homo Sovieticus.* But, he said, if I had met him in those
days and asked what his citizenship was, he would not have said
Soviet. "I would have said Lithuanian. It was a very strong feeling."

Early in 1968, Kuzmickas became a member of the Communist
Party. In part this was a matter of convenience; in order to teach
philosophy, he had to be a Party member. This was the way the
regime tried to defend against heresy. But there was another factor.
The appearance of "socialism with a human face" in Czechoslovakia
raised hopes that Soviet communism, too, might move in that direction. When, instead, Moscow sent tanks to crush Prague's Spring,
those hopes wilted. "It was very hard, very negative," Kuzmickas
said, sighing, twenty-odd years later, at the recollection.

By becoming a philosopher, Kuzmickas placed himself at one
of the aneurysms of Soviet control of thought in Lithuania. The
country's tradition of academic philosophy was a long one. Vilnius

University, one of Europe's oldest, had been a Jesuit institution. Although the Communist Party vetted all the appointments to philosophy positions at the university and other academies, the people who did the first round of vetting were Lithuanian communists, and they put competence ahead of ideological purity. This was partly a function of Lithuania's small size. By the 1970s, the original communists who had come to power on the heels of the Soviet Army were gone, either dead or retired. In their places men of Bronius Kuzmickas's generation began to appear. Everyone with an education knew everyone else with an education, and they all knew who the competent people were. The chairman of the philosophy department at the university, for instance, was a professor named Eugenijas Meschkauskas. His wife was a minister in the republic government. He knew Antanas Snieckus, the leader of Lithuania's Communist Party until his death in 1974. Meschkauskas, I was told by one of his protégés, "was able to attract the best people, not mediocrities." Because of the general impoverishment of the country, Lithuanian professors never had their own offices. An entire department might share a room with a battered common table and a couple of small desks. These rooms, like the one Meschkauskas presided over at Vilnius University, became little islands of free debate.

The philosophers' acts of rebellion hardly seemed likely to lead to a revolution. Kuzmickas, for instance, worked throughout the 1970s on the publication of a multivolume anthology, in Lithuanian, of American and Western European philosophers of the nineteenth and twentieth centuries, most of whose works gather dust in their native lands. In Lithuania the publication was a political event. Party reactionaries condemned it as a dangerous flirtation with bourgeois ideology. But the local Party organization did not stop it. The Lithuanian intelligentsia affirmed its right to a limited amount of free expression. And, Kuzmickas recalled, "there arose a conviction that this was not enough, and we must do more."

* * *

The generation coming along behind Kuzmickas, although it had never lived in an independent Lithuania, almost instinctively picked up the ideas its elders had had to repress. In the autumn of 1968, when the American sprinters Tommie Smith and John Carlos raised their black-gloved fists in protest above the victory stand at the Mexico City Olympics, one of the countless millions who watched on television was a twelve-year-old boy in Vilnius named Arvydas Juozaitis. Juozaitis was himself a budding athlete. At the age of eight, he had taken up swimming to strengthen and straighten a curved spine. The image of the two black Americans using the Olympics to call attention to the complaints of their people kindled an idea in Juozaitis's mind. Someday he might be able to use swimming to focus the world's attention on Lithuania.

Improbably enough, Juozaitis grew to be tall, broad-shouldered, handsome—and a world-class swimmer, one of the ornaments of the Soviet amateur sports machine. From the age of fifteen, he lived the life of a professional athlete. Except for his schoolwork, he devoted all his time to training; he spent his vacations in special sports camps. And in 1976 he qualified for the Soviet Olympic team in his specialty, the one-hundred-meter breaststroke.

When he arrived in Montreal, Juozaitis found that the world, at least as it was represented by the sportswriters and fans at the Olympics, knew little and cared less about Lithuania. Many people, in fact, referred to him as a Russian, as if the word *Russian* applied to anyone from the Soviet Union. He had brought with him a sweat suit, black with gold trim, with the word *Lithuania* across the back; it was a souvenir from an internal Soviet competition. He often wore it to workouts instead of the national team's uniform sweatshirt with the Cyrillic *CCCP* across the back. His coaches treated it as an eccentricity they could afford to indulge in one of their best athletes, a young man who seemed, in every other respect, to be the paragon of Soviet youth.

In the finals of the one-hundred-meter breaststroke, Juozaitis finished third, behind an American named John Hencken and a Scot named David Wilkie. He was one of the first Soviet male swimmers ever to win an Olympic medal. The dream born in 1968 moved within his grasp. He needed only to wear his Lithuanian jacket on the victory stand to force the world to learn the difference between a Lithuanian and a Russian.

But in those days, Mikhail Gorbachev was still a provincial apparatchik, and *glasnost* was just another Russian word. Juozaitis agonized for hours over his decision. In the end, he wore the jacket with *CCCP*. "I was afraid of what would happen," he told me, when we first met in the fall of 1989. "I would have been pushed out of my university, and my parents would have lost their jobs. . . . I wasn't strong enough to do it." He carried a lesson away from the experience. "Without a strong organization and support, you can't accomplish something great. One man is too weak."

Juozaitis took his medal, went back to Lithuania, and never swam competitively again. He took an undergraduate degree in economics, then switched to philosophy. He wrote his dissertation on nineteenth-century German philosophy and joined the staff of the Lithuanian Academy of Sciences, where Bronius Kuzmickas already worked. And a dozen years after the Montreal Olympics, a dozen years after the publication of Western philosophers in Lithuania, the time finally came to put to use what Juozaitis had learned about the need for people to stand up together and support one another against Soviet power.

By the spring of 1988, *glasnost* and democratization had been the proclaimed Soviet policies for three years, but Lithuania was only beginning to stir and to show signs of political activity outside the purview and approval of the Communist Party. One group of Vilnius intellectuals had begun to devote its energy to the restoration of old houses and buildings in the center of the city. In theory this activity had no political connotations. But, as in Romania, Hungary, and the rest of Eastern Europe, urban design questions were in fact political, and the people who concerned themselves with the preservation and restoration of old, precommunist structures were saying, obliquely, that they still revered the values and traditions of an age that had been discredited and superseded by the glorious Soviet epoch.

Concern for the deterioration of the urban fabric led naturally to concern for the deterioration of the whole Lithuanian environment. In February 1988, a group of young scientists, led by a boyish, blond physicist named Zigmas Vaisvila, formed the republic's first club of environmentalists, called *Gemmias.* "We started off with discussions of things like the pollution of the Baltic, and the nuclear power station at Snieckus [a new city named for the old Party leader]," Vaisvila recalled two years later. "They were simple activities—collecting signatures and so on."

This time the connection to Lithuanian politics was clear, and the environmentalists' activities soon attracted the attention of the local KGB. "I would get called and invited to meet with them at a restaurant, or in a square," Vaisvila said. "The main idea they wanted to give was that I would have a lot of trouble if I continued." But, unlike in past eras, this time there were no deportations, no disappearances. The KGB confined itself to informal attempts to intimidate the growing group of Lithuanian activists. That effort failed.

At about the same time, an economist named Kazimiera Prunskiene was organizing a group of colleagues to talk about self-sufficiency for Lithuania. Prunskiene, at the time forty-five years old, is a plump, fair, blue-eyed, and pleasant woman with close-cropped, light brown hair, the mother of three nearly grown children. Like Bronius Kuzmickas, she was a communist of convenience. "I joined the Party in 1980," she told me in Vilnius in March 1990. "It was entirely pragmatic. Without membership, I could not travel abroad and work with foreign scientists. Being a member, I've been able to spend about nine months in West Germany over the past ten years."

She did not, at least to me, stop to take note of the irony in what she had said. The Soviet system had forced her to join the Party as a way to defend its orthodoxy. Instead, membership had given her a means to go abroad and study alternative economic ideas. To her, it was an inanity not worth mentioning, just one of many that the system had forced on Lithuania. She did worry, however, that I would portray her as a communist. "You shouldn't exaggerate the importance of our membership in the Communist Party," she said, speaking of herself and other independence activists. "To me, socialism isn't a very attractive word. I stand for the transformation of the Soviet model which is called socialist into a market economy moderately regulated by the state along the lines of a European social democratic system."

Prunskiene had many friends in Estonia, the third of the Soviet Union's Baltic republics; she had defended her doctoral dissertation at the university there. Late in May 1988, she invited two prominent Estonian economists, Ivo Raig and Mikhail Bronshtein, to Vilnius for a seminar. The agenda was supposed to be economics, but it quickly became political. Activists in Estonia had already organized a Popular Front, and the idea quickly spread among the Vilnius intellectuals. Three of the younger and more daring men among them, including Zigmas Vaisvila, called a meeting for June 2 in a hall at the Academy of Sciences on Vilnius's main street, at that time still called Lenin Prospekt.

On June 2 several hundred people crammed into the meeting place. The organizers had to remove a table from the stage and allow the extra people to sit on the floor. Ostensibly, the meeting was about bureaucracy and how it was strangling *perestroika,* but the discussion soon spilled over into a broad critique of Lithuanian life, about the problems in government, in the environment, and in the economy, about the need to rein in the KGB, about the tyranny of the Party. There was no overt talk of independence, but the meeting was a pivotal event. Like the environmental demonstration that galvanized the little band of progressives in Ventspils, the meeting showed everyone in Vilnius that those who fundamentally disagreed with the status quo were not just isolated dissidents. They were the mainstream of Lithuanian intellectual life.

Another meeting occurred the next night. It was, Vaisvila recalled, a hot summer evening, and the temperature in the overcrowded hall quickly rose. The heat was not the only thing making people uncomfortable. They all knew that a Lithuanian popular front was the logical next step. It would be an organization that would support Gorbachev's economic and political reforms as well as incorporate issues such as the environment and urban preservation. Eventually, they all realized, it could become the Lithuanian independence movement. And, for just that reason, no one was prepared, as the evening dragged on, to move for the creation of an organization.

Finally Vaisvila got the floor. "I just said that everyone knows what we're here about, knows the main idea. But we were afraid of the name, the title *popular front.* All right, I said. We'll call it something else. Maybe *Sajudis* [which in Lithuanian means simply "movement"]. And I said, let's elect a group of people, whom we know from their writings and speeches, to head this group." He began to suggest the names of people to sit on the organization's board, including Kuzmickas, Juozaitis, Prunskiene, and about thirty others. The meeting, by acclamation, adopted his proposal. *Sajudis* was born. Within eighteen months, running on a pro-independence platform, it swept to a crushing victory over the remnants of the Lithuanian Communist Party in the republic elections of February 1990.

Although it had almost immediately engaged the loyalty of the Lithuanian population, *Sajudis* remained, as it was founded, an organization of intellectuals. No one epitomized this more than the man who became its leader, Vytautas Landsbergis. Landsbergis, named after a grand duke who led Lithuania to a brief period of medieval grandeur and empire, was the son and grandson of Lithuanian intellectuals. His grandfathers on both sides were active in the movement that led to the country's independence in 1918. His father was an architect who fled the country at the end of World War II and lived through the Cold War years in Australia. According to the propaganda spread by the Communist Party before the 1990 election, the elder Landsbergis was a Nazi sympathizer who signed a statement welcoming the Germans into the country in 1941. That was partly true, Vytautas Landsbergis's supporters said; the elder Landsbergis had welcomed the liberation from Soviet rule that the Nazis brought. But he was no Nazi, they went on. In fact, he had sheltered Jews and partisans the Nazis were looking for. Nevertheless, the old family connection with the Germans probably explains some of the deep dislike Moscow felt for him.

Vytautas Landsbergis became a musicologist at Vilnius University. He specialized in the work of the turn-of-the-century Lithuanian composer Mikalojus Ciurlionis. Just as in Latvia, the work of perpetuating the native music had distinct political connotations. Orthodox communists condemned Ciurlionis as a bourgeois nationalist. By specializing in his music, and teaching it to a new generation of Lithuanians, Landsbergis tacitly rejected Soviet ideology.

But Landsbergis had no direct political experience until the foundation of *Sajudis.* He looked and acted, in fact, much more like a music professor than a politician. (According to one widely told anecdote, he had once devoted a great deal of time at a *Sajudis* meeting to the question of which key the national anthem should be sung in.) In his late fifties, he is of average height and build, although his body has a soft, doughy look. He wears thick glasses, baggy suits, and a Vandyke beard, and his eyes, set close together, seem to be perpetually squinting.

Had the Lithuanian system required a direct popular election, Landsbergis might not have become his country's leader. He is a poor speaker, with stooped shoulders and a melancholy air, who sighs deeply before beginning an address, as if the opportunity to rally his audience is a burden that only a profound sense of duty could bring him to shoulder. At one point, while the Lithuanian Parliament was debating whom to elect as the leader, someone prevailed on Landsbergis to go outside to a courtyard where several hundred people had gathered, despite a cold drizzle. Landsbergis stepped outside, and someone draped a coat over his shoulders. Someone from the crowd gave him flowers. He smiled shyly and, with a cramped, awkward little motion, waved a couple of times. Then he went back inside, saying nothing. A poll taken by a Lithuanian newspaper in 1990 found that he ranked only sixth or seventh among prominent Lithuanians in public popularity. But within the councils of *Sajudis,* his fellow intellectuals appreciated his patience and ability to conciliate conflicting views. And it was they who would choose the country's leader.

They brought to this decision a remarkably sanguine view of Lithuania's prospects. I spoke at length about this to yet another of *Sajudis*'s philosophers, Arvydas Sliogeris, in the philosophy department office at Vilnius University, a room of scarred walls, heavy pillars, and oil paintings. The university was closed that day, in observance of March 8, International Women's Day. The election process, which involved runoffs in some constituencies, was almost over. It was clear that *Sajudis* would win enough seats to pass whatever legislation it chose in the new Lithuanian Supreme Soviet. What was not clear, of course, was what Moscow would let the Lithuanians get away with. So I asked Sliogeris how he assessed the Russians.

"We don't hate the Russians," he replied. "They're an unfortunate people."

Sliogeris regarded the entire history of Russia since 1917 as a colossal, irremediable error for which generations of Russians yet unborn would have to pay. "I don't know of another people that has destroyed itself the way the Russians have over the last seventy years," he said. "Stalin cut off the roots of the country. They destroyed the countryside and the peasantry. They forgot how to work, and now they don't know what work is. If they hadn't had so many natural resources to exploit, they wouldn't have gotten as far as they did, and those resources are disappearing. It was self-destruction, and, if there is a God, He can't forgive that."

Sliogeris did not believe Gorbachev, or anyone else, could arrest or reverse this decline. "They need a critical mass of people who can work and manage and think, and Stalin destroyed that," he said. This, he felt, would force the Russians to let Lithuania go. "They wouldn't let us go if they could avoid it, because it's too important to them to be a great power," he went on. (Like many of the Muscovites I spoke with, Sliogeris assumed that Russia's status in the world would somehow be tied to its ability to hang on to its empire.) "But they have to reckon with the West." Like most *Sajudis* strategists, Sliogeris assumed that the West would require at least a superficially peaceful Soviet policy toward Lithuania as a condition for the trade and technology exchanges that Moscow needed for any rational economic recovery plan.

Whatever it did, Sliogeris felt, Russia would decline, and probably break up. "There isn't really a Russia, or a Russian people," he said. "Just Moscow and the provinces. The Moscow bureaucracy is cosmopolitan; it tries to control everything. But the Russians have lost their roots. That's our strength. We're still a people with roots." He felt that the Soviet Union, like an unstable isotope, would break up into those elements that were irreducible. First the republics, such as Lithuania, would break free. Then, he imagined, Siberia, Leningrad, and other pieces of the Russian mosaic would break off. Russia would revert to what it was at the end of the era of Tatar power six or seven centuries ago, a collection of principalities. It would go through periods of anarchy and dictatorship. But it would not be able to maintain an empire again for a long time, if ever. Lithuania, as a consequence, had come to the most fortuitous moment in six centuries for the revival of its independence.

Based on such assessments, nearly all *Sajudis* strategists assumed that Moscow would react to a Lithuanian bolt for independence with an economic blockade rather than with tanks. To an outsider, Soviet economic sanctions seemed a powerful weapon. A paper prepared by a special commission of the old republic Supreme Soviet, and published by *Sajudis*'s English-language newspaper,

The Lithuanian Review, laid out the extent of the republic's dependence. Lithuania imported 97 percent of its fuel from the Soviet Union. It imported all its cotton, metals, tractors, and automobiles. Equally important, it paid for those imports either with goods or with rubles, and it paid prices much lower than world market prices. To replace its imports from the Soviet Union, Lithuania would have to multiply rapidly its exports to the world market in order to earn the hard currency that market would demand. In the interwar independence period, the country had earned its living as a supplier of agricultural products, such as butter, to the industrial nations of Western Europe. But the European economy had changed dramatically in fifty years. In 1990 the Western European countries competed for ways to export the surplus farm products their own well-subsidized farmers produced. There was no apparent market for Lithuanian farmers to exploit.

Still, the *Sajudis* leaders professed not to be too worried about a blockade. In part, Kazimiera Prunskiene told me, this was because the Soviet economy worked so badly in the best of circumstances. "In a certain sense there is already a blockade because of the general chaos in the Soviet economy," she said in early March. Suppliers in the rest of the Soviet Union no longer responded to orders from Moscow's central planners to deliver goods to enterprises in Lithuania or anywhere else. When they did deliver, they demanded goods, rather than rubles, in return. Some suppliers in Russia and the Ukraine, she said, had taken it upon themselves not to cooperate with Lithuanian enterprises. But in an economy where nothing worked, who could tell the difference?

Prunskiene professed to believe that reason and enlightened self-interest would prevail in the economic relations between Lithuania and the rest of the Soviet Union. Russian factories that needed Lithuanian components or food would deal with Lithuanian suppliers. "Ties that are natural and profitable for both sides should be preserved," she said. "Moscow would be acting on the basis of emotions, or ambition, if it tried to break the ties between Russia and Lithuania or the Ukraine and Lithuania. And that will hardly be possible when there are parliaments in Russia and the Ukraine which are democratically elected and trying to establish their own sovereignty. Moscow would be behaving very unsensibly if it didn't permit cooperation and take advantage of our strengths for the common interest."

Prunskiene's position had an obvious anomaly. Lithuanians had watched Moscow's seventy-year pursuit of an economic policy, communism, that nearly all of them felt was profoundly mistaken, if not irrational. For most of those years, they had suffered from that policy. Yet, particularly during the 1990 election campaign, they told the public that they expected Moscow to behave rationally toward them, to base its policies on a cold calculation of economic interests, as they strove for independence.

In truth, there was another reason behind the calculations of the *Sajudis* leaders. They felt very strongly that nothing the Soviets might do to retaliate for a Lithuanian effort to secede could be worse than what the Soviets had done to them and their families when Soviet power was established. I spoke to a *Sajudis* leader named Kazimieras Antanavicius one rainy morning at his office in the Lithuanian Academy of Sciences complex, on the banks of the Neris, the turbid river that flows briskly through the center of the city. Antanavicius, a pale, black-haired man in a loose-fitting suit, had been born during the last years of Lithuanian independence, in 1938. His father had served in the czar's army during the First World War, then joined the Red Army, "because Lenin promised Lithuania independence." After the war, he settled on a farm of 150 acres near the Baltic and had ten children. When the Soviets collectivized agriculture in the late 1940s, his Red Army service didn't help him. He was branded a *kulak* and sent, with his wife, to Siberia. He had only enough warning to send his children to hide in the homes of poorer neighbors.

At the age of ten, Kazimieras Antanavicius was left more or less on his own in a starving land. He and a sister two years older stole potatoes, scrounged shelter, and somehow survived. After ten years in Siberia, his parents returned during the Khrushchev thaw of the late 1950s. Not only had they survived their exile, they had amassed a nest egg of fourteen thousand rubles. Their old land had been turned over to a collective farm, but they managed to get a piece of it back and used their savings to build a small house. Antanavicius's father lived to be eighty-six and his mother ninety. Antanavicius had in the meantime managed to get an education, despite being deprived of his childhood. He did it in part by telling school administrators that his parents were dead; dead parents were politically preferable to exiled, *kulak* parents. Antanavicius became a construction engineer, then got a doctorate in construction management, although he had to wait for three years after completing his dissertation because the Party refused to certify his reliability.

Given all that, Antanavicius shrugged when I asked whether Lithuania could survive an economic blockade. "It wouldn't be fearful," he said. "We won't be hungry."

The *Sajudis* leaders got mixed signals from the two capitals whose opinions weighed most heavily in their calculations, Moscow and Washington. Through 1988 and 1989, the Kremlin alternated between harsh and conciliatory messages. Gorbachev deserved some of the blame for this. In August 1989, after the independence groups in all three Baltic republics combined to stage a massive protest against the secret protocols to the 1939 Molotov-Ribbentrop Pact, the Communist Party issued a withering denunciation and threatened to intervene. But Gorbachev was on vacation at the time, and when he returned, he held a conciliatory meeting with the Communist Party leaders of the three republics, calling for dialogue. The official who was believed directly responsible for the harsh attack, Politburo member Viktor Chebrikov, ex-chief of the KGB, was summarily retired shortly afterward.

Gorbachev seemed sometimes to concede the legitimacy of the three republics' desire for independence and to suggest that, under the right circumstances, they could have it. In December 1989, at the close of a brief visit to Vilnius, where he could see and feel the depth of pro-independence sentiment, he drove to the airport with Algirdas Brazauskas, the leader of the republic's Communist Party. According to a source who spoke to Brazauskas shortly afterward, Gorbachev said he understood Lithuania's feelings and requested only that the Lithuanians proceed gradually and cautiously.

Even after the first round of elections, on February 24, 1990, he remained conciliatory, Kazimiera Prunskiene recalled. "When we spoke to Mikhail Sergeyevich on February 27, he didn't threaten us with a blockade. On the contrary, he twice mentioned the necessity of further cooperation on the basis of mutual understanding and two-sided interests," she said. "He said that there would definitely be difficulties, and it would be worse for both sides [if Lithuania declared independence], but he didn't belabor the point."

Perhaps at this point Gorbachev failed to realize how firmly *Sajudis* was set on restoring independence and thought that a friendly approach might persuade the Lithuanians to stay in the Soviet Union. No doubt the *Sajudis* leadership heard more or less what it wanted to hear when he spoke. In any event, Moscow sent no direct and unambiguous message that it would deem a Lithuanian secession effort intolerable.

In Vilnius, the actions of the KGB reinforced the idea of Soviet vacillation. The KGB seemed to have given up trying to intimidate people and attempted, rather wearily, just to keep an eye on them. I spoke one day with a veteran of the independence struggle, Antanas Terleckas. Unlike Kuzmickas, Landsbergis, and the other Vilnius intellectuals, Terleckas had never accepted even a tacit accommodation with Soviet power. In the 1950s and again in the 1970s and 1980s, he spent time in jail and in Siberian exile for dissident activities. When he was released in 1987, he moved into a little two-family cottage at the end of a dirt lane outside Vilnius. The KGB rather blatantly installed a series of young agents in the apartment on the second floor. Terleckas continued his activities in the Lithuanian Freedom League, an organization that considered

Sajudis far too moderate. One day Terleckas confronted the KGB colonel he believed was responsible for his surveillance. When, he demanded, was the KGB going to withdraw its spies? When would it recognize the policy of *glasnost?*

The KGB officer didn't try to deny that he had agents living upstairs in Terleckas's house. He simply replied, "What difference would it make to you?" Terleckas, when he recounted the incident, regarded that reply as a sign of the KGB's arrogance. I took it another way, as a sign of resignation, an acknowledgment of the fact that, in the late 1980s, the KGB could no longer intimidate Lithuanians.

As if to confirm this, in late 1989 trucks began to roll at night out of the KGB headquarters on the Vilnius street that once was called Lenin Prospekt but had just been renamed for Gediminas, the medieval duke who built the Lithuanian state. There were rumors that the KGB was transferring its local archives to safer storage in Moscow. Two *Sajudis* leaders who had become members of the republic's government went to KGB headquarters and demanded to see the archives. "We were shocked," one of them, Romualdas Ozolas said in a report published in *The Lithuanian Review.* "We saw empty shelves and rooms full of empty boxes. We estimated that at least ten thousand individual files were missing." It was all very reminiscent of the last days of American influence in cities such as Saigon and Tehran. And it hardly suggested that Moscow believed any longer in its ability to control events in Vilnius.

The Lithuanians also received mixed signals from the United States. In their view, the American attitude was critical. The United States had, ever since 1940, refused to recognize the legitimacy of Soviet control over Lithuania and the other two Baltic republics. A Lithuanian legation continued to operate in Washington, and every year Congress passed a Captive Nations Resolution that called for the liberation of the Baltic states. Those gestures may have seemed like anachronistic Cold War symbolism to many Americans, but in Vilnius they had helped nurture the belief that Lithuania might again be free. No one in *Sajudis* in 1990 had any illusions about American soldiers coming to their rescue. But they could read the newspapers as well as anyone. They knew how much Gorbachev had invested in improved relations with the West. They assumed that suppression of Lithuanian independence would damage those relations, although they were not certain how much.

Early in March, a Lithuanian delegation traveled to Moscow to see the American ambassador to the Soviet Union, Jack S. Matlock. Matlock, a veteran foreign service officer, had a reputation as a hard-liner with the Soviets. He had served as an adviser to President Reagan during the most vituperative months of Soviet-American hostility, in the mid-1980s. If any American diplomat might have been expected to encourage Lithuanian hopes for support from Washington, it was Matlock.

Matlock instead delivered a lesson in realpolitik, according to two delegation members with whom I spoke after they returned to Vilnius. He told them that a Lithuanian government declaring itself independent without Soviet consent could not expect to get diplomatic recognition from Washington. Moreover, it could not expect much in the way of economic assistance. The United States always offered humanitarian assistance to starving people, he said, and the Lithuanians could expect that much. But nothing more.

Nevertheless, the *Sajudis* leaders tended to hear what they wanted to hear. The chargé d'affaires at the legation in Washington, Stasys Lozoraitis, sent a message saying he had been encouraged by what he heard from his contacts within the administration. Maybe, the *Sajudis* leaders thought, Matlock was giving them the views of only one faction. Maybe, they thought, there were other levers that would move the administration. "Public opinion plays a role in the West, and we can raise our voices and cry out to the whole world. And in Congress you have a group supporting Baltic independence, which will exert some influence on the government," *Sajudis*'s executive secretary, Virgilius Cepaitis, told me.

* * *

Within Lithuania, by early 1990, the Communist Party had ceased to be Moscow's agent, as a result, probably unintended, of Moscow's democratic reforms. The reforms meant that the Lithuanian Communist Party would have to compete with *Sajudis* to stay in power. In order to do that, the Party had to respond to the popular will. And that made its transformation inevitable. Starting in 1988, the Party shucked off most of the leaders that Moscow had installed in both the pre-Gorbachev and post-Gorbachev eras. The Party leader became a barrel-chested, gray-haired industrial manager named Algirdas Brazauskas, who looks and acts a bit like a physically tougher Tip O'Neill. Brazauskas announced that he too favored independence. Late in 1989, he and his allies in the revamped Party announced plans to sever it from the Communist Party of the Soviet Union.

That left only a rump faction within the Party loyal to Moscow. Lithuanians derisively called it the "Night Party," because its adherents could only find places to meet at night. Whatever credibility it might have had vanished when it became clear that the bulk of this group's members were ethnic Poles and Russians, minorities that in Lithuania made up about 15 percent of the population. Unlike the Latvians, the Lithuanians had an overwhelming majority of the population in their republic. Because of that fact, they often seemed not to care what the Poles or Russians thought.

The Polish-Lithuanian relationship had been a touchy one for centuries. In its 1990 manifestation, it brought out some of the least attractive, to an outsider, aspects of *Sajudis.* In medieval times the Polish and Lithuanian royal families had intermarried and cooperated against their common enemies in Germany and Russia. Lithuanians at times were kings of Poland. But, beginning with the Union of Lublin in 1569, Poland became the dominant partner, and over time the Polish aristocracy came to view Lithuania as its hinterland. By the close of the eighteenth century, Russia had taken control of both countries. But when the Russian empire collapsed at the end of World War I, one of the first actions of the newly independent Polish state was the invasion and occupation of much of what is now southeastern Lithuania, including Vilnius. The Soviets, ironically, restored this territory to Lithuania when they and the Germans dismembered Poland in 1939. The composition of the population, however, did not change as rapidly as did title to the land. Poles, who constituted about 15 percent of Lithuania's population before World War II, still accounted for about 7 percent in 1989; they were a majority in some of their traditional lands southeast of Vilnius.

Sajudis's relations with the Poles tended to produce nasty little quarrels in which neither side looked particularly democratic. On the one hand, the Poles' elected leaders could be counted on to complained loudly about their lack of political and cultural autonomy whenever Moscow television wanted to broadcast something negative from Vilnius. The Lithuanians, on the other hand, seemed incapable of even small conciliatory gestures. *Sajudis* published several newspapers, including one in the Russian language for the republic's Russian population. It could not get around to publishing a newspaper in Polish. *Sajudis* leaders generally took the position that if any of the republic's Poles wanted to receive their higher education in the Polish language, there were lots of good universities in Poland they could apply to, but they should not expect instruction in their native tongue at Lithuania's universities. After Lithuania's Catholic hierarchy liberated Vilnius's venerable cathedral from communist servitude as an art museum, it decreed that Mass in the cathedral would be exclusively in Lithuanian, never in Polish. After all, *Sajudis*'s Cepaitis told me, the Poles had not permitted Mass in Lithuanian when they controlled Vilnius and the cathedral.

This was one of the small manifestations of *Sajudis*'s tendency toward intolerant nationalism that worried some of its original supporters. Bronius Kuzmickas, when I spoke to him shortly after the February 1990 elections, said he wished that *Sajudis* had not won so easily. The lack of opposition, he feared, would only accentuate that tendency. Kuzmickas stifled those misgivings, however, and prepared to take his place among the *Sajudis* deputies in the new republic Supreme Soviet.

When I arrived in Vilnius, I expected to find Arvydas Juozaitis sharing in the postelection elation, and in the thick of *Sajudis*'s debate on independence strategy. We met in front of the gloomy old mansion that houses the Lithuanian Writers' Union and walked to a crowded cafeteria on Gediminas Prospekt. We stood in line for about five minutes and got a couple of cups of muddy coffee. I asked him what he was up to. Along with about a half dozen friends, he replied, he recently had founded a weekly newspaper, called *Siaures Atenai,* "The Athens of the North." He spoke proudly of the things they had published in their first issues: an essay by Czeslaw Milosz about the blitzkrieg in Poland and an abridgment, in Lithuanian, of Francis Fukuyama's essay on the triumph of liberal democracy and the end of history.

But although technically he remained a member of *Sajudis*'s governing council, Juozaitis had all but completely withdrawn from its activities. When I asked him why, he replied that it had begun to manifest "undemocratic tendencies." Some of its leaders, he feared, wanted to transform it from a movement into a nationalist party, like the faintly fascist nationalist party that had suspended Lithuanian democracy in 1929 and ruled until the Soviets drove it out.

It seemed, at first, absurd. *Sajudis* had used exclusively democratic means—peaceful rallies, protests, the ballot box—to achieve power in Lithuania. But Juozaitis was not the only person thinking this way.

Vitas Tomkus, the young editor of *Respublika,* a popular newspaper founded in 1989 with *Sajudis* sponsorship, had also parted company with the movement's leaders. He produced a lively, slightly yellow newspaper that did not flinch from suggesting that some *Sajudis* members, like the members of the old Communist Party hierarchy, were not above using their offices to enrich themselves. As a result, *Sajudis* had condemned him. Virgilius Cepaitis, when I asked him about *Respublika,* stated flatly (but without evidence) that "control of that paper has been seized by the ideological department of the Communist Party." To Tomkus, that was just another sign that *Sajudis*'s leaders did not understand pluralism. "Their idea is that while Lithuania is an occupied country, it is not possible to criticize *Sajudis,*" Tomkus said. He worried that "we are destroying Bolshevism, but we are building another bolshevism."

Arvydas Sliogeris expressed these fears in a more scholarly way in an article published just before the elections. *Sajudis,* he wrote, had committed a fundamental mistake by making national independence, rather than democracy, its highest priority. In the minds of *Sajudis*'s leaders, of course, there was no conflict; they believed they were working for both. But, Sliogeris pointed out, the politics of nationalism tend inherently to be both impatient and antidemocratic. Nationalism elevates the national charismatic rituals and symbols—the flag, the anthem, the human chain across the Baltic states—above democracy's gradual and mundane pragmatism and compromise. "The ritual goal requires from each person striving for it unconditional submission and unwavering adherence to the ritual," he wrote. "Whoever deviates from the ritual is denounced as a heretic."

The fact that Sliogeris published his article in a *Sajudis* newspaper suggested that the Lithuanian movement still tolerated a certain amount of heresy. But I thought of his warning about the potential conflict between nationalism and democracy, and about the tactical pitfalls to which nationalism can lead, many times in the ensuing days, when Lithuania made its bolt toward independence.

After the elections of February 1990, and the runoff round (in districts where no candidate received a majority) on March 10, *Sajudis* calculated that its candidates had won 95 of 133 seats, a majority sufficient to amend the republic's constitution. The *Sajudis* leadership faced a critical decision. There was no question that they would seek independence; any doubts about that had been resolved by the balloting, in which candidates who advocated separation trounced the few candidates who warned that it would be rash. Rather, the choice was over the means to independence. "There are two paths," Cepaitis summed up for me in the days between the election and the convening of the new Supreme Soviet. "One is to negotiate with Moscow on giving us more or less independence. The second is to declare the restoration of our state and to negotiate with Moscow as a state."

Advocates of the second path made a case based on international law. Lithuania, they said, had never voluntarily given up its sovereignty. The Soviets had illegally occupied and annexed it. In *Sajudis*'s view, that annexation had neither moral nor legal legitimacy. Therefore, it was not a question of declaring independence; Lithuanians had done that in 1918. It was not a question of seceding; Lithuania could not secede from a country to which it did not legally belong. The Supreme Soviet elected in 1990, they argued, would be the first freely elected representative body since the occupation. It could and should pick up where the last legitimate Lithuanian government had left off.

That case appealed to the *Sajudis* leadership on three grounds. Politically, it sidestepped the question of a referendum. In Moscow, the USSR Supreme Soviet was considering legislation setting out a procedure for secession, and referenda played a critical role in that bill. In Lithuania, *Sajudis* could no doubt easily win an overwhelming majority for secession, although it was not clear that the minority populations, particularly the Russians and Poles, would not give embarrassing majorities to remaining in the Soviet Union. In Estonia, and especially in Latvia, with greater minority populations, the prognosis was even less clear. Yet, if Lithuania were to hold an independence referendum, it would be very difficult for Estonia or Latvia to avoid one.

Second, the *Sajudis* leaders knew that as they prepared to convene Lithuania's new Supreme Soviet in Vilnius, Mikhail Gorbachev was getting ready to convene an extraordinary session of the Congress of Peoples' Deputies in Moscow and to ask it to amend the constitution to create a strong presidency, tailored to his requirements. Some *Sajudis* leaders felt it was important to act before Gorbachev acquired his new powers, lest he be tempted to declare direct Moscow control in the republic and prevent them from fulfilling their independence mandate.

Most important, the case for "restoration of our state" appealed to the logicians and philosophers in *Sajudis* as a logical and philosophically appropriate solution to the problem posed by the Soviet annexation of Lithuania.

No one with whom I spoke in the *Sajudis* leadership approached the problem as a politician might. That was natural enough; almost none of the *Sajudis* leaders had much experience in politics. A politician would have at least assessed the issue of Lithuanian independence from the point of view of the other party involved, Gorbachev. A politician would have sought a strategy designed to induce Gorbachev to calculate that it was better to let Lithuania go than to hang on to it. Such a strategy would probably require giving Gorbachev some sort of fig leaf, in the form of a process which suggested that Moscow still exercised some control over its dominions. The *Sajudis* leaders, though, often seemed to act on the assumption that their fate would be decided not in the Kremlin but at the International Court of Justice in The Hague.

Sajudis decided to convene the new legislature as soon as legally possible, a couple of hours after the polls closed for the runoffs. The day had been a strange one. At first light snow was falling. By noon a wind from the Baltic had blown the clouds away, and it was bright and sunny. By midafternoon snow was falling again. The skies cleared again in the evening. A crisp breeze blew, and there was a full moon.

The Lithuanian Supreme Soviet is housed in a new three-story building of white stone on the banks of the Neris, about a mile from the center of Vilnius. Other new government buildings, none of them particularly graceful, are linked to it in a bureaucratic complex. The building, until that day, meant little or nothing to most Lithuanians. Spiritually, the capitol of the country was the four-story brick tower that Gediminas built in the fourteenth century on a high bluff a mile or so upstream. (Vilnius, like Moscow, grew up around a fortress on readily defended high ground near a river.) When flying the red, yellow, and green Lithuanian flag became legal again in the autumn of 1988, Gediminas's Tower was where Lithuanian patriots first went to raise it. But Gediminas had failed to include an auditorium in his tower, so, the newly elected deputies gathered at the government complex the communists had built.

As it happened, I got a ride to the opening session in a group that included Kazimiera Prunskiene. When we arrived, perhaps five hundred people had gathered in the courtyard of the legislative building, which is shaped like a U with its open end facing the river. Carrying candles, Lithuanian flags, pro-independence signs, and even a sign that said PRUNSKIENE FOR PRESIDENT, they surged gently toward her as she got out of the car, smiling. We could hear the muffled sound of gloved hands applauding her. Smiling even more broadly, she walked toward the front door through an aisle that the crowd formed for her. *"Laisves!* [Freedom!]" someone shouted. The people took up the chant. *"Laisves! Laisves!"* Other deputies, coming along right after Prunskiene, heard the same chants. In a little while, the people started to sing Lithuanian folk songs, in clear, high, church-choir tones, their pale faces glowing in the light of their candles and the moon.

Inside the hall, the dominant color was amber; the amber trade was the first commerce of the Baltic peoples. The seats were made of blond wood, upholstered in amber cloth. Behind the rostrum hung a huge amber-colored tapestry, and embossed on it, in the same color, were the Soviet hammer-and-sickle seal and the letters *LTSR,* which, in Lithuanian, stand for Lithuanian Soviet Socialist Republic. The deputies to the new legislature occupied only the first five rows of seats. The rest were taken by spectators: bureaucrats from the Lithuanian government, guests, and foreign correspondents. I saw no Russian correspondents, however. To the Moscow press, this would be almost a nonevent, and what coverage it received would be determined not by reporters on the scene but by officials in Moscow.

The deputies, almost none of whom had served in a legislature before, took their preliminary duties very seriously. They earnestly debated how many deputies should be required to force a roll call vote, rather than a vote taken by holding up their deputies' identification cards and letting the chairman count them. There was an electronic voting apparatus, with scoreboards mounted high on the wall, but no one seemed certain how it worked.

The first real item of business was the election of a chairman, who would serve as the leader not only of the legislature but of the republic as a whole. Although *Sajudis* had won an overwhelming majority, the voting would be by secret ballot. No one knew for a certainty what the *Sajudis* deputies would do in the privacy of the voting booth. The next morning they got to it, a bit hesitantly. When the temporary chairman opened the floor for nominations, no one said anything for a while. Then a woman stood up and nominated Romualdas Ozolas, the deputy chairman of *Sajudis* (and yet another philosopher). Ozolas nominated Landsbergis. Someone else nominated the Communist Party leader, Algirdas Brazauskas. The nominations seemed to be, in contrast to those at an American nominating convention, completely unscripted and the rhetoric unpolished. Speakers gripped the lectern tightly, spoke in monotones, delivered a few sentences, and sat down.

The deputies took a break. In the hallway, a group of foreign correspondents besieged Brazauskas. According to some polls, as well as to what I had been hearing on the streets, Brazauskas was the most popular and respected politician in Lithuania, even though his party had been trounced by *Sajudis.* "He's more *tolkovy,*" one old woman said to me. The Russian word she used literally means "sensible," but it has the connotation of knowing how to use one's elbows, of being, perhaps, better suited to handle a negotiation with Mikhail Gorbachev. Brazauskas has the bearing of a leader, being tall and robust, and his position of relative privilege helped him project an image of competence. In the entire legislature, he was the only deputy with a decent-looking suit. Yes, he told one reporter, Gorbachev had told him that Moscow might demand $18 billion in compensation for its lost industrial plant should Lithuania secede. Of course, he added, Lithuania would have its own compensation demands. Had Moscow been pressuring for postponement of a decision on independence? Yes, he said, there had been calls, to him and to others, suggesting that the Lithuanians do nothing rash and come to Moscow to talk things over. He would not say who had placed them. (In fact, other sources said, a leader of the USSR Supreme Soviet had called Landsbergis with that request.)

When the deputies reconvened, all the candidates besides Landsbergis and Brazauskas withdrew. Brazauskas spoke first. A month before, in an interview with *The Lithuanian Review,* he had refused to say when Lithuania should restore its independence; he spoke then only of a "long, hard road." But by this time he knew which way the wind was blowing. "The restoration of the independence of the state of Lithuania is our immediate task," he said. He promised to support that and to negotiate with Moscow for the removal of Soviet troops and "real economic independence." Then he returned to his seat. The temporary chairman gently reminded him that he would have to answer questions from the deputies. This, presumably, had not been on the agenda of Lithuanian legislatures under the ancien régime. Brazauskas, slightly redder in the face, returned to the lectern and fielded some questions. What concrete plans did he have for achieving economic independence, a vehemently pro-secession *Sajudis* deputy demanded. Negotiations with Moscow, Brazauskas replied, were the only way he could see. "Maybe the deputy knows some other way," he added. "Let him present it."

Then it was Landsbergis's turn. He moved slowly to the podium, wearing a baggy gray suit, and, characteristically, heaved a deep sigh before he began to speak. As he talked, he rocked slightly, back and forth from the microphone, and he concluded his address even faster than Brazauskas had. (Neither man, nor anyone else in the legislature, seemed interested in taking advantage of the television cameras present to address a wider audience. Lithuanian democracy, obviously, had yet to progress to the point where television skills define a politician.) Lithuanians' common goal, Landsbergis said, was to restore their own state and to be free people in a free land. "We are standing on the threshold of historic change," he concluded. "I think I can contribute. I will seek peace, harmony, and concord of all nations living in Lithuania." But in the question session, Landsbergis said that he saw no reason to establish a second university in Lithuania to educate Poles. If they wanted an education in Polish, he concluded, let them go to Poland.

The deputies went solemnly to cast their ballots, quite aware that Lithuania would be choosing its leader via a democratic process for the first time in three generations. They filed downstairs to a sunken lounge off the building's lobby. The balloting committee had set up a table, and as each deputy picked up his ballot, a committee clerk stamped it to validate it. Then the deputy walked into one of two booths, made of a wood frame draped in bright yellow cloth. There he (only a handful of deputies were women) might cross one or both names off the ballot, leaving either the name of his favored candidate or a blank ballot, which counted as an abstention. Coming out of the booth, he dropped the ballot into a wooden box. After lunch the committee chairman announced the results. Landsbergis had 91 votes for and 42 against. Brazauskas had 38 votes for and 95 against. Four people had voted against both candidates, but it hardly mattered. Landsbergis had held the *Sajudis* vote together. He was Lithuania's new leader, and the first noncommunist ever to head a government in the Soviet Union.

The deputies rose for a standing ovation. Landsbergis stood, eyes downcast, and nodded. He moved to the chairman's position and spoke. "I don't know how even to address you," he said. "We are friends and colleagues, people sharing the same fate. The fate of this land unites us." An elderly woman, a survivor of Stalin's camps, came down from the spectators' gallery by prearrangement. She had embroidered a purple ceremonial sash for Landsbergis, following a Lithuanian custom of presenting a sash to someone about to embark on a long journey. She draped it over his shoulder and tied it at the hip. On it were the words "May success accompany you, may God accompany you, and may God save you." Landsbergis stood for a moment with this odd garment on, looking quite embarrassed. The photographers in the hall clustered around him, their cameras clicking and whirring. After a moment, he took the sash off and waved them away.

Landsbergis made a gesture toward unity by asking Brazauskas to become one of his deputy chairmen. He knew that Brazauskas had already said he would not accept such an offer. Brazauskas, evidently a proud man, did not change his mind. "The results of the voting were not in my favor. The majority of the legislature has voted against me," he said. "It would not be fitting." Later, in the corridor outside the meeting hall, I asked Brazauskas when it had become clear to him that he would lose. "As soon as they announced that there would be free elections to the Supreme Soviet of Lithuania," he said, and walked away. Landsbergis nominated three *Sajudis* legislators as his deputy chairmen, including Bronius Kuzmickas.

With their strength conclusively established, Landsbergis and *Sajudis* moved forward with the rest of their hastily planned agenda. A few weeks before, in *The Lithuanian Review,* most *Sajudis* leaders had assumed that the movement would not try to declare independence for several months after the election. Only Landsbergis had suggested what would happen. "A great deal will depend on the general political situation in the Soviet Union, which may even make us act more quickly than we would like," he had said then. After that interview, Gorbachev had announced his plans to create a powerful presidency, including the power to rule by decree anywhere in the Soviet Union. The Congress of Peoples' Deputies was about to convene in Moscow, presumably to give him what he wanted. The *Sajudis* leadership had become convinced that delaying action might risk the opportunity to act. The laws they intended to enact had been drafted hastily, and reporters got copies on odd scraps of paper, some in Russian, some in English.

The five bills on the agenda reflected the work of *Sajudis's* lawyers, who carefully structured them to create a legally impeccable bridge from a territory occupied and administered for fifty years by the Soviet Union to a free state. First, the deputies resolved that they had been given a mandate in the recent elections to "restore the Lithuanian state and to reflect the sovereign will of its people." The deputies marked paper ballots; then Landsbergis read the name of each and asked him to confirm his vote. Of the deputies, 126 voted for the resolution. Six, all representing the Polish population, abstained. One Polish deputy, Stanislav Peshko, explained to me later that the Poles had abstained because they felt the new order *Sajudis* was creating failed to protect their rights.

The next resolution renamed the state the Lithuanian Republic, dropping the words *soviet* and *socialist* from its title. And it adopted as the official seal and symbol of the new republic the silhouette of a legendary Lithuanian knight, Vitas. The passage of this resolution provided the occasion for some theater. As soon as the vote, 133–0, was announced, a plain amber-colored curtain was raised to cover the old hammer-and-sickle seal behind the rostrum. As the symbol of their subjugation disappeared, the deputies stood and applauded. The crowd of several hundred people standing under a cold rain in the courtyard outside the hall surged forward and tore the copper version of that seal, which was about four feet in diameter, from its place above the lintel of the front door. Once the old seal was on the ground, they tromped on it for a moment, then tossed it contemptuously to the floor in the lobby. Someone later carted it unceremoniously away, while others worked to mount a silk-screen version of Vitas, the Lithuanian knight, above the lintel.

By this time it was getting late, but Landsbergis and the *Sajudis* leadership pressed on. They asked the deputies to consider the last three resolutions as a package. The first was the historic document, and changes were being made in the draft until its introduction. It declared that "expressing the will of the people, the Supreme Council of the Lithuanian Republic resolves and solemnly proclaims the restoration of the exercise of the sovereign rights of the Lithuanian state, infringed in 1940 by alien aggression. From this moment, Lithuania again becomes an independent state."

The second element in the package was a lawyer's document. It reinstated the 1938 Lithuanian constitution in an effort to link the 1990 legislature's authority with that of the last sovereign Lithuanian government. The final portion of the package suspended the 1938 constitution and replaced it, temporarily, with a patchwork of new Lithuanian and existing Soviet laws. Since 1940, of course, much had changed in the world; television, for instance, had been introduced. The old Lithuanian legal code had not envisioned such things, and it would take time to draft and enact Lithuanian laws to cover them. In the meantime, some Soviet law would continue to apply.

When the debate opened, surprisingly, no one stood up and declaimed about the course of human events or even the iniquity and fate of the Soviet Empire. No one, except for one of the Polish deputies, even questioned the wisdom of an abrupt declaration of independence. This stemmed, I thought, in part from what Arvydas Sliogeris had written about: that tendency of a nationalist movement to make obeisance to the ritual goal the ultimate political priority. But it also reflected what I had found in Latvia. Among members of both nationalities, there was no point in debating the wisdom of independence. The desire to be free from the Soviet Union was something that Latvians and Lithuanians felt at an emotional level beyond the influence of debate.

Instead, the deputies picked assiduously at seeming nits in the package, such as whether the new legal framework should provide for local government elections every three years or every five, or whether an individual could serve on both a local council and a national council. What had promised to be a dramatic, emotional event instead became rather turgid. As the evening wore on, reporters in the press gallery could be seen nodding briefly off to sleep.

Midway through the debate, Landsbergis recognized some visitors: Lev Shemayev and Sergei Kovalyov, both members of the democratic, anticommunist movement within Russia. "I want to congratulate you," Kovalyov said. He is a thickly bearded man who had spent time in prison for his dissident views. Recently he had been elected to the Supreme Soviet of the Russian republic. "You are creating a miracle. But let's not be too optimistic. In my country [Russia], you may get an unfriendly response. They talk about how they freed Lithuania from the Germans and built its economy, not about how they deported one-third of its population to Siberia. But they're not the real Russians. A true Russian bears the guilt for what other people of his nation have done. Forgive me; forgive us all."

Finally, at half past nine, the deputies voted. They marked paper ballots. After the ballots were collected, Landsbergis opened each and read each deputy's name. The deputies stood as their names were called to affirm their votes. The six Polish deputies again abstained. All the rest voted for independence. "I congratulate you. The act passes," Landsbergis said. Then, again by prearrangement, a massive red, yellow, and green Lithuanian tricolor that had been furled on the floor below the plain amber curtain rose slowly behind the podium. A recording played the Lithuanian national anthem. The deputies, previously so solemn, clasped hands and raised them over their heads, chanting *"Lietuva! Lietuva!* [Lithuania!]"

After the cheering died away, the deputies lined up proudly to sign a ceremonial copy of the declaration of independence they had just enacted. I saw Justas Paleckas standing off to one side, observing. His father, also named Justas Paleckas, had been a left-wing journalist in 1940, when the new Soviet overlords of Lithuania had selected a government to their liking. The elder Paleckas had become the first acting president of the country and then had served for many years as chairman of the republic's docile Supreme Soviet. His son had been a journalist and Soviet diplomat before returning to Vilnius as one of the leaders of the local Communist Party apparat. He is a tall, gray-haired man with a chiseled face and a reputation for acute intelligence, and he had adopted the pro-independence position in time to be elected to the new legislature and to maintain cordial, if guarded, relations with *Sajudis.*

I asked Paleckas how his father, who died in 1980, would have reacted to the evening's events.

"I think positively," Paleckas said. If my question irritated him, he managed to conceal it.

Even though he had helped to found the Lithuanian Soviet Socialist Republic?

"You have to know the history of Lithuania," Paleckas replied. "Then, there wasn't a man in the world who could have prevented what happened. He could only try to make it a little milder, a little less inhumane."

Had his father, and the other Lithuanians who cooperated with the Soviets, really believed in communism?

"Well," Paleckas replied, drawing the word out. "I think he really believed. So did a lot of intellectuals at that time who didn't know all the facts that have only recently become widely known. [He was referring to the details of the crimes of Stalin and other Soviet leaders.] Even though I, for instance, worked as a diplomat in the West for a long time and had access to a lot of facts and sources, I thought it [the accusations] was all propaganda. But it turns out it was true."

He himself, Paleckas said, still believed in the ideals of social justice and equality, of a sensibly organized society. But he no longer believed that the Communist Party responded to those ideals. So he was supporting independence and would sign the declaration, though not without a touch of cynicism.

"You know," he said as we watched the deputies file past the declaration and sign it, "fifty years ago, they lined up just like that to sign the declaration asking admission to the Soviet Union."

Outside the hall, in the courtyard, I found no such cynicism. Although it was almost midnight, several hundred people were still standing there, their faces glowing in the light of the candles they held, bearing witness to what had happened inside. One of them had an accordion, and he played folk songs about mountains and forests, Lithuanian boys and Lithuanian girls. The people swayed and sang along. One woman, sixtyish, dressed in a traditional Lithuanian peasant's costume trimmed in red, yellow, and green, told me what she recalled of the day when Lithuania had passed under Soviet control: her teacher had disappeared and all the children had cried. She would, she said, remember this day as clearly as she did that one. "Give our regards to President Bush!" a grizzled old man shouted happily when I told him where I was from. In a few days, Mikhail Gorbachev would react angrily to what had happened in Vilnius and begin an escalating series of sanctions designed to force its retraction. George Bush would decline to extend diplomatic recognition to the new Lithuanian government. But the people in the courtyard hardly cared, as they sang their songs, held hands, and swayed gently in the cold rain.

THE TRANS-CAUCASUS

September 1990

On the border between the Soviet republics of Armenia and Azerbaijan, rocky streams and dried up branches furrow the withered, brown hills. Peasant villages cling to the sides of the narrow, blacktop roads like beads on a string. The border snakes over the ridges and around the streams and roads, and near the neighboring villages of Baganis, in Armenia, and Baganis-Airum, in Azerbaijan, an outsider can barely tell where it is, or has been. Rows of cement fence posts meander across some of the scrubby meadows, marking unsuccessful efforts to agree on a line. An old, red stone church with the characteristic Armenian drum-and-conical dome, topped by a cross, seems to mark the eastern boundary of Armenian land, but the people who live around it now are Azerbaijanis. In late summer, when I visited the two villages, I found only one reliable marker: a squat, green armored personnel carrier with a machine gun mounted in the turret, stationed by the Soviet Army on the road between the villages, at the edge of Azerbaijani territory.

Until the era of *glasnost,* Soviet power suppressed border disputes and enforced the observance of proletarian internationalism among the villagers who worked on the vast state farms called *sovkhozi* on both sides of the line. In Baganis and Baganis-Airum, weddings best illustrated the kind of amity that resulted. "We went to their weddings, and they came to ours," a man named Allakhverdi Poladov, who used to live in Baganis-Airum, told me. But when I asked if he would permit his daughters to marry Armenians, he laughed harshly and replied, "God forbid." Azerbaijani boys, he explained, might marry Armenian girls, if they were pretty. But on both sides of the border, a girl most often moves into the household of her husband's family, and an Azerbaijani girl who moved in with Armenians was considered lost.

Azerbaijanis and Armenians both tend to have black hair, brown eyes, and complexions that range from sallow to olive. I asked Poladov how he and his fellow villagers told the two groups apart. "Their noses are very long and hooked," he said. "And their faces are dark and unpleasant." Everyone around us, in an outdoor tea garden, laughed in agreement. They were all Azerbaijanis, but I heard almost the same words, and the same hard laughter, when I posed the question to Armenians.

By the spring of 1990, tension between the two republics had grown feverish, and neither Moscow nor the governments of the two any longer had the strength or the inclination to enforce proletarian internationalism. The paved road from Yerevan, the Armenian capital, to Noyembryan, a provincial Armenian seat, crosses into Azerbaijan at several points near Baganis. During the winter, Azerbaijani farmers along the road had taken occasionally to blasting away with their shotguns at passing Armenian cars and trucks. On March 22, the eve of an Azerbaijani spring holiday called Novoruz, they did so with particular gusto, shooting up a convoy of trucks and wounding several people in a Volga sedan. Someone got on the phone to Yerevan and asked for help.

The help arrived at about two o'clock on the morning of March 23. Several cars full of Armenians armed with Kalashnikov assault rifles and shotguns arrived in Baganis via a dirt road that avoids Azerbaijani territory. Before dawn they slipped across the border to

Baganis-Airum and murdered eight Azerbaijani villagers, burning about twenty homes. The bodies of one family, including an infant, were found burned in the embers of their home. By the time troops of the Soviet Ministry of Internal Affairs arrived in Baganis-Airum, the attackers had fled.

The soldiers, known as internal troops to distinguish them from regular Soviet Army troops, set up some checkpoints along the border, but they could not pacify it. Shootings and kidnappings continued through the summer. In mid-August, Azerbaijanis stopped an Armenian car attempting to cross through Azerbaijani territory. They took one hostage, but the second occupant of the car escaped and sounded the alarm. Within hours, dozens of heavily armed Armenian guerrillas, whom the Azerbaijanis call *sakkallilar,* or bearded ones, began to filter into Baganis. On August 19, a battle erupted.

I heard about it from one of the soldiers manning the armored personnel carrier stationed between Baganis and Baganis-Airum. He was a slightly built, nineteen-year-old sergeant from Tashkent named Yefim Liberman, dressed in camouflage fatigues and a blue-and-white striped T-shirt. Sergeant Liberman carried his Kalashnikov casually slung over his shoulder, and he had successfully cultivated the bored but dangerous look of the combat veteran at rest. On the nineteenth, he said, at the border checkpoint between Baganis and Baganis-Airum, the internal troops had stopped a Kamaz truck. Liberman had heard the Azerbaijani version of events, in which the truck's passenger, without warning, opened fire on the troops. (In the Armenian version, the nervous truck driver for some reason tried to run the checkpoint, whereupon the internal troops shot him in the back.) From the Armenian hills ringing the checkpoint, the *sakkallilar* had opened fire in return. The internal troops asked the army for help, and Liberman's unit was sent to the checkpoint.

"We got here about eleven in the morning," Liberman said. "There were sixteen internal troops here; their sergeant had been wounded, and a senior lieutenant was dead. We called for help to the staff headquarters down the road. But they said they couldn't send anyone because they were under fire. At first, the Armenians were firing with automatic weapons. Then we noticed that their weapons seemed to be getting heavier." Liberman pointed to the crest of a high ridge to the west. "They had cannons up there and grenade launchers." Behind him stood the blackened ruins of a metal trailer and a farmhouse that the internal troops had used as a dormitory. The Armenian guns had destroyed both.

The battle continued for eight hours that day, with the soldiers holding their position and the Armenians firing on them from the high ground. Liberman saw trucks kicking up dust plumes on the dirt roads atop the ridges; he assumed that they were bringing ammunition and reinforcements to the Armenians. Early in the afternoon a white, unmarked helicopter, which he identified as a type sometimes used in Soviet agriculture, landed on the ridge, presumably bringing more reinforcements. Liberman said he ordered his men not to fire at the trucks or the helicopter. "Civilian transport," he said, rolling his eyes. The next day, Liberman's unit was assigned to another position, but the fighting around Baganis and Baganis-Airum continued for three days. Since that time, the army had patrolled the border roads, periodically setting up checkpoints. I asked Liberman what would happen if the troops withdrew. "I'm afraid to say," he replied. "There would be a war, a real war. We're like U.N. troops here."

My escort, Kasum Aliyev, the second secretary of the regional Communist Party organization, walked back up the road from Liberman's position with me, eager to show all the damage the Armenians had inflicted. He pushed open a rusty metal gate, and we walked into a peasant's home. The Armenian fire had blown away the roof of the four-room house and left a hole in the side of the barn. The summer kitchen, under a shed roof attached to the house, was strewn with rubble. Down the road a little farther, the village library was in similar condition. Aliyev poked with his toe at a mound of books that lay in a pile of glass shards and chunks of concrete. He turned over the Azerbaijani edition of *The Collected Speeches of M. S. Gorbachev,* volume 1. He laughed, sarcastically. "Marx and Engels are in there, too," he said, pointing to another pile of books inside.

Outside the library, a low, green T-72 tank, the kind that Pentagon officials used to warn might roll across Western Europe, stood parked in a shallow trench, its long gun pointing at the Armenian ridge across the border. Next to it, in a slightly deeper trench, were a few flowers and some bloodstained rocks. They marked the spot where Senior Lieutenant Aleksandr Lipatov had failed to keep his head down on August 19. We drove up the road a little farther, to the village's Muslim cemetery. The brown grass was charred black, and some of the old, mossy tombstones had been turned over. "They came on August 22, just after the soldiers had temporarily withdrawn," Aliyev said. "They set fire to all the houses still standing, and to this cemetery. I could show you the Armenian cemetery," he went on, voice rising. "We haven't touched it. But in Armenia, they've destroyed everything Muslim!"

We drove on to an intermediate school that the army had commandeered for its local headquarters. A soldier had created a guard post out of a rusty pipe and an old steel gate, mounting the pipe across the road to stop incoming traffic and the door over his head to stop incoming shells. In the school's dusty little playground stood two green cannons, mounted on wheels, each with a barrel about twenty feet long. They were scarred by bullet marks, with wires hanging out of holes in their metal skins. On the other side of the school, a platoon of about sixteen soldiers in fatigues and the floppy green hats that Soviet soldiers wear in hot climates were going through an inspection. The senior officer present was a lieutenant named Boris Bobikin, who had the brass belt buckle with a tank on it that signifies membership in the Soviet Army's armored units.

The guns in the courtyard, Bobikin explained, were one-hundred-dred-millimeter cannons that the Soviet Army had retired about twenty years ago. Instead of destroying them for scrap, though, the army had distributed them to state farms, which used them to shoot rainmaking chemicals into clouds. During the August battle, his unit had counted eighteen cannons firing in the hills above the two villages. They had disabled two of them by firing at them from a helicopter, then sent tanks up into the hills to tow them in. He did not know precisely where the cannons had come from, or where the Armenians had found the shells to fire from them, although the KGB had sent an investigator to try to trace them.

It was getting dark, and Aliyev took me back to Kazakh, the regional capital, in the white Volga that was one of the perks of his Party position. Kazakh was a farm town, where cows occasionally grazed near the main street. Piles of onions and melons spilled out of the grocery stores and kiosks; in contrast to what would have happened in a Russian city, no one had lined up to buy them. Kazakh's poverty lay in a lack of other supplies. Several building projects had simply stopped for lack of materials to finish the interiors, and weeds were growing in the concrete shells. Only the regional soviet, or governing council, had the requisite priority to finish a building, and its new headquarters gleamed, down to the marble staircase. After trying a couple of restaurants that had already closed, Aliyev found one with tables set up in a grove of trees by a small creek, each in its own little clearing. Light bulbs strung through the tree branches provided illumination. As we walked to our table, diners, all men, rose to greet and shake hands respectfully with Aliyev. In some parts of the Soviet Union, the Party has lost power. But in Kazakh, it retains control.

A waiter brought a bottle of vodka, some thick, chewy bread, a salty white cheese called *pendyr,* and roasted Azerbaijani dishes: chunks of lamb and beef, eggplant, tomatoes, peppers, and an aromatic tripe. I asked Aliyev whether there were any Armenians living in the town. "There were about two hundred," he said. "They worked in trade, spare parts, restaurants, wherever there was money. They lived a lot better here than they do now in Armenia. In Baku, they were all millionaires."

I knew that over the last two years both Armenians living in Azerbaijan and Azerbaijanis living in Armenia had been subjected to massive *izgnaniya,* a Russian word that means "explusions" but carries the connotation of being physically chased out. Aliyev confirmed that this had happened in Kazakh, but he hastened to add that it was not done barbarously, as in Armenia, but in . . .

He hesitated, looking for the right word.

"In a civilized way?" I suggested.

He nodded. "Yes, in a civilized way. Our youth wanted to burn them. We didn't allow that. Our police protected them, but told them to leave. They did. Some of them even stayed a month or so until they'd sold their houses."

A few minutes later, Aliyev asked me to turn off my tape recorder. He poured some vodka and proposed a toast: "To the day when Azerbaijanis get out from under the heels of the Russians, sell their own products abroad, buy weapons, and have sons to avenge what has happened here."

A week later, in Yerevan, I arranged to drive with a young economist named Samuel to the same border region but from the opposite direction. The road from Yerevan to Baganis passes over the resort country near gleaming, blue Lake Sevan and then up over some rugged, brown hills and along rushing, clear streams. Along the sides of the road, we could occasionally see peasants standing beside the carcass of a sheep, ready to sell meat to city people who had despaired of finding any in the state stores. But Samuel barely noticed the scenery or the meat sellers. He was looking for gasoline. The main freight line from the rest of the Soviet Union into Armenia runs through Azerbaijan, and, for the past year or so, the Azerbaijanis had often refused to allow trains through to Armenia, causing rampant shortages. Samuel had heard a rumor that the Baltic republics had contributed some gasoline to Armenia and sent it by a secondary rail line, but if so none of the gas had made its way to the few filling stations along the road. They were all shut; outside one of them there was a line of empty cars, whose drivers had apparently decided that this was the best place to leave their machines for the duration of the shortage.

But, like any Armenian still keeping a car on the road, Samuel was resourceful. He turned off the motor and coasted on the downhill stretches. He stopped at a taxi park to see if a driver might part with a little gasoline, but none would. When we passed a convoy of army trucks, parked by a roadside water pump, he stopped and asked if any of the soldiers were interested in selling a bit of gasoline. They might have been, they said, but their trucks ran on diesel fuel. In a town called Dilizhan he stopped next to a sign that advertised tire repairs, paid ten rubles to have his spare tire patched, then asked if anyone in town sold gasoline. There was someone in a house up the road, and we drove there. A woman answered the door. Her husband did deal in an occasional twenty-liter canister of gasoline, she said, but he had sold the last of his supply that morning. Samuel persisted. Well, she allowed, he sometimes kept a spare canister hidden away, but she did not know where it was. Samuel said that for a hundred rubles, he was sure she could find it. He was right. The price was twelve times the official pump price, but he was pleased with himself. "In this country," he said as we drove on, "you can buy anything if you have money. Even shark meat."

As we approached the border, Samuel stopped more frequently to ask directions, anxious to find the back road that went to Baganis without entering Azerbaijan. There were no road signs saying LEAVING ARMENIA, COME AGAIN, or WELCOME TO AZERBAIJAN. The only way to tell we were still in Armenia was the presence of pigs on the roadside; Azerbaijani farmers, being Muslim, don't keep pigs. Samuel waved down a gray-haired man driving a blue flatbed truck who said he was heading for Baganis as soon as he had dropped off a load of concrete. He offered to guide us and suggested that I ride with him. After a couple of miles, we stopped at a military checkpoint. The soldiers were as sloppy as most Soviet workers. They glanced in the back of the truck, said hello, and waved us on. We made a hairpin turn onto a rutted dirt road that wound up into the hills, then dropped, bouncing and rattling, toward Baganis.

Was it true, the trucker shouted over the grinding engine, that in America people couldn't go out in the streets after 6:00 P.M.?

In some places, I said.

He nodded sympathetically. "Things are going to hell around here, too," he said. "The Azerbaijanis are shooting people, and you can't find cigarettes anywhere. I think it's all Gorbachev's fault."

I asked why.

"He can't run the country," he shouted. "He's been married four times. Married, divorced. Married, divorced. How the hell can he run the country if he can't train a wife?"

Before I could ask where the driver had learned these previously undisclosed facts about Gorbachev's marital history, we were in Baganis. He dropped me off at the headquarters of the local *sovkhoz,* and I walked into the office of the director, a man in a blue windbreaker named Araz Yedigaryan, with coarse black hair and a nose shaped like the blade of a hatchet. I told him I had been in Baganis-Airum, seen the destruction there, and heard what the Azerbaijanis had to say about the Armenians. I wanted to know how the Armenians saw the conflict.

Yedigaryan nodded. "We don't deny that there's destruction over there," he said. "But you need to hear the roots of it."

For Armenians, the roots begin in 550 B.C., when Greek historians first recorded the presence of an Armenian kingdom in what is now eastern Turkey, on the plateau dominated by Mount Ararat, the peak where Noah's Ark, according to legend, came to rest. The Armenians established their kingdom by displacing a people called the Urarti, and their neighbors named them after a king called Armas. Armenian power reached its apogee in 95 B.C., when a king called Tigran the Great began a campaign of conquest that eventually subdued virtually all of Asia Minor, from the Caspian to the

Mediterranean, from the Caucasus to Palestine. That, however, only brought Tigran into conflict with another expanding empire, Rome, which ended Armenia's run as a great power in 66 B.C. Armenia's kings and princes became vassals and buffers for the empires of Rome, Byzantium, and Persia. Early in the fourth century of the Christian Era, at the command of their king, the Armenians became Christians, the first people to embrace that faith as a nation.

Turkish-speaking people entered the area much later. They were nomadic herdsmen from the dry steppes of what is now Mongolia. In the eleventh century, a Turkic band called the Seljuks swept out of the east and conquered nearly all of Asia Minor, Baghdad, and Damascus, laying the foundation for the Ottoman Empire. They adopted the Arabs' religion, Islam.

These conquests scattered the Armenians. In the Ottoman Empire, they formed one of the non-Muslim *millets,* or communities, and many of them moved to Constantinople and entered commerce. Others moved to Tbilisi, in Georgia, or to cities in southern Russia. At the beginning of the nineteenth century, according to figures compiled by the historian George Bournoutian, the Armenians constituted no more than 20 percent of the population of the khanate of Yerevan, the capital of the present Armenian Republic. According to Turkish sources, they had declined to minority status as well in their homelands in Anatolia.

Meanwhile, the Turkic herdsmen followed their warriors and settled on the conquered land. In the lowlands west of the Caspian Sea, they gradually assimilated a people who had lived in the Persian orbit, whose land was known as "the land of fire," perhaps because the local oil was used to light temple fires (*azer* in Persian). They became the forebears of the present Azerbaijanis, although, until the present century, they were called simply Tatars or Caucasian Turks, and their language was considered a peasant dialect of the Turkish spoken in the Ottoman Empire.

Deliverance of a sort for the Armenians came via the southward expansion of the Russian Empire. By the eighteenth century, the long process of ending the Turkic dominion over Russia and the Ukraine had acquired its own imperial momentum in persistent attacks on the declining Ottoman and Persian empires and the annexation of their lands. In 1801 Russia began incorporating, by force of arms where necessary, the independent khanates that had broken away from Persian rule in what is now Azerbaijan. They called this area the Trans-Caucasus because it lies, from their point of view, across the Caucasus Mountains. By 1828 Russia had swallowed, if not absorbed, all the territory within the present Soviet Trans-Caucasus, dividing the Azerbaijani people in two. The greater part of the Azerbaijanis remained in Persia; today they constitute Iran's largest ethnic minority.

The Armenians and the Russians were natural allies in this imperial venture. The Armenians saw the Russians as Christian Europeans who might protect them from the Muslim, Asiatic Turks and Persians. The Russians saw the Armenians as an industrious people who would be loyal and productive subjects in an alien land. They invited the Armenians scattered around the region to return to their ancestral lands. Many thousands did; others took advantage of the czar's patronage to settle in Baku, where the discovery of oil in the late nineteenth century created a boomtown. Armenians, being better educated and more accustomed to commerce, gained control of a disproportionate share of the local oil wealth. They tended to hold white-collar jobs, whereas the Azerbaijanis held the menial jobs in the oil fields. This competition for wealth and movement of populations exacerbated the natural tension between the two communities. And it further complicated the modern question of who has an ancestral right to what land, particularly in the territory known as Karabakh.

The Khanate of Karabakh straddled the eastern edge of the historically Armenian plateau and the plains below it. During the years between the arrival of the Turks and the arrival of the Russians, its rulers had been Muslims, and its population had been largely Muslim. But in the plateau area, known as Mountainous

Karabakh and roughly the size of Delaware, the local rulers continued to be Armenians, who offered political fealty to their Muslim khans in return for a degree of local autonomy. Although the Armenians considered Mountainous Karabakh a part of their patrimony, the Muslims had a legitimate claim as well. They formed a majority of the population in the khanate as a whole; their shepherds used its highlands for summer pasture. The Russians might have solved the problem, from the Armenian point of view, by drawing their provincial boundaries in a way that united Mountainous Karabakh with other historically Armenian districts around Yerevan. But they kept, essentially, the old khanate boundaries, forming a *gubernia* called Elisavetpol that included both Mountainous Karabakh and the plains below. It seemed a matter of minor consequence. Everyone belonged to the same empire.

That, of course, was hardly the only loyalty tugging at both nationalities. Azerbaijanis were divided among Shi'ites and Sunnis. The Armenians had a strong attachment to their national branch of Orthodox Christianity, which had kept their language and culture alive through centuries of political subjugation. And, as the nineteenth century went on, the European idea of the right of nations to self-determination and statehood attracted intellectuals in both communities.

The Russians occasionally found it convenient to exploit these divisions. In 1837, when Azerbaijani Sunnis rallied to a rebellion organized by a Daghestani named Shamil, the Russians organized Azerbaijani Shi'ites to help crush them. By the turn of the century, the Russians had begun to have problems with Armenian nationalists, who resisted imperial orders that established Russian as the language of school instruction and pressured the Armenian church to merge with Russian Orthodoxy. The Armenian unrest crested in 1905, a time of general Russian upheaval, when much of the army was off fighting Japan. The czar's agents responded by inciting a pogrom.

"We, the Muslims, were told by the administration: 'You have been economically enslaved by the Armenians. They are arming themselves and plan to create their own state. One day they will do away with you. The Armenians were told that the idea of Pan-Islamism had put down deep roots in all strata of the Muslim community and one day the Muslims would massacre them,' " an Azerbaijani leader of the time recalled. The pogrom began in Baku after an Armenian nationalist killed an Azerbaijani. Azerbaijanis from all over the province moved into Baku to exact revenge, and the violence spread quickly; the czar's police studiously failed to stop it. By the time the massacres ended, fire and pillage had destroyed the town of Kazakh and almost four hundred other villages, both Armenian and Azerbaijani. Between three thousand and ten thousand people had died.

The bloodshed was worse in Turkey. As the Ottoman Empire entered its final years, rising nationalism among both Turks and Armenians destroyed the equilibrium that had existed under the old *millet* system. The Armenians in Russia organized nationalist parties with the goal of creating a state of their own in eastern Turkey. The Young Turks who came to power in 1908 had their opposing goal: a pan-Turkic state stretching from the Mediterranean to Mongolia. The Armenians and their patrons, the Russians, were the principal obstacle to its achievement. In 1895 a tax dispute became the pretext for the massacre of perhaps 100,000 Armenians by Kurds and Turks in eastern Turkey.

When World War I broke out, Armenians in Turkey called unsuccessfully for the Ottoman Empire to remain neutral. Instead, it joined the Central Powers against the Allies and Russia, hoping to conquer the Trans-Caucasus, seize its oil, and unite the Turkish-speaking peoples. Armenians in Russia saw their opportunity: Russia would bring Ottoman power to an end, and they could build their state on the ruins. The Turks, under Enver Pasha, took the initiative, moving toward the Trans-Caucasus in 1914. But the Russians, with the open assistance of Russian Armenians and, perhaps, the covert assistance of some Turkish Armenians, threw them back and entered Turkey.

The Turks had no trouble identifying a scapegoat for Enver's failed campaign. In the spring of 1915, the Turkish government determined to remove the Armenian population from the war area to the deserts of what are now Syria and Iraq. Disinterested accounts of what happened thereafter are rare, but there is little doubt that the Turks and Kurds who executed this decision simply exterminated hundreds of thousands of Armenians, including women and children. A missionary from Germany, Turkey's ally in the war, wrote a letter recounting a part of the deportations: "They have marched them off in convoys into the desert on the pretext of settling them there. In the village of Tel-Armen (along the line of the Bagdad Railway, near Mosul) and in the neighboring villages, about five thousand people were massacred, leaving only a few women and children. The people were thrown down wells or into the fire." When it became evident that the Turks were slaughtering the Armenians, not simply moving them, the American ambassador to the Sublime Porte, Henry Morgenthau, sought an audience with the minister of the interior, Talaat Pasha. As soon as Morgenthau broached the subject, he recalled in his memoirs, Talaat responded angrily: "The Armenians are not to be trusted. Besides, what we do with them does not concern the United States."

This trauma, involving the loss not only of a significant part of the national population but also of its ancient homeland, became and remains the core of Armenia's national consciousness, always referred to as the Genocide of 1915. The Turks, as all Armenians know, have never apologized for what happened, or offered reparations, or even acknowledged that anything occurred beyond the unavoidable brutality of warfare.

Two years later, the collapse of the Russian Empire thrust a brief period of independence on the Azerbaijanis, the Armenians, and the third major Trans-Caucasian nation, the Georgians. (Many smaller nations live in the area as well.) At first, the three nations tried to band together in a Trans-Caucasian Federation. But that soon dissolved, in part because each element chose a different patron among the warring Great Powers, and in part because they could not decide how to divide their territory. Azerbaijan wanted to retain all of Elisavetpol *gubernia*. Armenia insisted on a revision of the boundaries that would have transferred Mountainous Karabakh to its sovereignty. That was hardly the only dispute. R. G. Hovannisian, in his history of the Armenian Republic, had to devise eleven types of cross-hatchings for a map that showed the various territorial claims and counterclaims in the region. After the federation split into three republics, the territorial disputes escalated into warfare and pogroms. Armenians slaughtered thousands of Azerbaijanis early in 1918. The Azerbaijanis, with the help of an invading Turkish army, slaughtered tens of thousands of Armenians a few months later. By the time the Red Army moved across the Caucasus Mountains in 1920, none of the three exhausted republics could resist. And none of the Great Powers cared to help them.

During these years, the Armenians tried twice to have third parties award them control of Mountainous Karabakh. In 1919, when British troops occupied the region, the British commanding officer, Col. D. I. Shuttleworth, supported the appointment of a temporary Azerbaijani governor for the territory and denied the requests of the local Armenians for unification with the Republic of Armenia. In 1921 the Armenians appealed to the Caucasian Bureau of the Communist Party to transfer Mountainous Karabakh to the new Armenian Soviet Socialist Republic. The bureau met on July 4 of that year, with Joseph Stalin present as an interested, but nonvoting, observer from Moscow. Its seven members voted four to three to transfer Mountainous Karabakh to Armenia, pending a plebiscite of its Armenian inhabitants. But the next day, the bureau reversed itself and decided to leave the region in Azerbaijan, though granting it broad autonomy. One Armenian historian with whom I spoke, L. A. Khourshoudian, hypothesized that Stalin twisted arms overnight to reverse the original decision, for reasons rooted in his twisted character. But records that would prove his thesis either never existed or have yet to come to light.

For the next sixty-seven years, Soviet power stifled periodic

Armenian efforts to raise the question anew. Stalin's regime enforced silence through terror. After his death, Moscow struck a new, tacit bargain with the two republics. The bargain required the local Communist Party leaders to suppress overt manifestations of nationalism or dissent. In return, Moscow allowed them to enrich themselves. The corruption of communist rule in the Trans-Caucasian republics was legendary. My driver in Armenia, Samuel, stopped at one point to buy a couple of cartons of cigarettes under the counter in a café; he paid twenty rubles a carton, fourteen over the legal price. The seller, he mentioned, would face two choices if caught: he could spend three years in jail or pay a fairly standard five thousand rubles in bribes to have the charges dropped. In Azerbaijan, almost everything was for sale. In Baku, I met a young nationalist named Azaddin Gyulmamedov. He told me that, at an earlier and more naive stage in life, he had applied to join the Communist Party, only to be told that securing approval for his membership would require a bribe of five thousand rubles.

Gyulmamedov, along with many other Armenians and Azerbaijanis, told me stories that suggested how, during the years of Soviet power, their people had carefully picked their way between submission and resistance to the state's promotion of Soviet values and Russian culture. "My father was a truck driver and a Party member," he said. "We moved to Baku in 1962, when I was a year old. He drove an oil pipe truck for a while, and then he became a policeman in 1969. At home, we always spoke Azerbaijani. Some of my relatives advised him to send me to Russian school, as a better way to get ahead. [Baku had schools where the main language of instruction was Azerbaijani and schools where the teachers spoke Russian.] But my father said that if I went to Russian school I would become Russian a bit, and he didn't want that. So I went to an Azerbaijani school, although at home he always helped me study Russian. He used to say the only thing the Russians had taught us was how to drink." At that point, a redheaded man with bleary blue eyes, looking very Russian and very drunk, although it was not yet noon, stumbled up to the car we were sitting in, stuck his head in the window, and mumbled a request, in Russian, for spare change. Gyulmamedov gave him some. "You see," he said to me. "God sent him to prove my point."

All of this has left the present Azerbaijanis insecure about their place in the world and suspicious of outsiders' intentions. Many of the people I met in Baku urged or warned me to write objectively about them. Many felt that both the Soviet press and the foreign press, under the influence of "the Armenian lobby," had portrayed them unfairly and that the world was rife with anti-Azerbaijani conspiracies. I visited one morning with a prominent Azerbaijani intellectual, Aidin Mamedov. He had a large, well-lit office in his capacity as director of a center for literary translations. He was also deputy director of the local Karabakh Committee, deputy director of a magazine called *Soviet Turkology,* and a candidate for the republic's Supreme Soviet. Mamedov, like nearly all Azerbaijani men, wore an open-collared sport shirt to work. He has a broad face, thick, gray hair, a mustache, and a few gold incisors. He spoke a slurred, accented Russian, usually blurred further by an "Azerbaijan" brand cigarette in his mouth. I asked him about the Turkic-Azerbaijani worldview and national character.

He responded by telling me that in the nineteenth century the Turkish world and Turkish culture had been one of the principal interests of German social scientists. "They knew it was a leading ethnic force," he said, adding that the Germans were well known for producing some of the best social scientists, artists, and philosophers in the world, even though they had made an obvious mistake with Marx. I asked why he had answered a question about Azerbaijani culture with a reference to German social science. "Because the German mind studies what is necessary and important," he said. To him, the interest of the Germans certified the validity of Turkish culture.

"All Turkish culture is based on nomadic culture," Mamedov went on. "The Turkish races are distinguished by the nomad's warlike quickness of mind and temper. They're very swift and impetuous. It's a natural gift. The Turks move fast and decide strategy on the run, unlike the Europeans, who sit and plot strategy. The Turks always had the blitzkrieg."

Western writers frequently cite the number of Muslims in the Soviet Union and speculate that the central authorities in Moscow must be worried about the spread of Islamic fundamentalism in their southern republics. In Azerbaijan, however, there was little evidence that Islam was a central factor in the anti-Soviet unrest. Over the years of Soviet rule, the state had dominated the mosques, and compromised them. There were only a few operating in Baku. Moreover, the Islamic fundamentalists of the Middle East are either Arabs or Persians. Dissident Azerbaijani intellectuals, seeking an ideological underpinning for their opposition to Soviet control, had turned instead either to Western social democratic concepts or, more frequently, to their ethnic identity, which predates Islam. Aidin Mamedov fell into the latter group.

Mamedov maintained that the Azerbaijanis' true history, and that of all the Turkic peoples, had been distorted by historians from other nations, particularly Russians. "The Russians hate the Turks because the whole Slavic world was under the Mongols," he said. "Their ideological machine fights against a unified Turkish world. You're Azerbaijani, you don't have any relation to Turkey. You're an Uzbek, or you're a Kazakh, or you're a Tatar [other Turkic nationalities in the Soviet Union]. Now they're manipulating the Turkish peoples against one another. There's fighting between brothers in Ferganah, in Osh [Soviet Central Asian sites of recent ethnic unrest]. Why? Imagine, if the Turks had a unified image of themselves. How many people would be unified under the Turkish banner? In Bulgaria and Yugoslavia, there are Turks. In Moldavia, the Gagauz are Turks. And then Turkey, the Crimean Tatars, the Azerbaijanis, the Kazakhs, the Bashkiri, the Uzbeks, the Kirgiz.

There are 50 million in the Soviet Union, 20 million in Iran. In the world altogether, about 100 million. You can imagine the strength. So they tell us we're not Turks. We're just Turkish speaking. It's a theory that serves the imperial interests."

These anti-Turkish, imperial interests, Mamedov told me, lay behind the new Soviet foreign policy and Mikhail Gorbachev's design for a common European home, a home designed to keep the Turks out. "To Europe, the Turkish people are a threatening demographic force. There's a historical experience, Jenghiz Khan and so on. Strategically, the construction of the European home is predicated on the possibility of the unification of the Turkish people. There's a division of roles here. And who has what role—Mr. Bush, Mrs. Thatcher, and Gorbachev know that. They know. We only guess."

The Armenians I met were not so prone to conspiracy theories, but they saw their history as an open wound, an injustice awaiting redress. The most important monument in modern Armenia sits atop a hill called Tsitsernakaberd, or the Castle of the Sparrows, a mile or two from the center of the city. On clear days, the site affords a view of Mount Ararat, across the border in Turkey. The monument itself is simple and impressive. It consists of a steep, bifurcated, metal pyramid rising abruptly from the ground at the end of a long concrete plaza. Next to it are twelve massive stone slabs, arranged in a circle and tilted to form an open dome around a gas flame. All the stone and metal surfaces are blank; there are no words etched anywhere.

The government of Armenia permitted the construction of the monument in 1965, only after thousands of Armenians dared to march and protest to commemorate the fiftieth anniversary of the massacres in Turkey in 1915 and to demand some sort of official recognition of those events. Given the politics of the time in the Soviet Union, permitting the construction of the monument was a major concession. The government tempered it by prohibiting the erection of a relief sculpture showing suffering people that the designers had wanted to build along the concrete plaza. The monument is entirely abstract. Nevertheless, Armenians know exactly what it is about. The bifurcated pyramid, a young woman named Hasmik Khourshoudian told me, represents the bifurcated peak of Ararat. The twelve stone slabs represent the twelve Armenian provinces lost in Turkey. They tilt over the flame as if bent over in grief, representing the grief of the nation. The flame, of course, is the memory of those who perished. Khourshoudian was surprised when I pointed out the absence of explanatory words on the monument. She could not remember where or when she had learned its symbolism.

At Yerevan State University, I dropped in one day on the chairman of the psychology department, a man with a round, florid face and a trim beard named Ruben Aguzumtsyan. Like many Soviet psychologists, he specialized in industrial efficiency. He had first become an electrical engineer and then a psychologist, and his research concerned ways to design working environments that help people operate complicated machinery such as ships or airplanes more effectively. When I asked him about the Armenian national character, he replied that he was not a specialist in that subject, but he did have a few general opinions.

The exigencies of climate and terrain, he said, had forced Armenians to become smart and hardworking; otherwise they could not have survived. "Just to live, a man has to expend enormous energy, because the territory is steep and mountainous and the plains where it's possible to live and grow things are very small. People have had to carry dirt on their backs up mountainsides, spread it out, then plant something. It's hellish work." The long history of strife and suffering had further tempered them, he added.

I asked how Armenians conveyed that history, particularly the history of 1915. "It's hard for me even to remember how I learned about it," he replied. The Soviet educational system, he said, offers only a sketchy history. "They don't tell lies, but they don't tell the whole truth, either." One of his graduate students brought me a seventh-grade history text. It contained only a page or so on the killings of Armenians in Turkey in the 1890s. "It's all correct, but it's not enough to really understand," Aguzumtsyan said. "We get a lot more than that, of course. We have a fine tradition of education by parents on national themes. Every Armenian family considers it an obligation to have sources on the history of the nation—books, literature. Even the littlest kid, in general terms, must know the history of the nation. It reflects a self-defense mechanism, self-preservation."

I asked how this preoccupation with history and genocide affected Armenian attitudes toward the contemporary Turks, and particularly the Azerbaijanis. "This knowledge has never led to any negative positions toward other nations," Aguzumtsyan replied quickly. But later that afternoon, as we walked toward the Castle of the Sparrows, Hasmik Khourshoudian suggested otherwise. "When I was growing up," she said, "the worst thing you could call a person was 'Turk.' "

The Armenians interpreted *perestroika,* one of them told me, as a promise by Moscow that "all the old deals would be reexamined." In the Trans-Caucasus, that effectively meant a return to the fractious status quo before Stalin clamped his lid on the Karabakh question. During the years of Soviet power, the Azerbaijani governments in Baku had done what they could to discomfit the Armenian population in Mountainous Karabakh, despite its formal autonomy. In 1930 they redrew the territory's boundary to separate it physically from Armenia. They rigged the television reception tower for the region so that the people could watch broadcasts from Baku, not from Yerevan. They closed Armenian churches. Although the schools taught in the Armenian language, they taught the history of Azerbaijan, not Armenia. The water supply became polluted, so the region had twice the rest of the Soviet Union's incidence of stomach illness. "I don't know of a more neglected oblast in the country," I was told by Arkady Volsky, who for a time in 1989 and 1990 was the Supreme Soviet's special viceroy in the region. "In their subconscious, they [the governments of Azerbaijan] were always thinking, 'the worse the better,'" he said. Volsky described Azerbaijani attitudes toward the Armenians of Karabakh as "a psychosis." Late in 1987, the Armenian population of Mountainous Karabakh began to agitate for separation from Azerbaijan and unification with Armenia, signing petitions and sending delegations to Moscow. At the same time, the Armenian intelligentsia in Yerevan was probing the new freedom to dissent promised by *glasnost.* As in other republics, the dissident movement in Yerevan began as an environmental protest; the demonstrators calculated that the government would find it hardest to rationalize repressing a rally in favor of clean air and water. Their small initial demonstrations went unpunished, just as the news of the renewed dissent in Mountainous Karabakh began to circulate. Silva Kaputikyan, a writer, remembers rising at a Communist Party cell meeting within the republic's Union of Writers on February 15, 1988. Kaputikyan has been publishing verse, essays, and children's literature in Armenian since the 1940s, writing first about love and, since her marriage had ended, increasingly about love of country. She was then seventy-one years old, stout, grayhaired, and cheerful. Her books have been translated into Russian, English, and other languages, and she is a woman of enormous prestige and popularity in her country. She urged the writers to break their silence and support their brethren in Mountainous Karabakh. They did, by sending a letter to Gorbachev. And, on February 20, the regional soviet, or council, of Mountainous Karabakh voted formally to seek incorporation into Armenia.

This Armenian request for a border revision represented the first time since the launching of *perestroika* that a nationalist movement had challenged, in a principled way, the existing order in the Soviet Union. Gorbachev responded, characteristically, with contradictory signals that suggested he had yet to come to grips with the divisions within his own government and with the inherent conflict between his desire for the democratization of Soviet life and the long repressed grievances of the country's national minorities. In Moscow, Gorbachev faced a conservative faction within the Politburo, led by Yegor Ligachev, that insisted on a tough response, denying the possibility of border changes without Azerbaijani consent. On February 21, the Politburo issued a stern statement rejecting the Armenian demands and condemning them as "extremist."

The Politburo statement inflamed the people of Yerevan. "When our people heard this unjust definition, the movement quite lost patience," Silva Kaputikyan recalled. The number of demonstrators in the Opera Square swelled until there were, according to some reports, between seven hundred thousand and a million in the streets, and the city was paralyzed by general strikes. (Crowd estimates from both Armenia and Azerbaijan in 1989 and 1990 doubtless suffered from exaggeration. The squares in which the demonstrators gathered are simply not big enough to hold the numbers reported. Yerevan's Opera Square, for instance, measures roughly 360,000 square feet. Packed like a subway car at rush hour, it could hold only about 120,000 demonstrators. Nevertheless, the numbers were massive.)

It was a pivotal moment. Ligachev, in an interview more than two years later, told me that he and the conservatives believed Gorbachev should have stood fast by the principle in the Politburo declaration. "If we had," he said, "things would have turned out differently." But the local Armenian Communist Party had lost control of the situation. Forcing the Armenians to give up their claim on Karabakh would have required a military crackdown that would jeopardize much of what *perestroika* was trying to accomplish.

Instead, Gorbachev handed the ball to the man who was then the leader of the Politburo's liberal wing, Aleksandr Yakovlev. Silva Kaputikyan recounted what happened next. "On February 25, I suddenly got a telephone call from Moscow," Kaputikyan told me.

"A friend of mine answered it, and she said, 'My God, it's Yakovlev on the phone.' I'd known him for a long time. When I was visiting Canada, he was the ambassador there, and I was his guest. He's a very literary man, you understand. He thought I could somehow rein in the people. You understand? He said the people were in the streets and I should 'put out the fire.' I said that before I might have been able to, but after the television broadcast that malevolent [Politburo] resolution, I can't. He said, 'Who can?' I said I didn't know. I was very nervous. I talked about how for three hundred years we had looked to the Russian people when we were dissatisfied and never turned to others. We had looked to the Russian people with love, I said, but apparently you pay less attention to love than to hatred from the Turks. That was my spirit, and we had a very sharp conversation for a half an hour. And as we finished, he said, 'When you're in Moscow, drop by.'

"That night Zori Balayan [another prominent Armenian writer and activist] called and said Yakovlev would receive us tomorrow and that I should fly to Moscow as soon as I could. The next morning I flew to Moscow, and, by that evening, we were in Yakovlev's office. We talked to him for three or four hours. He talked again about how the fire had to be put out. I said, 'How can you put it out, you haven't promised us anything? Maybe if the president sees us, even for fifteen minutes.' He said he would try to arrange it. Then Gorbachev called, and we left the room while they talked. When we returned, Yakovlev said that the next day at nine o'clock, Gorbachev would see us for half an hour."

The next morning, Gorbachev worked hard to charm Silva Kaputikyan. "He told me, 'I love your poetry, and when they found out at home that I would be meeting with you, Raisa Maximovna asked me to convey a greeting,' " Kaputikyan recounted. Gorbachev mentioned particularly a poem she had written in the 1950s called "Secret Ballot," about a Party member who agonizes over his choice in a Party election. "I told him, yes, I had written that poem during the Khrushchev time, when there was a little renaissance. We talked

196

to him for an hour or a little longer and told him everything about the outrages in Mountainous Karabakh. He said, 'Everything will improve. I promise reforms in Karabakh. I'll take it under my personal supervision. As Silva said, there will be a "little renaissance" there.' "

I asked her whether Gorbachev had promised to transfer Mountainous Karabakh to Armenia. "No, he didn't," she replied. "He said, 'There are nineteen such national problems and we can't solve them separately. There has to be a general solution, and we'll make sure those autonomous republics receive more freedom. I'll create great conditions for the flourishing of culture and the economy.' "

Gorbachev apparently calculated that his flattery and promises would gain him a respite from demonstrations in Yerevan, and, indeed, when Kaputikyan returned that evening to Yerevan and told the crowd at the Opera Square what had happened, they voted en masse for a moratorium on demonstrations. But in making her report, Kaputikyan, seized by the romance of the day, said that the Armenians had triumphed. "I meant that we triumphed morally," she explained to me, many months later. "We Armenians are accustomed to drawing inspiration from defeats. We still celebrate battles we lost. It's a very interesting part of our psychology. Even if we're defeated, if we've defended our Christian faith and principles, a defeat can inspire us to live and go on to victory. And that's what I had in mind. We triumphed morally." Unfortunately, the broadcast reports of her speech failed to convey the nuances of Armenian psychology. In Azerbaijan, her words were taken, briefly, to mean that Gorbachev had caved in to the Armenian demands. Many Azerbaijanis felt that a piece of their homeland was being stolen from them.

The Azerbaijani city of Sumgait, on the edge of the Caspian Sea about thirty miles from Baku, like Ventspils, is one of the industrial wastelands that Soviet planners in Moscow have inflicted on the outlying republics. It is a new city, built up over the last thirty-odd years to serve the Soviet petrochemical industry, a city of smoke-stacks and pipelines and occasional clouds of noxious gases. Work-ers from all over the country moved to Sumgait in its early days, among them the parents of Marina Pogosyan, a young Armenian woman whom I met in Yerevan.

"My parents were from Mountainous Karabakh," she told me. "My mother finished pharmacy school in Yerevan, but to get a job in Karabakh she needed permission from Baku; that was necessary for anyone who completed her education in Armenia. While she was in Baku trying to get it, they gave the job to an Azerbaijani. Sumgait was just getting started, and there were a lot of jobs and apartments. She was already married, so they moved there. My father worked in furniture making. She was a pharmacist. I was born in 1968. We lived in the Third Microrayon in a factory area of five-story apart-ment houses.

"I went to Russian schools and from the second grade also studied Azerbaijani. At one time, they say, there was an Armenian sector in the school, but it was closed. We spoke Armenian at home, but, among my friends, we spoke only Russian, even when everyone was Armenian. Maybe we were shy or uncomfortable about Ar-menian. We studied in the same classes, of course, and there was no formal division among Armenians, Russians, Azerbaijanis. But there was always a sense that we were Armenians. Maybe behind your back you'd hear something nasty, or an expression the Azerbai-janis had: 'You're a good person, too bad you're an Armenian.' If a fight broke out in school, for whatever the reason, if the fighters were from different nationalities, it would quickly become Armeni-ans for Armenians and Azerbaijanis for Azerbaijanis. The relations were all right on the surface, but neither side tried to go further. Still, I thought, okay, we're in a unified country, the Soviet Union; we'll live in harmony, et cetera, et cetera. I believed in that. I was in the Komsomol, and I wanted to be a Party member." I asked her about the golden crucifix she wore around her neck. "I didn't wear this then," she replied. "I started wearing it after what happened. Now I go regularly to church."

On February 25, when Aleksandr Yakovlev placed his call to Silva Kaputikyan about the demonstrations in Yerevan, Marina Pogosyan had heard rumors that Armenians in Mountainous Kara-bakh were demanding independence, "but the central press said nothing, the television said nothing. Even among ourselves, we didn't speak of it. Then, the next day, there was a gathering of Azerbaijanis in the square in front of Lenin's statue, across from the city Party committee. It was a small group at first, then it got bigger. I heard that there was someone, an Azerbaijani, who came from Armenia and said they're beating and burning Azerbaijanis there. [This was not true; there had been an incident in Mountainous Karabakh, Arkady Volsky told me, a few days before. A crowd of Azerbaijanis, intent on opposing the resolution seeking unification with Armenia, had marched on Stepanakert, the capital of Mountain-ous Karabakh. They had confronted a crowd of Armenians and the police. Two Azerbaijanis had been killed, one by a stone and one by an Azerbaijani policeman.] Still, I figured, okay, they have rallies in Stepanakert, why not here?

"On the twenty-seventh, a Friday, a friend of mine warned me to stay inside over the weekend. Still, I went to work—I taught in a nursery school—and walked home. That afternoon, there was another Azerbaijani rally, and then crowds of people went through the shop area where Armenians worked and broke windows and smashed things. I heard cries of 'Death to Armenians! Blood for blood!' It was mostly young people, and the police didn't stop them. Late that night, we had gone to bed when we heard yelling on the street, and through the window I saw thousands of people in a mob marching through the street, mostly dressed in black, carrying clubs and Turkish flags with the half-moon. They were yelling, 'Get out! Armenians are killing our people and you're sitting here! We must purge our city!' "

Still, Pogosyan did not believe that the violence would turn murderous. It did, after the word spread that the Armenians had declared "victory" following their meeting with Gorbachev.

"The next day we went to a neighbor's in the building for her birthday party," Pogosyan continued. "We talked about what we had seen, but we thought it was just young hooligans. Then a neighbor boy came in, all pale. We asked him what was happening, and he said, 'You don't know? They're killing and burning people out there, breaking into people's apartments.' We called the police, and they said, 'Stay where you are. You're not the only ones. We can't help you.'

"A Russian neighbor came to us and invited us to wait in her apartment. There were about three families with her, fifteen people. We spent the whole night there. The mob came and knocked on our door. But she went outside and told them that we were not there, that a week ago we'd moved. A few times after that, they passed by and broke into neighbors' apartments. By that time, no Armenians were home. So there were no killings, but there was a lot of destruction. They threw the chairs and the dishes out the window."

Marina Pogosyan and her family survived for two more nights by hiding in the basement, close to a container of gasoline. They vowed to set themselves on fire rather than let the mob take them. "I had absolutely no hope that we'd survive. I figured they'd kill us all sooner or later. The mob came again, but, on Monday, soldiers came in tanks and took us to the Party committee building. They fed us and announced that we could leave to other cities if we wanted. They let us get our money and a few other things, then we went to the airport and flew here to Yerevan."

She had been fortunate. According to Armenian counts, the mobs had killed thirty people by stabbing them, stomping them, or burning them. In one case, widely publicized in Armenia, a crowd seized a thirty-seven-year-old woman named Lola Abakyan, stripped her naked, and took her out into the street. They forced her to dance, then slashed at her breasts, burned her body with cigarettes, raped her, and killed her.

* * *

The bloodshed at Sumgait ended any chance to settle the Armenian-Azerbaijani dispute as Gorbachev had said he hoped to do, by creating a "little renaissance" for the aggrieved Armenians in Mountainous Karabakh. Within a week of the pogrom, a group of Azerbaijani intellectuals at the Academy of Sciences in Baku founded a group called the Scientists' Club of Baku that would, over the next eighteen months, grow into a mass movement called the Azerbaijani Popular Front. Among its first priorities was the retention of Mountainous Karabakh. In Armenia, the ad hoc Karabakh Committee that had helped organize the February demonstrations soon became the Armenian National Movement, dedicated to securing the right of the Armenians in Mountainous Karabakh to secede and join Armenia.

The distribution of population between the two republics guaranteed continuing strife. Both republics had gradually been growing more homogeneous during the Soviet period, as subtle pressure induced Armenians to leave Azerbaijan and vice versa. But at the time of Sumgait, roughly half a million Armenians still lived in Azerbaijan, counting Mountainous Karabakh. Almost 200,000 Azerbaijanis, mostly farmers, still lived in Armenia. Beginning with Sumgait, a series of *izgnaniya* started a steady flow of refugees in both directions.

Not even membership in the ruling *nomenklatura* could protect someone. In Baku, I spoke to the deputy director of the Azerbaijani State Committee on Refugees, Museib Imamaliev. Until the troubles began, he told me, he had been one of the highest-ranking Azerbaijanis in Armenia, the chairman of the executive committee of the regional soviet in Vardenis, an agricultural area east of Lake Sevan with a minority population of around forty thousand Azerbaijanis. His father had been first secretary of the rayon Party organization. He spoke fluent Armenian and had good connections in Yerevan. He lived in a four-room house on a state farm called Shafag, a few miles from Vardenis.

One day in November 1988, he recalled, the first secretary of the Party organization in Vardenis called him into his office. "He said the people were gathering and that they would chase me out. He said I should leave right away. I said, 'What's happening? They have nothing against me.' And he said they would kill me because they were angry about Armenians being expelled from Kirovabad. In a matter of hours, there were ten thousand people on the street, yelling 'Get out, Turks!' I tried to call the police, the Central Committee in Yerevan, the Council of Ministers. My phones suddenly didn't work. I called together the people who had worked for me. They said I should go, or they'd be killed, too.

"Then they took me out through a back door and put me in a car. It wasn't my black Volga; it was a Zhiguli. The deputy director of the police department was driving, and he took me home. A crowd of about a thousand people surrounded the house, yelling and throwing rocks. The police protected us, but they didn't disperse the crowd. It was like that for two days. The phone hadn't worked, but then suddenly it rang. It was Vladimir Movsissyan, the deputy director of the Council of Ministers at that time. He said the people didn't want me, I should resign. I refused. I told him I had been appointed by the first secretary of the Party, and I would only resign if he asked me to. So they organized a police car to take me to Yerevan. I went to the Party headquarters, but the first secretary refused to see me. When I went back outside, the car was gone."

Imamaliev had no way to get back to Vardenis. He bought a plane ticket to Baku and eventually sent a helicopter back to fetch his family. The other Azerbaijanis in the region fled on trains or in cars, until none were left. In Baku, Imamaliev traded his house for the apartment of an Armenian steelworker who had decided to leave Azerbaijan. At that, he was lucky, he told me. More than 160,000 Azerbaijanis had fled from Armenia by the end of 1989, and many wound up in Baku, living in dormitories, or hotels, or wherever they could find a roof.

Gorbachev and his advisers responded to the crisis with a mixture of assistance and intimidation. In March 1988, Arkady

Volsky went to Stepanakert to assess the situation. Volsky is the type of bluff, friendly Russian who addresses a visiting American with the intimate second-person pronoun *ty* within the first fifteen minutes of conversation. A metallurgical engineer, he made his career in the Soviet automotive industry. Late in the Brezhnev era, he became the Central Committee staff member in charge of auto production. Yuri Andropov noticed Volsky when, in 1982, he became general secretary and began purging the Brezhnev cronies and pushing ahead people like Gorbachev. Volsky became Andropov's assistant for industrial issues. His career suffered a setback after Andropov died in 1984 and Konstantin Chernenko presided over a brief revival of Brezhnevism. But since Gorbachev's accession, Volsky had been given a number of responsible jobs in both the Supreme Soviet and the Central Committee.

He occupied an enormous office in the warren of Party apparat buildings just off Red Square, but he displayed a skeptical, lightly mocking attitude toward what once were sacred dogmas. "Our founding fathers in 1917 were romantics," Volsky told me at one point, explaining how the border between Armenia and Azerbaijan was set. "They thought it didn't matter where the borders were, that the proletariat would triumph all over the world and the borders would fade away by themselves. But the proletariat didn't win all over the world." He paused. "Thank God." He laughed and, looking at the standard portrait of Marx on the wall, excused himself for his small blasphemy. Then he walked over to a wall map and pointed to the way the Azerbaijani and Armenian populations overlapped. What the romanticism of the founders of the Soviet state had done in the Trans-Caucasus, he said, was "idiotic."

Volsky returned to Moscow from Mountainous Karabakh in 1988, made his report to the Supreme Soviet, and was promptly sent back again, this time as a mediator. When the situation deteriorated still further, in January 1989, the Supreme Soviet decided to dissolve the local organs of government in Mountainous Karabakh and run the area through a commission headed by Volsky. He and one aide moved to Stepanakert and worked hard to fulfill the promise Gorbachev had made to Silva Kaputikyan. They stayed for a little more than a year, until the Supreme Soviet voted to return most authority to Azerbaijan. "We opened the television tower to receive Armenian broadcasts; we opened Armenian schools and gave them Armenian textbooks. We opened an Armenian theater and gave two churches back to the Armenian community. We even opened three religious communities for the first time in seventy years of Soviet power. We declared disarmament within the region, and we took the cannons away from the *sovkhozi,*" Volsky recalled. "Unfortunately, outside the region, in Armenia and Azerbaijan, they didn't do the same. And the situation remained tense."

At first, the authorities tried to intimidate the growing nationalist movements in both republics. In March, after the initial spate of demonstrations in Yerevan, troops moved ostentatiously through the streets, and helicopters buzzed the Opera Square. Leila Yunosova, one of the founders of the Baku Scientists' Club, recalled that plainclothes police rather openly followed the club members and photographed their occasional meetings with visiting journalists. The local Communist Party refused to allow the group to register as a political party, even though its platform was quite moderate, calling for continued Azerbaijani loyalty to the Soviet Union.

The police in Armenia arrested the leaders of the Karabakh Committee in December 1988 and sent them to jail in Moscow. Levon Ter-Petrosyan, one of those arrested, recalled that he spent his time in a cell block in Matroskaya Tishina, an old Moscow jail. "We were constantly interrogated," he said. "They were trying to make a case against us for inflaming national enmity. They went over all of our speeches, which they had on videocassettes. But they couldn't find any real evidence that we had inflamed national enmity. We were released on May 31, 1989."

On the heels of this evidence that the central authorities were no longer prepared to use the courts as a railroad, politics in both Azerbaijan and Armenia opened up considerably. In Baku, the members of the Scientists' Club, who by now called themselves the Popular Front, managed to convene a conference in a hall that one of them had rented, ostensibly for a wedding reception. Two buses of police came, Leila Yunosova recalled, but they did not break the meeting up. By this time, however, a more militant element had entered the dissident movement in Azerbaijan, and the Popular Front showed signs of splitting into two wings, moderates and radicals. The moderate candidate for leader of the Front, a writer named Iosif Samedogli, lost a raucous, contested vote to a radical representative, Abulfaz Aliyev, who, one of his supporters proudly told me, had spent time in jail in the Brezhnev years for espousing pan-Turkic ideology. The new leaders of the Popular Front mobilized the small army of refugees in Baku, and a growing number of supporters, in a series of mass demonstrations, strikes, and blockades of the railroads leading to Armenia.

At this point, in the view of the moderate wing of the Front, a curious thing occurred. They began to sense that the Communist Party leaders in Azerbaijan were prodding the movement to become more radical and nationalistic. Leila Yunosova recalled a meeting that autumn between the Front leaders, who were still seeking official recognition for their group, and Viktor Polyanichko, the second secretary of the republic Communist Party. Polyanichko told them that their program was too European, that it needed to draw more on Azerbaijan's Islamic and Turkic traditions. "It was a ploy to discredit us," Yunosova said.

As winter set in, the mood of the refugees in Baku grew angrier. The radicals in the Popular Front called for more strikes, more railroad blockades. There was talk of a putsch against the Party if it failed to support the militant course. Strangely, the Azerbaijani government chose to grant television access not to the Popular Front moderates but to the radicals. Tofig Gazymov, a physicist who had helped found the Front, told me that he and some of his moderate colleagues pleaded for a chance to go on television to urge people to stay away from a mass rally called by the radicals for

January 13, 1990. They were refused. Instead, on the evening of January 12, several radicals, including Aidin Mamedov, appeared on television, calling for the protection of Azerbaijani sovereignty against the Armenians and recalling the injustices that Azerbaijan had suffered. A member of the city government, who participated in the program, said the council would distribute apartments being freed by fleeing Armenians to people who were on the city's normal housing waiting list, a decision certain to inflame the refugees, who wanted the Armenians' apartments for themselves.

Small bands of Azerbaijani men had already been terrorizing the Armenians of Baku, banging on their doors and warning them to get out of town. The next day, this small-scale terrorism erupted into a pogrom. Although it coincided with the Popular Front's mass rally in Lenin Square, the accounts I heard, from both Azerbaijani and Armenian witnesses, suggest that it broke out independently of the Popular Front.

Abram Kazaryan is a short, stocky old man with oily gray hair; he had a few days' worth of stubble when I met him in Yerevan. He was wearing blue pants, a plaid flannel shirt, and a floppy fedora. In an American city, he might have been panhandling, but in Yerevan he approached me because he had heard that an American journalist was looking for people who had lived through the Baku pogrom. He pushed into the room I was using and, assuming a gruff air of authority that clashed with his clothes, demanded to see my identification. Only after I complied did he begin to answer my questions.

"I'm a military pensioner," he said. "I served in the army for forty-five years, and my rank was lieutenant colonel. I lived in Baku from 1920 until this year. I had an apartment near the stadium. I lived alone. My son had lost his job and moved away.

"The pogrom started on the tenth of January. A man came to my door and said, 'Leave, old man. Your time is up. Your people have left, and you should leave.' If he had been alone, I'd have chased him away. But there were three of them. I said, 'I'm an old man, I have no place to go.'

"On the twelfth, about twenty of them came, and they broke down the door. I tried to fight them and yell for help. A neighbor came, and they ran away. On the morning of the thirteenth, I went to the police and filed a complaint. They said, 'Okay,' and did nothing.

"I stayed at home and tried to prop the door up as best I could, but there was nothing to repair it with. That evening, at six, they came again. They rang the bell and knocked. I could see there were a lot of them in the courtyard. I put my coat on and went to open the door. As I got there, it came down on me." Kazaryan walked to the door and showed me how he had tried to ward it off with his arms.

"It fell on me," he said. "I think they had an ax. There were four of them, and then it seemed like forty. They beat me and threw me on the floor and started trampling me. They broke three ribs, right here"—he pointed to his side—"and threw me down the stairs. I lost consciousness. When I opened my eyes, they were carrying my things away—the rugs, the TV, everything. My pockets and clothes were torn, and they'd taken away my documents. Two of them stood guard over me to keep me from running away. I said to them, 'Why are you beating up an old man?' They didn't answer. They put me into a car and took me to a movie theater and threw me into a basement with some others. We were there for a day and a half.

"Then finally they put us on a bus and took us to the harbor. They had a steamship there with room for about 350. They put 1,500 people on it. We were like dogs. And we sailed off, and after a day we got to Krasnovodsk [in Turkmenistan, on the eastern shore of the Caspian Sea]. People met us there and gave us food."

Kazaryan was evacuated to Yerevan and spent about six weeks in a hospital, recovering. He had no money and no place to live. Eventually, the Armenian State Refugee Committee found him a bed in a workers' dormitory, but he was unhappy with it. As we talked, his voice lost its tough edge and grew sad, slow, and pathetic. This was not the way he had envisioned the last years of his life. "I'm a war veteran," he said, almost in tears. "We're human beings. We need help."

By all accounts that I heard in both Baku and Yerevan, the Armenians got no help from the Azerbaijani police during the pogrom. Azaddin Gyulmamedov, the young Azerbaijani whose father had been determined not to send him to a Russian school, told me he was working as marshal for the Popular Front at its rally when someone came to the podium and informed him that Armenians were being beaten in the city's residential quarters. "We went to see what was happening," he recounted. "We saw these guys in the streets. I don't know who they were. Drug addicts, maybe. They had sticks and clubs and lists of Armenians and where they lived. They wanted to break down the doors of Armenian apartments and chase them out. The police didn't do anything. They just stood and watched. Same with the soldiers [internal troops] who had weapons. We asked them to help. There were about a dozen soldiers and ten of us. There were about twenty in the gang. But the soldiers wouldn't help. They said, 'You can do it yourself, Blackie. We're not getting involved.' "

The pogrom against the Armenians had largely run its course after four days. According to official totals, 56 people died, the vast majority of them Armenians; the Armenian population of Baku, once 200,000, fell to nearly zero. But the mobs remained on the streets. Thousands of Russian residents, feeling unsafe, began leaving the city, and a crowd surrounded the building that houses the Central Committee of the Azerbaijani Communist Party.

Only at that point did the Soviet Army intervene. Late in the evening of January 19, the troops arrived, without warning and not gently. According to the accounts assiduously compiled by the Azerbaijanis, the troops shot at buses and civilian cars, and into apartment windows. Their tanks crushed cars and people who got in the way. By the time the occupation was complete, 130 people had been killed by the troops and 600 injured. The Azerbaijani Supreme Soviet commission investigating the events calculated that another 20 or 30 deaths were related to the occupation, such as that of a young woman who took poison after her husband was killed.

The troops established a martial law regime that included censorship of the press and a prohibition on political gatherings without the permission of the military commanders. The Azerbaijanis created a martyrs' grave site in a shady hillside park overlooking the Caspian Sea and buried eighty of the victims in a long, single row, with their pictures mounted on wrought-iron frames over their graves. By September, the troops and their armored vehicles had all but disappeared from the streets. But perhaps two dozen Azerbaijanis had made the long, sweaty climb to the grave site on the day I visited. They walked silently past the row of portraits. An old man chanted prayers.

The authorities' evident disinterest in stopping the pogrom in its early stages, along with the suggestions that they had goaded the Popular Front into more radical positions, raised a number of questions. I asked for and received an opportunity to put them to Ayaz Mutalibov, first secretary of the Communist Party of Azerbaijan and president of the republic. Mutalibov had been prime minister during the January events. He rose to the head of the republic's government when his predecessor took the blame for failing to prevent the disorder. The Central Committee occupied a new, red stone office building on a hillside with a fine view of the sea, in a neighborhood of old Beaux-Arts buildings left over from the nineteenth-century oil boom. Mutalibov's suite of offices, on the seventh floor, was decorated in the style that might be called Soviet Power, with herringbone parquet floors and red runners, long, polished conference tables, and huge, empty anterooms. He greeted me in a small reception area and led me to a couple of black, upholstered divans in a room next to his office.

Mutalibov, who was then fifty-two, is a communist leader of the traditional type, an engineer who entered Party work after proving himself as an industrial manager. During our long conversation, he expressed regret over the passing of many old Soviet institutions, from the high prestige of the engineering profession to the authority of the KGB, and skepticism about the reforms that have taken their place.

"What do you do with a guy who is born to break things, steal, not work?" he asked me at one point. "Dialogue? Hm? Why in the United States do people fear like fire a tax audit? Because the auditor can catch Spiro Agnew. Here, all order has stopped. We used to have the KGB, this giant monster. Now, there's no KGB. There's no Ministry of Internal Affairs. They don't do anything."

An aide laughed and said that the KGB had become part of the Ministry of Culture. Mutalibov laughed in agreement. "Ministry of Culture," he nodded. "They've become the opposite of what they once were."

He was responsible, he said, for introducing market reforms into Azerbaijan's economy, but he doubted that many people wanted such changes. "We say, 'Okay, there will be privatization,' but there are quite a few people who say, 'I don't want that, I don't need it.' You tell them there will be villas, and Cadillacs, and Mercedes, and they don't care. They just want—" He tapped his index finger against his throat in the standard Soviet sign language for drunkenness, laughed harshly, and went on.

"You have to take such people into account," he said. "If you call law and order dictatorship, then I'm for dictatorship." He slapped the table. "They're for anarchy!" If he had his way, Mutalibov said, he would reintroduce toughness into the system and tell the people, "Enough. We have to work."

When I raised the question of the pogroms, Mutalibov said he thought they had been planned and provoked—by the Armenians, in an effort to convince world opinion that their desire to tear Mountainous Karabakh away from Azerbaijan was justified. When I asked how he knew this, he replied that he had no evidence. "We just don't have the documents to unmask them. But when there is a special commission, and I believe there will be, then it will all be found."

I asked why the authorities had encouraged the radicals in the Popular Front, rather than the moderates.

"It wasn't because we wanted to bless the radicals," he said. "No, at that time, the radicals had taken control of the Front, and the public had the opinion that they were the ones representing the Front. They demanded access to television, and we gave it to them." He shrugged, as if he considered the matter unimportant.

I asked why the police had failed to stop the pogrom in its early stages.

"They're just traffic police," he said. "They couldn't do anything, and there weren't enough of them."

I asked Mutalibov how many Ministry of Internal Affairs troops had stood by and watched the killing.

"I don't remember," he said.

I told him I had heard that there were a few thousand in Baku when the pogrom began.

"Well, yes," he said. "About six thousand in the barracks."

Why, I asked, had they not intervened?

"We didn't have the right to give them orders," he said. "Today, we have the right to command internal troops on our territory. But we just got it."

Had he not telephoned Moscow asking for orders?

"We not only telephoned. We sent a mass of telegrams to Moscow. They were top secret. It's too bad you can't read them. But if you could, you could see that we asked for five thousand Ministry of Internal Affairs troops, well armed. We said, 'Give us help. We've got a pogrom, you need to save the situation.' " Mutalibov and his aides suggested that Moscow might have been reluctant to authorize force against the pogrom because of the backlash against the use of troops to break up a demonstration in Georgia in April 1989.

But the Azerbaijani leader's account was directly contradicted by Arkady Volsky when I spoke to him a few days later in Moscow. Volsky had been in Mountainous Karabakh at the time, monitoring the situation in Baku and in Moscow closely. When I told him what Mutalibov had said, he responded bluntly.

"That's a lie. I'll say openly that Moscow responded on the day after the troops were requested. Before that, I called several times to the leaders of the republic and said, 'What are you doing? Make a request!' I called Gorbachev ten times and said, 'Send troops!' He said, 'I don't have a request.' It's another question as to whether it was necessary to wait for a request. I don't think it was. But Gorbachev is a very tactful person. The request came only when the Azerbaijanis began to kill their own people. Then they asked for troops to be sent in."

It was impossible, barring access to the archives in both Moscow and Baku, to know who was telling the truth. Most members of the Popular Front with whom I spoke believed fervently that Moscow had let the pogrom continue in order to win international support for the repression of their growing separatist movement. But Moscow must have foreseen that the long-term result of the military occupation would be even stronger Azerbaijani determination to be independent. Even President Mutalibov, who supported Gorbachev's intention to preserve the Soviet Union on a looser, confederated basis, told me that independence was, perhaps, the next stage in Azerbaijan's development, a generation or so in the future.

It seemed to me that the real beneficiaries of the January events in Baku were the leaders of the local Communist Party. The pogrom, by getting rid of Baku's Armenians, largely solved their most pressing domestic problem, finding housing and work for the refugees. The pogrom and the ensuing occupation discredited the Popular Front. To many Azerbaijanis, particularly in rural areas, the violence and destruction seemed organically linked to the Front's radicalism of late 1989 and to its mass demonstration on January 13.

Under martial law, the Front could not freely call rallies or hold meetings to help organize its support and explain its positions. By September, the Front was demoralized and divided. It failed even to nominate candidates in most of the republic's districts for the fall election to the Supreme Soviet. Its leaders, one of them told me, were afraid they had alienated the important class of economic managers and were not even certain whether to continue to call for the independence of the republic.

Mutalibov, meanwhile, took a strong stand against Armenian claims to Mountainous Karabakh. The solution to the conflict, he told me with vehemence, was "a very simple one: stop telling us what to do in Karabakh." He advocated the creation of a special, well-armed police detachment to act as border troops against Armenian incursions. It is not surprising that the local Party won a resounding victory in the balloting at the end of September.

In Armenia, the Communist Party proved beyond salvage. With its residual strength in rural districts, the Party managed to elect a paper majority to the republic Supreme Soviet in the spring 1990 elections, although it could not elect a single candidate in Yerevan, the center of the republic's intelligentsia and the stronghold of the Armenian National Movement. But the Party had for too long been content to recruit men primarily interested in bribes and their own careers. Once the Supreme Soviet convened in August and began to vote for a government, these men put wet fingers to the wind and gradually deserted the Party first secretary to support the National Movement's leader, Levon Ter-Petrosyan. On the final ballot, only 24 of 161 communists remained loyal to the Party, and Ter-Petrosyan became the republic's leader.

When I visited Yerevan in September, the Party still occupied the most imposing building in town, a palace of massive pilasters and Doric capitals, set in a private park, surrounded by a wrought-iron fence. It was the only building I saw in Yerevan still flying the red flag of the Soviet Union. To enter the grounds, a visitor still needed to apply for a pass from a uniformed clerk who sat in a glass booth with a hole cut in it at waist height, designed so that the petitioner had to bow to address him. But it was like Versailles after the fall of the Bastille; the trappings of power were lingering after power had departed. I spoke with Stepan Pogosyan, the new secretary in charge of ideology. People were resigning from the Party in large numbers, he told me, and it had no program at the moment. "We don't try to supervise anything anymore," he said. "We've learned our lesson." He and the remaining apparatchiks were thinking of holding a referendum among the remaining members to decide whether to continue calling the organization the Communist Party of the Soviet Union or to seek some more palatable identity.

The communists left Ter-Petrosyan an unenviable situation. The periodic railroad blockades in Azerbaijan had exacerbated the general chaos of the Soviet economy. Although no one was starving, and there was ice cream in the city's sidewalk cafés, many things were scarce. My hotel in Yerevan had no hot water, and the management shut the power off for a few hours every afternoon to save energy. I spoke with the manager of an Armenian-American joint venture that was supposed to be manufacturing plastic pipes and plumbing supplies for use in the reconstruction of the areas damaged by the 1988 earthquake. The joint venture had yet to get started, he told me. There were no materials to build a factory, and Moscow had informed him that, because of marketization reforms, it could not guarantee a supply of raw plastic. Of the first five Armenians I met, three wanted to emigrate. The other two wanted to fight the Azerbaijanis.

On some Yerevan streets, Kalashnikov assault rifles, hijacked from government weapons stores or bought on the black market, were as common as briefcases. The men who carried them belonged to a variety of guerrilla armies, like the one that raided Baganis-Airum. The largest of them, the Armenian National Army, had occupied a fortified house, with spiked tire traps in the street outside, about two hundred yards from Lenin Square, in the center of town. As Ter-Petrosyan assumed office, his first task was controlling the guerrillas. He sent an emissary to the Armenian National Army house one morning, and they shot him dead on the street. Ter-Petrosyan formed a new, heavily armed police unit of two thousand men. The Armenian National Army leaders surrendered. The rest of the guerrilla units, recognizing Ter-Petrosyan's government as legitimate, submitted to its authority and were formally disbanded.

But that did not mean they turned in their weapons. "We've so far collected very few weapons," Ter-Petrosyan told me one afternoon in his office at the Supreme Soviet. "But we haven't paid attention to that. Our attention was fixed on the destruction of these structures." I asked him how many guerrillas there were. "The numbers in the press—forty thousand, fifty thousand—were largely myth," he said. "In all of Armenia, in all those groups, there were no more than five thousand or six thousand men."

Ter-Petrosyan, like several of the nationalist leaders who came to power in 1990 in Soviet republics, springs from the segment of the intelligentsia that specializes in the culture of its republic. Vytautas Landsbergis studied Lithuanian music; Ter-Petrosyan had worked in the Matanadaran, the repository of ancient Armenian manuscripts in Yerevan. He is a tall, stooped man, with a drooping left eyelid, an indoor pallor, and no apparent muscles in his arms or neck. He wore a short-sleeved shirt, with the collar unbuttoned and his tie pulled down, and he compulsively smoked a Finnish cigarette called Milde Sorte, frequently snuffing one out before it was done and immediately lighting another one.

Since making the switch from leader of a movement to leader of the republic, Ter-Petrosyan had found himself taking positions that struck more fervent nationalists as soft. He advocated, and the Supreme Soviet accepted, a Declaration on Independence rather than an immediate rupture with Moscow. It merely announced the beginning of a process, of indefinite length, leading to statehood. Even after independence, Ter-Petrosyan said, Armenia would favor some kind of Common Market–style affiliation with the Soviet Union and would be happy to consider a military alliance. More conscious than many Armenians that contemporary European institutions take a dim view of irredentism, he told me that Armenia had no claim on Mountainous Karabakh. "It is a question of self-determination for Mountainous Karabakh," he said. "We support that right. Nothing more."

It was not hard to find more militant Armenians. Across Marshall Bagramyan Prospekt from the Supreme Soviet, a group called the Republican Party had established quarters in an old, gray stone mansion it had seized from the Armenian Union of Architects. A red, blue, and orange Armenian tricolor hung from a flagpole mounted on the facade, over a seal that featured an eagle and a sword. Inside, I met Levon Akopyan, a teacher at Yerevan Polytechnic Institute and a member of the party's governing board. We sat down under a map of the Middle East that showed, in a broad pink swath, the lands that had belonged to Armenia under Tigran the Great two millennia ago. Modern Armenia would settle for somewhat less than this, Akopyan assured me: eastern Turkey, Mountainous Karabakh, and Nakhichevan, which is also now part of Azerbaijan. "We have our rights, we have our land, and we'll get it back," he said, sternly. "If the world doesn't become moral and give it back to us, then we'll use force, as much as we can."

His party had begun, he told me, as a military organization, called the Army of Independence, with several thousand men under arms. When Ter-Petrosyan's government had declared the dissolution of the various guerrilla groups, the Army of Independence had formally complied, becoming a civilian party. Its soldiers had either taken their weapons home or smuggled them into Mountainous Karabakh.

I asked him what would happen to the Turks now living on those lands the Armenians meant to regain.

"There has to be a decision that they leave, somehow," he said. "I think the Armenian people, given their independence, will flourish and be strong, like Israel, and we'll solve those problems. Nature created the nation. The idea that there could be a mixing of the nations is vulgar."

Ter-Petrosyan, when I mentioned this conversation to him, dismissed the militants. "Such people exist," he said. "They try to raise their issues in the press and in parliament. We easily persuade the people that this is all harmful."

But he had no more plausible suggestion to make about how the conflicting claims to the land might be peacefully resolved. It seemed to an outsider, I said, that there was only one solution that might be acceptable to all involved: to improve the conditions of life inside Mountainous Karabakh so that living there would be as acceptable for Armenians as living in Switzerland is for the French-speaking people there. Ter-Petrosyan said he did not think such a solution was possible. "I don't think the prerequisites exist, that there's a sufficient level of civilization," he said. "I'm not talking about Azerbaijan, particularly. I'm talking about the Soviet Union. The Soviet Union isn't Europe. There are still feudal relations here, real feudalism, psychologically. That's why I don't think so."

Psychologically, in fact, the people in both republics seemed intent on preparing for war, on erasing objective traces of the other, and on forming an image of the enemy that served as a receptacle for all their loathings and frustrations. In Azerbaijan, one of the main streets used to be called Shaumyan Prospekt, after an Armenian who was one of the leaders of the first communist government in Baku. It has been renamed Azerbaijan Prospekt, and an Azerbaijani journalist told me, quite earnestly, that "recent research" had disclosed that Shaumyan was not such a loyal disciple of Lenin after all and didn't deserve a street named for him. An Azerbaijani publishing house this year reprinted thirty thousand copies of a 1904 tract about Armenians that begins by asserting that they are descended from Jews and commenting on the breadth of their foreheads.

In Yerevan one night, a friend took me to see a pile of rubble behind an apartment building at 22 Ulitsa Knunyantsaya. It had been, he whispered, a small and simple Azerbaijani mosque back in the days when Azerbaijanis still lived in Armenia. Then, during the cycle of pogroms and *izgnaniya*, the Armenians of the neighborhood had descended on the mosque and torn it apart with picks and crowbars; a bulldozer had come to level the pile. I went back a few days later and spoke with residents of the building, who confirmed the story.

Once in a while, after listening to an Armenian passionately list the uncivilized and genocidal acts of the Azerbaijanis against his people, I would mention the destruction of this mosque. Almost invariably, the response was an indignant denial that such a thing could have occurred. Even Rafael Papayan, the chairman of the new Supreme Soviet's commission on human rights, a man who served several years as a political prisoner in the pre–*glasnost* days, insisted that such a tale must be "disinformation. Absolute disinformation. The only mosque that was in the city is still preserved, and I can show you where it is." He was not lying; he simply did not know what had happened. It was not the sort of thing the Armenian press would report. It was not the sort of thing the people of Yerevan would talk about among themselves. To do so would threaten their self-image as the civilized victims.

About the only leader I met on either side who seemed to retain any objectivity was the Armenian poet Silva Kaputikyan. "As a writer, as a principled person, I feel that one of our losses is that somewhere, our philosophy of life was compromised, particularly with the young people," she told me one day. "Now they're preaching a different philosophy, of violence. They think that you have to reply to a Sumgait with a Sumgait. In some of the border villages, our young people have started to act just like they [the Azerbaijanis] did with us in Sumgait. I consider this our very great loss. And it continues to this day."

Back in Baganis, I told Araz Yedigaryan, the Armenian *sovkhoz* director, that I had heard a fair amount about the roots of the conflict. He nodded. Unfortunately, he said, the kind of kidnapping and hostage taking that had preceded the battles in March and August was beginning again, a situation he blamed on the Azerbaijanis. "We'll take it up to here," he said, gesturing with his hand to his neck, "and then the Armenian guerrillas will come again."

As it happened, the Popular Front and the National Movement had agreed to a hostage exchange that afternoon on the road between Baganis and Baganis-Airum. We got into Yedigaryan's olive green, Jeeplike car and drove down the road toward Azerbaijan. A few hundred yards from the border, we passed a cluster of a dozen dark-haired Armenians on the side of the road. They were the friends and relatives of an Armenian from Noyembryan whom the Azerbaijanis had kidnapped four days previously. We drove a bit farther down the road, to within sight of the checkpoint that the Armenians had destroyed in August. Another group of people stood, talking. One of them, in a gray shirt and gray pants, looking like a schoolteacher on his day off, was the Azerbaijani Popular Front leader from Kazakh. Another, a strapping, blond Byelorussian soldier with two bullet clips taped to his Kalashnikov, was supervising the transfer.

The Armenians walked cautiously down the road into Azerbaijan, to a green Zhiguli, where they satisfied themselves that their hostage was inside the car. They walked back. The Azerbaijani asked where his countryman was.

"They're feeding him," one of the Armenians cracked. It is an old Soviet custom to feed and fatten up a prisoner just before he is released.

The Byelorussian laughed out loud. "Feeding him," he repeated, shaking his head.

After a couple of moments, a car drove up, and several people got out. In their midst, surrounded, was a young man with a full beard, his head held high. They walked down the road toward the Azerbaijani side. Another group got out of the green Zhiguli and walked toward the Armenian side. In their midst was a thin, middle-aged man in a blue sport shirt. The two groups met and made the exchange, then walked back to their respective sides of the border. The freed Armenian looked haggard, and his hands trembled as he lit up a cigarette.

"We want this to be the end of it," the man from the Azerbaijani Popular Front said, before he walked back to his side of the border. But neither he nor any of the people on the Armenian side looked as if they expected that it would be.

"In my family," an Armenian with the Russified name Boris told me, "if a relative were taken hostage, I would tell my children about it, and they would tell theirs, and it would not be forgotten for two hundred years."

ROMANIA

November 1990

Nearly a year after its revolution, Bucharest looked much as it had when I left. By day the streets remained littered and grimy, and lines formed outside stores selling meat, milk, or butter. By night it was a dark city, still short of light bulbs. In the traffic median on Balcescu Boulevard, the makeshift memorial the students had erected to honor their dead had become more or less permanent: several large wooden crosses, decorated with icons and dates, and a black metal contraption to hold candles, all enclosed by black ribbon the way yellow tape encloses a police crime scene. On the sidewalk, a few old women had gone into business selling the slender, amber candles that had appeared simultaneously in December 1989. The benefits the revolution had brought to the city seemed almost marginal. On long tables near the subway entrances, vendors hawked some of the dozens of new, weekly newspapers that had sprung up, and restorers' scaffolding had appeared around some of the old, Beaux-Arts buildings that Nicolae Ceausescu had allowed to decay. The state television network began to broadcast a twice-weekly West German soap opera that gave a fascinated country a glimpse of Western glitz and glamour. And along the Piata Victoriei, not far from the seat of the new government, I saw a poster advertising the imminent appearance of a topless ice show.

When I went to see Gabriel Andreescu, the circumstances could not have differed more from those of our first, furtive meeting in August 1989. The political group that Andreescu had helped establish in the first days after the revolution, the Group for Social Dialogue, had flourished. Its members had commandeered a nineteenth-century mansion on the Calea Victoriei, a few blocks north of the epicenter of the revolt, the Palace Square. The house, one member told me, had been built by a Romanian duke for his mistress. Nicu Ceausescu, the dictator's son, had taken a fancy to it and spent millions of lei restoring its crystal chandeliers, its grand staircase, and its pale blue walls with their flowery, ornamental trim; the building had a very elegant, French flair. Nicu had used it for the headquarters of an international youth foundation that had served primarily to provide him with pretexts for foreign vacations. In January the Group for Social Dialogue had simply moved in. And, after occasional run-ins with city authorities, its tenancy had become more or less undisputed. Very quickly, it had grown from an informal gathering of erstwhile dissidents to an institution, with telephones and secretaries. Its members met regularly with the representatives of international human rights organizations. It published a weekly newspaper called *22*, after the date in December when Ceausescu fell. It even had a logo, an arrangement of the letters *g, s,* and *d*. The membership had decided to employ a couple of full-time, paid staff members. And Gabriel Andreescu became one of them.

When I walked into his office, he looked just as he had: short and slender, almost fragile, with thick eyeglasses and hair brushed straight back from his high forehead. He quickly apologized and said that he would have to postpone our talk, because an emergency had arisen. The government, in a round of price increases, had multiplied the cost of paper by a factor of six. Books, he told me, might in the future cost as much as one hundred lei, which was a day's pay for many Romanian laborers. Some of the new newspapers might not be able to survive. The Writers' Union, in its mansion up the street, had called an urgent meeting of paper consumers to plan a protest, and he had to represent the group. We agreed to meet later that day.

When we did, most of the staff had gone home. We sat in a room with several empty desks, and I asked him to tell me more about the group's origin.

In the beginning, he replied, the group had consisted of thirty-two intellectuals, all of whom had suffered, to some degree, under Ceausescu. Some, like Andreescu, had spent time in jail for dissent. Others, like Stelian Tanase, the editor of *22,* had been unable to publish much of what they had written. The members generally had earned reputations as men who refused to compromise themselves. As a result, they enjoyed great moral authority. Immediately after the revolution, seven of them served on the council of the National Salvation Front. Some of them signed contracts to do research projects, such as public opinion polls, for government ministries. But as time passed, the Front's reliance on old communists and old methods had alienated most of them. Only a couple of the members, including Minister of Culture Andre Plesu, still supported the government.

In the spring of 1990, the election campaign had presented the Group for Social Dialogue with a dilemma. Few of them cared to see the Front win. Few of them had any respect for the opposition parties that had emerged. The two most prominent, the Liberal Party and the National Peasant Party, were relics of the pre–World War II era, suddenly revived. Most of their leaders were also old, old enough to have participated in politics before the Second World War. Each of them nominated for president someone who had not lived in Romania for years—the Peasant Party candidate, Ion Ratiu, for fully fifty years, and the Liberal Party candidate, Radu Campeanu, for sixteen years. Against this weak opposition, the Front deployed all the advantages of incumbency, including control of the national television network and the ability to reduce the workweek and raise the pay of Romanian laborers.

"Thousands of people came to us and wrote to us and said you must do something," Andreescu recalled. "Our group had furious meetings and debates about this problem—should we get involved in political competition? None of us were members of a party. That was a rule. We could not be active in a party because we try to maintain a perfect independence from political interests. This status of the conscience of the public is our most important asset. We didn't want to affect our image by political involvement. But finally, very late in the campaign, some of us decided to run as independent candidates for the new Parliament."

This devotion to a privileged, elite status surprised me, but it comported with the traditional role of the intelligentsia in Romania and much of Eastern Europe. It was a fact that where Eastern European opposition groups, before 1989, had dented the Communist Party's monopoly of power, they had done so when intellectuals climbed down from their ivory towers and united with workers and peasants. This had been the genesis of Poland's Solidarity in the 1970s—a fusion of Warsaw intellectuals with factory workers in Gdansk and other cities. (That union, not coincidentally, seemed to unravel in 1990, when the Gdansk electrician Lech Walesa ran for president against his erstwhile Solidarity comrade Tadeusz Mazowiecki, a writer.) But the more traditional attitude for Eastern European intellectuals involved a certain condescension, bordering on scorn, toward those who worked with their hands. When I met Stelian Tanase, the editor of *22,* he was wearing a red-and-white Solidarity lapel button, a gift from someone in Poland. But when I asked him about the Romanian coal miners, he replied simply, "They are savages." He had reason to resent the coal miners, of course. But he seemed totally oblivious to any contradiction between his attitude toward them and his lapel button.

In the elections on May 20, not surprisingly, the National Salvation Front crushed its opposition. Ion Iliescu, the erstwhile Party functionary who had taken power in December, received 85 percent of the votes for president. The Front's candidates won two-thirds of the seats in the new Parliament. The second-place party was the

Hungarian Democratic Union, which drew on the suspicion of many Hungarian Romanians that Romanian nationalists would be no more sympathetic to them under the Front than they had been under Ceausescu. Foreign observers noticed some irregularities in the balloting. But everyone involved, including the defeated Romanian opposition parties, conceded that even without the alleged cheating, the Front would have won easily. Gabriel Andreescu, who late in April had become a candidate in Buzau, the city of his exile, got about 5 percent of the votes in his campaign for a seat in the Parliament.

Despite his popular mandate, Iliescu showed few signs of becoming more liberal or tolerant of opposition. His government formed a new agency called the Romanian Information Service, an intelligence agency under the direct control of the president. Although the Securitate had formally been abolished, it appeared that the new agency was its direct descendant, minus a few of the more thuggish types, who had been purged in secret proceedings. Only a handful of Securitate agents were publicly tried, and then only for what they did during the December revolt, not for their prior activities. The new agency refrained, at least initially, from the torture and intimidation of dissenters that the Securitate had specialized in. But its mere presence was enough to concern many intellectuals.

I asked Andreescu if he had encountered any of the men who used to watch and interrogate and beat him.

"I saw one of them in April near University Square," he replied. "He had obviously been sent there to spy on the students who were occupying the square in protest against the government. He saw me, and suddenly he looked up at the sky, I guess hoping that I wouldn't recognize him. I understood the situation was very difficult for him, and I decided to say nothing.

"Then, about five weeks ago, I saw another one, one of the gentler ones I had had contact with. It was on the street, not far from here. He walked up to me and said, 'You know me, of course,' and shook my hand. I said, 'Okay, how are you?' He said, 'I now work for the Romanian Information Service. I want to say that, of course, you know we didn't agree with the [Ceausescu] regime. We had to do what we did, but we didn't agree with it, and now we can be real professionals.'

"He asked if he could phone me," Andreescu went on. "I said he could, and he told me his real name was Dinest. But I haven't heard from him since."

The Group for Social Dialogue had invited the director of the new intelligence agency to come and talk. "He wanted to come," Andreescu said. "He came and said they want a new reputation for this service. We asked him about tapping telephones and intercepting mail. He said they didn't do that anymore, although it was possible that former Securitate people were still doing it."

Andreescu believed otherwise, based on things that happened to him. Someone had sent him a letter from France, inviting him to a meeting in Strasbourg on October 1, 1990. The letter was postmarked August 6, but it did not reach him until September 30, too late for him to arrange to go. Other Romanians with whom I spoke reported similar difficulties with letters and packages from abroad, although they were inclined to attribute them to corruption rather than political interference. The people who worked in the Bucharest post office had, long before the revolution, grown accustomed to opening letters and packages from abroad and pilfering anything that looked valuable. After the revolution, the easing of political restraints meant that many more foreigners sent mail to Romania. But the number of postal workers, and their venality, did not change. The result was that foreign mail was still opened and subject to theft. And it took longer to be processed.

But the most blatant example of the government's insecurity occurred in June. Throughout the spring a group of dissidents had been demonstrating in University Square, the site of some of the critical events of the revolution. The square is actually a major intersection in the heart of Bucharest. To the north stands the twenty-two-story Inter-Continental Hotel, where most foreign visitors to the city stay. Next to it is the National Theater, a graceful, modern building fronted by a lawn. Across Balcescu Boulevard are some of the central buildings of the city's university. They form a kind of half courtyard with a fountain. In the middle of the boulevard is the memorial to the slain students.

During the spring protests, a small group began a hunger strike, intent on bringing down the government. They pitched tents on the lawn in front of the National Theater and used the toilets in the nearby subway station. The protesters dubbed the courtyard across the boulevard a neocommunist free zone and decorated it with graffiti and wall posters. Each evening several thousand people would gather, and protest leaders would speak to them from a second-floor balcony on one of the university buildings. But after the election, on May 20, the number of demonstrators dwindled.

I spoke about what happened afterward with Sorin Dumitrescu, a reporter for *Romania Libera.* Before the revolution, the newspaper had been just another Ceausescu organ. But immediately after Ceausescu's flight, its staff staged a little revolution of its own and installed several former dissidents as editors. It became one of the liveliest newspapers in Romania and one of those most inclined to criticize the government. Dumitrescu had been a mechanical engineer before the revolution; he would have liked a career in law, but he had refused to join the Communist Party. After the revolution, he decided to try his hand at journalism, and he signed on as a thirty-one-year-old cub reporter. One of his assignments was coverage of the demonstrators in University Square. I met him in his office in the ugly, Stalin Gothic building, a gift from the Soviet Union, that still housed Romania's major publications. It had been formally renamed the House of the Free Press, but most people still called it Casa Scinteia, after the old Party newspaper.

"After the elections, the main organizations involved in the protest said they were leaving," Dumitrescu told me. "A different sort of crowd began to come at night, much smaller. They were not quality guys, not very clean. They liked to fight, not ideas. I can't say they were only Gypsies, but there were Gypsies among them.

I think some of them were infiltrators, who were sent to try to influence the action toward more violence.

"At four o'clock on the morning of June 13, the military police came with trucks and buses and cleared the square. I was asleep at the time, and I didn't hear about it until noon the next day. When I arrived, the whole place was blocked off by trucks and buses. The police would only let you pass if you could show that you worked there. I managed to get into the square through some alleys. On the lawn where the tents had been, there were some women from the city work crews digging and planting grass."

About an hour before his arrival, he told me, a group of workers from a factory in southern Bucharest, the Bucharest Heavy Machine Works, known by its initials as IMGB, had suddenly appeared in the square, chanting "IMGB makes order!" and smashing the windows in the university's architecture school. That had attracted a crowd, which, when Dumitrescu arrived, numbered about one thousand. They were massing on the northwest edge of the square, near the barricade of trucks and buses, shouting, "Down with Iliescu! Down with the Front!" Dumitrescu watched from the roof of the architecture school.

After several hours of standoff, at about 3:30 P.M., fighting broke out, Dumitrescu recounted. The protesters "pushed toward the police line like rugby players in a scrum and broke their line. More police, with shields and helmets and clubs, came, and they counterattacked. The people turned and ran, and some were trampled and beaten. The crowd started to throw rocks, and the police began throwing the rocks back. It was like the *intifada* on the West Bank. There were retreats and advances; lines moved back and forth. Then, after half an hour or so, some people in the crowd started to throw Molotov cocktails. I saw a policeman with his boots on fire, and then a bus caught fire at about 4:15 P.M."

Then he witnessed one of those odd events that feeds the conspiracy theorist who lurks in the minds of most Romanians. The police suddenly began to run away. "They left like spectators from a movie, all at once and in line. I'm not sure that it wasn't planned. Then all the buses and trucks were set afire. I left the square at that point and came back here to write my story."

I picked up the thread of what happened from Don Slaiman, an American labor organizer who was in Bucharest working for an international effort to help Romania organize free trade unions. Slaiman was at the headquarters of a trade union confederation called *Fratia* (Brotherhood), across the street from the police headquarters and the Ministry of the Interior, perhaps half a mile from University Square. From the *Fratia* windows he saw a mob chasing the police buses coming from the direction of University Square. Some of them tossed Molotov cocktails at the sprawling stone police headquarters; a small fire broke out, which, although it never threatened to burn down the building, was of enormous symbolic significance. The mob surrounded the Ministry of the Interior, which, in the Ceausescu years, had controlled the Securitate.

Slaiman heard shots and saw people fall. Snipers had taken up positions on some of the buildings around the plaza in front of the ministry. To Slaiman, it seemed as if each time the crowd showed signs of calming down, a sniper would kill someone, touching off more unrest. "They didn't wound anyone," he said. "They shot to kill, right in the head." Slaiman counted nine bodies, although the official death toll, announced later, was six. During the evening, Slaiman said, the police and the army both resumed helping control the mob. Tanks moved into the square where the snipers had been active to protect the Ministry of the Interior. Slaiman recalled that by three o'clock in the morning, the riot, if that was what it was, had begun to peter out. But by that hour the coal miners were already arriving in Bucharest from the Jiu Valley.

The Jiu River rises in the Carpathian Mountains about 150 miles northwest of Bucharest and tumbles southward toward the Danube. Many years ago it must have been a wild and lovely river, carving a path through rugged ridges, with forests of birch and pine clinging to their steep sides. But that was before coal mining became the economic staple of the valley. Now the water, when it froths over a rapid, is turbid and charcoal gray, and the sediment that collects in the crooks of the river bends is black. It is poor and rugged country, reminiscent of the coal-mining areas of West Virginia and Kentucky.

On a cold, bright Sunday morning, I drove out to the valley and turned off the main road toward a town called Vulcan, after the Roman god who commanded the earth's inner fires. A few hundred yards from the two-lane road, silhouetted against a ridge, I could see the steel superstructures of the mines, surrounded by a gray haze. Closer to the road stood a few peasants' cottages with small gardens, and row after row of three-story apartment buildings, laid out at precise right angles to one another, like enlisted men's housing at a military base. On the main street a couple of trucks had parked, and some men were standing inside them, selling limp green vegetables. All over the sidewalks, men had gathered in clusters of two, four, or more, talking and passing around bottles of *tuica,* the Romanian national liquor, a clear brandy made, almost always at home, from plums. Although it was barely noon, many of them were already drunk.

At one end of the little town stood a soccer stadium, its grass worn to bare earth at midfield. Many of the men of Vulcan were headed there to watch their local team take on a side from another mining town in the valley. In the little gravel parking area outside the stadium, I met Dumitru Jordach, a stocky, aging miner with blackened fingernails, who, like many others, had come to the valley after the communists collectivized his father's peasant farm, soon after World War II. He was forty-nine years old.

The work in the mines was hard, he said. The shafts stretched half a mile into the ground, and most of the coal was pried out with picks and shovels. Sometimes, in the "galleries" of the main shafts, a man could not stand up straight as he worked. In some he had to crawl. The stores in the town had no medicines, and the doctors in the area, all state employees, were notoriously quick to accuse an ill miner of malingering.

In the summer of 1977, Jordach said, he had taken part in one of the few serious protests of the Ceausescu era, a miners' strike. Ceausescu himself, then not quite as powerful as he would later become, came to Petrosani, the largest town in the valley, to settle it. The Jiu miners were, even then, considered a particularly important part of the labor force, the kind of proletarians that the Communist Party liked to consider its core constituency. Ceausescu, Jordach recalled, was so eager to settle the strike that he made concessions, including a six-hour day and a promise that none of the strikers would be punished.

As soon as the miners had gone back to work, Jordach said, Ceausescu began to break his promises. Strike leaders were arrested and sent to prison; Jordach said he served two years in a work camp. The Securitate gradually infiltrated the mine's work force with its agents, so that any further unrest could be dealt with before it reached the proportions of a strike. In 1982 the workday for miners went back to eight hours, and the mine management began to require them to work six or seven days a week to meet production quotas. "They pressured you to work on Sundays," Jordach said. "If you missed it, you were harassed."

The National Salvation Front, when it came to power, was clever enough to try to win the miners over. Under the Front, the workweek became five days, and the workday became six hours. Pay rose, and the miners won a cherished goal: a hazardous duty supplement, although they only got it if they worked every day they were scheduled to work in a given month. Soon miners were making, according to what I heard from many of them, about six or seven thousand lei a month, roughly twice the average wage in the country.

On June 13, Romanian television broadcast a particularly distorted account of what had happened in Bucharest, an account that showed all of the demonstrators' excesses and none of the police actions that had helped provoke them. President-elect Iliescu announced that a group of "fascist extremists" was making "an organized attempt to overthrow the government." And that evening, when the miners came out of the pits, their union leaders were waiting with bullhorns. Transportation was available, the leaders said, for any miners who wished to go to Bucharest to help protect the government.

Dumitru Jordach said he did not go, although he estimated that three-fourths of the miners did. As I walked around Vulcan, I had trouble finding any miner who would admit that he had taken the special government train to Bucharest that night. Perhaps they were simply suspicious of foreigners asking questions. Or perhaps they were no longer proud of what they had done.

Finally, in a restaurant in Petrosani, I shared a table with two men in their twenties. They were drinking a local cocktail made with cognac and a wedge of lemon, with sugar coating the rim of the glass the way salt coats the rim of a margarita glass. One of them cut the drink with some soda pop. After we had talked for a while, the older of the two, a man named Dumitru Semyon, acknowledged that he had joined the miners going to Bucharest on the thirteenth. He had seen the television reports about a possible government overthrow. He worried about losing the pay raise and the benefits the Front had given the miners. Still clad in his work clothes, including his helmet with the light mounted in it, he boarded the train. Many of his fellow miners, he noticed, were carrying clubs, axes, or crowbars.

Semyon's train, one of three, arrived at Bucharest's North Station in the early morning hours, just before dawn. A car with a loudspeaker, driven by someone who identified himself as a National Salvation Front representative, met them at the station and led them to the university area. No students were out on the streets, so the miners went into their buildings and dragged them out, beating them. Semyon watched, he said, as Marian Munteanu, a well-known student leader, was savagely beaten.

Then one of the Front "escorts" led them toward a market, where he said that Gypsy rioters were hiding. On the way, not coincidentally, they passed the headquarters of the National Peasant Party. The "escort" suggested that thirty miners enter the head-quarters and "search for weapons." The miners trashed the place. I heard accounts of how they trashed other sites, including the Liberal Party headquarters and the headquarters of other opposition newspapers and groups, including places that outsiders could only have found if someone familiar with Bucharest led them. They beat people on the street just because they happened to wear glasses or a beard. Several dozen showed up at the Group for Social Dialogue headquarters, bent on eviction, but Gabriel Andreescu was able to call a friend in the city government and win a ruling that the building belonged to the group.

During the two days they spent in Bucharest, trucks from the city's various food service enterprises delivered food to the miners. They camped out in one of the city's parks. And when they left town, Iliescu came to the station and thanked them. The miners went back to the Jiu Valley and, according to Dumitru Semyon, had to work an extra two days to make up for the time they had missed. But in July, he said, his mine had finally gotten its long-sought hazardous duty pay differential.

The most charitable interpretation I heard in Bucharest of what the Front had done suggested that Iliescu had panicked, had be-lieved that the street demonstrations could turn into a revolution, just as the Timisoara demonstration had in December. When he saw the police refuse to continue battling the mobs, this theory went, he called the miners in. More suspicious people believed that the Front, or elements in it, had deliberately provoked the incidents of June 13 to provide a pretext for calling the miners in, intimidating the pro-testers once and for all, and driving another wedge into the gap that already separated manual laborers and the intelligentsia.

The intervention of the coal miners did put a temporary end to the demonstrations in University Square, although by fall much of the graffiti was back, and the square again attracted small crowds of dissenters. As evidenced by Stelian Tanase's characterization of the miners as savages, the episode did reduce the likelihood of an anti-Front coalition. But in several critical ways, the Front apparently miscalculated.

Abroad, the miners' rampage damaged the reputation of the Front, perhaps irreparably. The United States, which had been neither supporting the Front nor dismissing it as a collection of unrepentant communists, tilted toward dismissal. No ranking U.S. officials attended Iliescu's inauguration. More important, the United States announced that it would maintain indefinitely some of the sanctions it had imposed against Romania during the Ceausescu era. This meant exceptionally high tariffs for Romanian exports to the United States and that Romania could not benefit from American government credits and trade promotion programs. Moreover, the United States maintained pressure on other Western countries not to grant easy credit to Bucharest.

And with the economy left by Ceausescu, Romania needed all the help it could get. Ceausescu, as Dinu Giurescu had observed, had truly believed in Stalinism, and his economic legacy suffered from all Stalinism's shortcomings. He had invested Romania's wealth in a relatively small number of huge projects, which looked neat and impressive in the government's annual plan and seemed to fulfill some kind of Stalinist conception of what an advanced economy looked like, with lots of heavy steel consumption and sinewy blue-collar workers. In reality, the projects of the Ceausescu era—or, for that matter, the entire communist period in the Soviet Union and Eastern Europe—proved to be elephantine enterprises, overburdened with workers, exquisitely unsuited for the transition everyone claimed to want to make, to a market economy operating on a Western level.

I rode out one morning to one of those enterprises, IMGB, the

Bucharest Heavy Machine Works, with a trade union organizer, Gheorgiu Ghimes. "Ih-Meh-Geh-Beh," as everyone in town referred to it, had been the source of some of the blue-collar thugs the Front had sent into University Square in June, before the arrival of the coal miners. It was a sprawling enterprise, an industrial complex of many buildings, with its own rail spur and subway stop. It made turbines, and electrical engines, and a variety of other metal products.

Ghimes, a short, curly-haired man in his forties, had been a worker at IMGB until after the revolution, when free union activity became possible. He gave me a quick tour of some of the plant, starting in an enormous building, perhaps 250 yards long and ten stories high. The building was cold and gloomy, lit primarily by shafts of light that fell through its scattered windows. The floor was made of dirt, and here and there small piles of coal were burning openly, used by the workers to melt paint or simply to keep warm; they made the air inside smoky. The floor was strewn with iron pots, ten feet high and twice as big around, that held molten metal. Behind them stood the ovens that melted the metal, perhaps thirty feet wide, some of them open and glowing red hot. From the ceiling a few cranes were suspended, making it possible to move heavy, hot loads from one end of the building to another. The centerpiece of the building was a green press, hundreds of tons in weight. A rough-hewn steel rod, perhaps six feet in diameter, glowing hot and destined to be a ship's propeller shaft, hung from chains at the bottom of the press. From a control room, a worker raised and turned the chains, manipulating the rod in the press. When he had it properly aligned, the press came down and squeezed the hot metal, trying to smooth it out. There were no computers to guide it, Ghimes said. Everything depended on the skill and eye of the man operating the press. It was, essentially, a big blacksmith's anvil. In another building, workers manned lathes that shaved excess metal off the rough rods and polished them. Most of them, as we walked through, were standing around, reading newspapers, or chatting.

Ghimes took me to the union's office in the complex's administration building. Two secretaries worked there, and one was typing letters on an old manual typewriter, even though a Romanian-made personal computer and printer stood in a corner of the room, covered with a sheet of plastic. Apparently they had no software for word processing. "We're still babies as far as computers go," one secretary told me.

In a conference room next to the union office, we met Toma Nuta, an engineer who had managed IMGB's exports and imports during the Ceausescu years and held the same job under the new regime. Nuta, an aging, heavyset man with bags under his eyes, gray hair, and drooping jowls, chain-smoked Bulgarian cigarettes. Quickly he ran down the statistics that defined the problems of IMGB.

Although it was relatively new, built in 1969, the factory's design was severely flawed. It employed sixteen thousand workers to produce what, in a German factory, he estimated might require about eleven thousand. Worse, it was designed to exploit that labor force. Although it had been communism's proudest boast that it ended the exploitation of labor, in fact the opposite was true. Ceausescu and his planners, in creating IMGB, built it even though it would consume huge and inefficient amounts of raw materials and energy. They counted on the fact that it could employ Romanian workers who, by Western standards, were paid almost slave wages. (The average salary at IMGB, under Ceausescu, was perhaps 2,700 lei per month. At the official exchange rate of the Ceausescu years, 9 lei per dollar, this amounted to $300 per month. The Front had adjusted the exchange rate to 35 lei per dollar, making the salary about $75 per month. And at the black market exchange rate of 100 lei or more to the dollar, the average wage came to less than $30 per month.) At those wages, even an inefficient plant could be "profitable" to the state and could produce a few exportable products that earned hard currency. IMGB had a deal with General Electric under which they received a license to produce some nuclear generating equipment in exchange for some of the products the factory produced. Nuta told me that in 1989 the factory's exports came to about $85 million, although some of that was in barter goods.

But in the Ceausescu years little or none of that hard currency came back to IMGB, Nuta complained. "There were no dollars here," he said. "We had to get approval from the government, sometimes from Ceausescu himself, to spend even as little as a thousand dollars. He wouldn't allow us to keep up with the world level. After you build these huge factories, you have to modernize them to make their energy consumption lower, to make them more efficient." Modernization required purchasing things abroad, such as graphite electrodes, and in the two decades since the plant was built, it had fallen further and further behind the rest of the world because it could not make such purchases. Nuta estimated that a South Korean plant would require 22 percent less energy to produce a turbine than IMGB needed. And energy was no longer cheap. Romanian coal was of poor quality. The Soviets were demanding hard currency for their oil, which used to go to Eastern Europe in return for barter goods or soft currency.

There were no politically palatable alternatives for IMGB. It could not continue to operate with huge and wasteful amounts of Romanian energy, unless the government was prepared to further deprive the citizens of Bucharest of heat and light. It could not export and earn money to buy modern equipment without continuing to exploit its labor force. That no longer seemed possible. In the more open, postrevolutionary political climate, trade union movements like Ghimes's were pressing for higher wages. And the Front, having taught the workers to march into the capital and crack heads, could hardly suppress the unions and risk having that violence turned against itself. Privatization of industries like IMGB was a problematic solution. Who would buy the stock? The old communist managers, or foreign corporations, were the only possible buyers. The Front had promised not to allow foreign capital to buy the country cheaply, and it would be politically suicidal to turn the ownership of the factories over to the managing class. Some Romanian reformers argued that the government should simply hand the stock to the labor force in return for its underpaid labor during the communist era. But the Front did not want to give up that much control. The compromise its economists were promoting would distribute 30 percent of the stock to the workers and leave 70 percent with the state. How that would solve any economic problems remained to be seen.

Nuta hoped that IMGB's "foreign partners" would help pull it out of the mire it was in. The company was talking about joint ventures with a variety of Western corporations. But thus far nothing had come of those talks, and as long as Romania was perceived as unstable, not much was likely to. The Front had agreed to allow plants like IMGB to keep half their hard currency earnings beginning in 1991. Nuta hoped that over time these revenues could be used to modernize the plant. Not many people I spoke to, though, thought that either the government or its factories would be given much time before the people grew tired of their unending sacrifice and exploded again.

None of the workers I spoke with at IMGB felt that any of the opposition groups or parties, including the Group for Social Dialogue, represented their interests. Several of them who had voted for Iliescu and the Front in May said they would not do so again, but that seemed principally because the government had just announced a round of price increases for food and clothing, without announcing a compensating pay increase. Don Slaiman, the American labor organizer, said he had found that most Romanian workers, once they felt free to voice their concerns, focused almost exclusively on immediate pay hikes. Even if their workplace was so unsafe that death and maiming were constant threats, they preferred to receive hazardous duty pay rather than press the government to improve safety standards. And there was no discernible movement toward an opposition that embraced both workers and the intellectuals who might have been able to articulate a sensible program for the future. The Group for Social Dialogue had just helped found a movement called the Civic Alliance, which was patterned after opposition movements in Czechoslovakia and other countries. But the only union it could persuade to join was the one that represented employees of the state television network.

IMGB was only one of many structures that Ceausescu and the era of the Soviet Empire had left behind which would influence Romania after both he and the empire had gone. The most dramatic example was the Boulevard of the Victory of Socialism, Ceausescu's hulking monument in the center of Bucharest. Whatever the people of the city might have thought of it as architecture, they had no choice but to complete it and use it, even though they gave the broad avenue a carefully neutral name: New Artery Boulevard. When I walked around, the stores and buildings that had in 1989 been Potemkin villages for the dictator's inspection were opening. Laborers were still trying to complete the House of the People. They had removed the spire Ceausescu had ordered, making the building look all the more massive and misshapen. Ministries were moving into the office areas, and families were occupying the apartments. Kids in ragged clothes played soccer next to the ornamental fountains on the boulevard, which had been left as dry receptacles for the fallen leaves.

I walked into one of the buildings, rang a doorbell at random, and introduced myself to the man who answered, a surveyor from Buzau named Bercau, who had moved to the capital a year earlier, just before the revolution. Rather proudly he showed me around the three rooms where he, his wife, and two daughters lived. Although the common wisdom was that Ceausescu had intended for the members of the *nomenklatura,* the Party elite, to live on his boulevard, the apartment was no larger or better appointed than many others I had seen in Bucharest. The *nomenklaturists* were the people who had enforced Ceausescu's madness, even though few of them believed in it. What would have been their gain for moving there? A little more heat? The right to turn on all the lights at night? It occurred to me that perhaps the most debilitating of Ceausescu's legacies was not that he had forced so many Romanians to kowtow to or cooperate with his despotism but that he had gotten them to do it so cheaply.

As the months passed without substantial improvement in the quality of their lives, many more Romanians came to believe in the various conspiracy theories that circulated in the country, all of which held that a cabal of disgruntled communists inside the Ceausescu regime had planned and staged a coup d'état in the guise of a revolution. Silviu Brucan, after falling out with the Front, actively fed these suspicions by giving interviews in which he detailed various plots involving himself and ranking military officers against Ceausescu that dated back to the early 1980s. But this was the same Brucan who, in January had insisted that the revolution was spontaneous and that the Securitate's repressive grip had prevented any conspiracies. It was probably no coincidence that the tales Brucan told later in 1990 all suggested that Iliescu had played no role in the underground muttering against Ceausescu. If such plots had existed, they never came close to achieving their goal. But the idea that there had been plots appealed to many Romanians because it gave them an easy way to explain what had gone wrong since Ceausescu's downfall.

Others simply slid into a depression more profound, in its way, than that which Ceausescu had inflicted. "I am not happy," a woman named Georgeta Moldoveanu, who worked for a Bucharest publishing house, told me. "I am confused. Before, there was just one big lie. Now there are many lies. There are so many things I don't know. I remember on December 22, I was so happy. I thought, finally, it was over. But it hasn't gotten better."

In March of 1990 Dinu Giurescu returned to Romania for the first time since his exile. He was part of a task force of American academics sent to Bucharest to explore ways of restoring contacts with his native land. "It was quite mild, and I remember thinking that two years earlier, when I'd left, I would never have believed I'd be back so soon," he told me. "Driving in from the airport, the first thing that struck me was the big apartment buildings on Piata Victoriei, which had not been touched by systematization when I left. I understood better the totalitarian mind, trying to impress people with size. I said to myself, 'Thank God! If Ceausescu had stayed another two years, everything would have been broken.'" He stayed in a friend's apartment around the corner from the site of his grandfather's old house. The sight of Ceausescu's huge apartment buildings where he had spent his childhood did not shock him, because I had taken some pictures in August 1989 and sent them to him. What did impress him was that so much remained the same in the old neighborhood, down to the cracks in the sidewalks.

Something had changed, however, within him. He had an American reentry permit in his passport, and a job waiting for him in Texas. He looked at postrevolutionary Bucharest differently from the way his old friends did. He saw fresh new newspapers, open debate, a little more light and heat. He saw reason for joy and optimism. His friends, however, the memory of the February intervention by the coal miners fresh in their minds, "were psychologically traumatized by the feeling that communism was back. They had expected an immediate, sudden change in everything, a new era of prosperity. They didn't realize that the people hadn't changed, and that prosperity is a most difficult thing to achieve. If you tried to tell them that significant changes had occurred, they would say it was easy for you to say, because you had a place to go in America."

Giurescu came back in May with another academic task force, and this time his old colleagues at the university offered him a full professorship in the Department of History and told him that if he came back, he could teach whatever he wanted. It was not an easy choice for him to make. His wife had established herself as a librarian in the United States and was beginning to teach Italian. His daughters had flourished there: one was in medical school and the other was studying for a master's degree in art history. They already thought of the United States as home, he realized. On the other hand, he told himself, "You spent sixty years in this country. Your father and grandfather taught history, and now you have a chance to teach Romanian students what happened under communism, and that will be better for them than teaching European history to American kids. Do it."

So Giurescu gave up his position at Texas A & M and agreed with his family that, for a few years at least, he would see them only in the summers and at Christmastime. In July 1990 he returned to Bucharest. He prepared a special lecture, which he called "The Confession of a Generation, 1944–1989," and delivered it at several universities around the country. In it he tried to explain how he and his peers had reacted to the communist takeover after World War II and why they had made the compromises they had. He abandoned medieval Romanian history, his specialty during the Ceausescu era, and taught two new courses. One was on the behavior of the Great Powers from 1938 to 1945. He hoped that from it his students would come to understand that Great Powers followed their interests and had no duty to help a minor power like Romania, that countries like Romania had to find their own way in the world. And he taught a domestic history course that covered the period from 1944 to 1947, when the communists had taken over. He very much wanted his students, who had been raised on Ceausescu's version of history, to know in detail the truth of how such a disaster had befallen their country.

LITHUANIA

December 1990

When I returned to Vilnius, nine months after Lithuania's declaration of independence, I found that most of the new government's leaders were out of town. Vytautas Landsbergis was touring Canada and the United States, where he met with President Bush. Kazimiera Prunskiene was in Germany. Bronius Kuzmickas had gone to Norway. All of them, of course, were intently seeking friends and allies in the West.

The ranking official in residence was Deputy Prime Minister Romualdas Ozolas. I called his office at the Supreme Council, as the Lithuanians now rendered it in English (rather than Supreme Soviet), and his secretary invited me to come by the following evening, when he would see me after a meeting with the Lithuanians who had been elected in 1989 to the Congress of Peoples' Deputies in Moscow. The congress would be convening later that month, and Ozolas had called the meeting to make sure that the "former deputies" understood Lithuania's posture of generally refusing to participate in governmental bodies of the Soviet Union.

A light snow had fallen into the early winter twilight and iced the sidewalks when I set out for the Supreme Council. The lights of the buildings on the embankments glinted off the black, cold waters of the Neris River. An embossed metal version of the Lithuanian symbol, Vitas the knight, had been mounted over the door to the Council building, replacing the silk-screen banner that the crowd had raised after tearing down the hammer and sickle on March 11. Inside a couple of policemen were watching television in the vestibule. I waited until Ozolas emerged from his meeting.

Ozolas is a wiry, bespectacled man in his early fifties, with coal black hair and a friendly smile. He was wearing a blue-gray, three-piece suit with socks that drooped toward his ankles. He invited me to ride with him to his office on the second floor of the Council of Ministers' building, about a quarter of a mile away. We walked out to the courtyard and climbed into the back of a white, chauffeur-driven Volga, the sort of car used by midlevel Soviet officials, that had been idling there. The Council of Ministers' building was deserted by that hour, save for a few guards toting Kalashnikov rifles and wearing what appeared to be Soviet Army uniforms modified by the addition of epaulets with the red-yellow-green Lithuanian tricolor. Ozolas's office suite had three rooms, a frayed yellow carpet, and some standard-issue, red Soviet furniture, including a cot that he used on nights when he worked too late to make it worth going home. He opened a small refrigerator in the reception room and offered me a choice of orange soda or cognac. Then we sat down to talk.

Like so many other *Sajudis* leaders, Ozolas had been a philosophy teacher before becoming a politician. He had become a Communist Party member at one point to advance his career, he told me, but he insisted that he had never believed fully in the Party's doctrines and that for the most part his goal had been to undermine the Party from within.

It seemed significant to me that so many of Lithuania's leaders were abroad, courting Western support, while none were in Moscow negotiating with the Soviet leaders. I asked Ozolas about that, and about the impression I'd had in March that despite

U.S. Ambassador Jack Matlock's warning to the contrary, the *Saju-dis* leaders had expected American recognition of their declaration of independence.

Ozolas nodded. "I remember the meeting with Matlock," he said. "It was a delicate conversation, one of those diplomatic speeches. Of course, his nonsupport was absolutely clear, but there were some doubts. It wasn't said that there would not be recognition."

(Ambassador Matlock, in a subsequent interview with me, confirmed the impression that I had gotten in March, that he had rather bluntly warned the *Sajudis* leaders to expect no American recognition. But he had not told the *Sajudis* leaders he could flatly rule it out, because the question at that time was hypothetical.)

Despite what Matlock had said, at least some *Sajudis* leaders continued to hope for American recognition. "We supposed that since Bush had not recognized the legality of the occupation, as a law-abiding man, a man who enforced laws, he would automatically recognize a people that had managed to rise and declare their freedom, that he would disregard everything else. It was one of our most terrible tragedies. We waited three days, around the clock, for something to be said in Washington. It wasn't. And after a week, when it became clear that nothing would come from Washington, then everyday life began," Ozolas said.

This expectation that somehow the West would bail them out and support their independence, as Western powers had supported the independence of the Baltic states in 1920, constituted, I thought, one of the chief miscalculations made by the Lithuanian leaders. They had predicated their strategy on the pattern their grandfathers had followed after World War I: taking advantage of a prostrate Russia, they would declare their independence, then count on Western support to help make it stick. The strategy had worked in 1918–1920, when the British, the Germans, and the Poles had helped the Baltic states. But it did not fully take into account several important factors of 1990. First, the sort of quick, low-risk military intervention that the Western powers had been willing to undertake after World War I (such as the British navy's rescue of Latvia's fledgling government from the Bolsheviks) was unthinkable against the Soviet Union. Second, and more important, in 1918–1920 the Western powers had wanted Bolshevism to die in its cradle. In 1990 they wanted *perestroika* to succeed, and they were loathe to help any separatists jeopardize its chances. The most the United States would do was point out to the Kremlin that armed repression of the Lithuanians would inevitably harm the cooperative relationship Gorbachev and his foreign minister, Eduard Shevardnadze, were trying to build.

Had they fully realized this, the Lithuanians might have tried a different approach, one oriented toward Moscow rather than toward the West. This would have been a Gandhian strategy of seeking ways to force the Russians to live up to their newly professed ideals of tolerance, nonviolence, and decentralization, of building independence gradually by taking more and more autonomy from the central government, all aimed at an ultimate, amicable separation. No one, of course, could have guaranteed that such a strategy would work. But it was never tried.

In Moscow, Gorbachev responded to the declaration of independence by gradually building up pressure to rescind it. At three thirty in the morning on March 23, a Soviet Army tank division rumbled into Vilnius and rolled past the Supreme Council building, where the legislature was holding an all-night, emergency session. Later that day, Soviet paratroopers helped the rump, pro-Moscow faction of the Lithuanian Communist Party occupy three local Party buildings in Vilnius. Two days later, the same forces occupied the capital's main Party headquarters and the Institute for Political Education, where some of the pro-independence newspapers had their offices. Two days after that, several dozen Soviet soldiers stormed into the Naujoji Vilnija Psychiatric Hospital and grabbed twelve

Lithuanians who had deserted the army before their required two years were up. Other troops rounded up other Lithuanians who had decided not to answer the Soviet draft call.

On March 30, Soviet internal troops dressed in police uniforms occupied one of the republic's nerve centers, the main printing plant in Vilnius, where virtually every Lithuanian newspaper is printed; their pretext was that the plant belonged to the pro-Moscow branch of the Communist Party and had to be protected. At the end of the month, Gorbachev issued a statement saying he would be willing to discuss the whole range of Lithuanian complaints and grievances, but only if the Supreme Council first repealed the March 11 declaration.

In the midst of this fearful turmoil and pressure, the *Sajudis* leaders faced the task of forming a government that had the authority to enforce its laws. Soviet power in Lithuania rested on four organs of coercion: the army; the state procurator, or prosecutor; the KGB; and the Ministry of Internal Affairs, which controlled the police and some uniformed troops, the so-called internal troops, soldiers trained for duty within the country, armed like light infantry, and authorized to wear police uniforms on duty. (The Moscow ministry was, at that time, organizing a special, all-volunteer division within the internal troops that wore black berets. But those troops had not yet been deployed in a violent situation.) The Lithuanian insurgents could take over the Supreme Soviet, rename it the Supreme Council, and pass all the declarations they wanted; they could take over the media and the schools to promulgate those declarations. But unless they controlled the organs of coercion, they would be a government on paper only.

Sajudis had lots of philosophers, but it had no soldiers or policemen in its leadership. To chair the parliamentary commission on internal affairs and defense, *Sajudis* turned to Zigmas Vaisvila, the young physicist who had emboldened his fellow intellectuals at the movement's founding meeting back in 1988. Vaisvila had gotten started in politics as an environmentalist; before *Sajudis* was founded, he helped launch the Lithuanian Green Party. He also, he told me, had taken the Soviet equivalent of an ROTC course while he was at the university and had spent three months in the army as a reserve officer. He was about as military a man as *Sajudis* had. I called Vaisvila, and he dropped by my hotel for lunch one Sunday afternoon.

The first thing the *Sajudis* leaders had tried to do, Vaisvila said, was appeal to the army. "They tried to ignore our request for contacts," Vaisvila said. "But finally we got in touch with the leader of the Vilnius garrison, and he came to see us. It was a very serious talk. We tried to ask him what he thought it meant when a country used its army for maintaining internal order, when it used force against unarmed people, when it took over newspaper publishing houses and entered hospitals. This is the argument we tried to make with them. But the answer turned out to be very simple. They are not the ones making the decisions. It's Moscow."

The office of the procurator, or prosecutor, constituted the next pillar of state authority in Lithuania, and here *Sajudis* had more success. The new government appointed its own procurator, Arturas Paulauskas. Moscow argued that his appointment was illegal and that the USSR procurator's office had the right to make the appointment. Its candidate was a Lithuanian loyal to Moscow named Antanas Petrauskas, who had previously been procurator of the Riga Military Command. But, unlike the army, the procurator's office in Vilnius did not have conscript troops from other parts of the Soviet Union. When both Petrauskas and Paulauskas attempted to assert their control, all but 7 of the 114 employees in the procurator's department vowed to be loyal to Paulauskas, the *Sajudis* candidate.

On March 30, ten Soviet Interior Ministry troops arrived at the procurator's office to enforce the claim of Moscow's man, Petrauskas. They secured him access to the building, but they could not force people to work for him. Petrauskas could give orders, but no one would listen. On April 5, fifty Soviet soldiers reinforced the occupation of the procurator's office. But Paulauskas simply moved his office to the Vilnius city procurator's office, and all the deputies and assistants remained loyal to him. Moscow was stymied.

With the KGB, *Sajudis* had less leverage. Before the elections it had staged a showy demonstration outside the KGB's headquarters to call attention to trucks leaving the building, apparently to remove the local KGB archives to a safer storage place in Russia. At that time, the republic KGB director had bluntly told them that the KGB answered to Moscow, not Vilnius. In the interim before the election, that director had been replaced with a Lithuanian who had spent the bulk of his career abroad, rather than in the KGB's internal apparatus. Vaisvila assumed that the Lithuanian communists had asked Moscow for the switch in an effort to show the voters that they could become masters of Lithuania's internal affairs. If so, it had not worked.

"The KGB in Lithuania is a little bit disorganized, split into different parts," Vaisvila told me. "One part is pro-Moscow, another is pro-Brazauskas, so to speak [meaning that it supported the faction of the Lithuanian Communist Party that favored independence], and another part is more interested in professional work and is very angry with the *nomenklatura* and its corruption."

Some of Vaisvila's new contacts within the KGB had begun to feed him information about corruption, and some of the allegations pointed at members of *Sajudis* itself. Vaisvila, who had a wide streak of revolutionary moralism in his character, publicized the charges he believed. "We announced it in the Supreme Council. We put it in the newspapers," he said. He seemed genuinely puzzled that this in itself had not been enough to get the accused to resign, that they had insisted that a fair trial would exonerate them and remained in their jobs. He told me confidently that in a democracy, charges of the sort he had made would have been sufficient to persuade them to quit. I thought of all the American politicians who had brazened their way through corruption investigations and tried to hold on to their offices even in jail; but I didn't argue with him.

Some of my contacts in Vilnius thought the KGB was manipulating Vaisvila. Whether or not that was true, it was clear that neither Vaisvila nor *Sajudis* could manipulate the KGB. When I asked Vaisvila how many men the KGB had in Lithuania, he admitted that he did not know. It was not information the KGB would give him. Despite the elections, the secret police, then, remained firmly under Moscow's control.

The uniformed police were more critical to the question of day-to-day control over the republic. The army was a blunt instrument whose use would entail substantial consequences for Moscow. The uniformed police were in many ways a more useful means of coercion. They were, ostensibly, under the control of the Ministry of Internal Affairs of the republic. But the Ministry of Internal Affairs in Moscow also had authority; it controlled the internal troops. Throughout the Soviet Union, the division of authority between the two was sloppily evolving in the direction of decentralization.

The first choice that Landsbergis, Vaisvila, and the rest of *Sajudis* had to make was whom to put in charge of the republic Ministry of Internal Affairs. The incumbent, Marijonis Misiukonis, had been appointed in 1989, during the period when the Lithuanian Communist Party, responding to public pressure and the imminence of elections, had tried to present a reform image. Misiukonis was a former KGB official, Vaisvila told me, who had been sent to Lithuania during the interregnum period of Yuri Andropov, a detail which suggested that he was at least opposed to the corrupt wing of the Party that had flourished under Leonid Brezhnev. And, for public consumption at least, he espoused some reformist ideas. "He had started to speak about depoliticization of the system of internal affairs," Vaisvila recalled. This was a little like a Republican police commissioner suddenly becoming an advocate of nonpartisan law enforcement after the Democrats win the local elections.

But, Vaisvila recalled, Landsbergis felt under intense pressure in those days, with the tanks rumbling regularly through the streets. "We had no wish to leave him in this position," said Vaisvila, speaking of the *Sajudis* stalwarts. "But unfortunately, Mr. Landsbergis decided we had no choice. He was afraid the militia would split into two parts, loyal and nonloyal to our republic, if we did not keep him." So Misiukonis was retained. But the *Sajudis* leaders could not be quite sure from whom their police chief took orders.

Events soon gave them reason to suspect. When the troops from Moscow's Ministry of Internal Affairs took over the republic's main printing plant, Vaisvila said, "we asked Misiukonis to defend the plant, and personally I had a lot of talks with him. But he said the militia was now a depoliticized force and could not be used to solve political problems." In fact, Vaisvila suspected, Misiukonis's police had helped the internal troops find and enter the printing plant and other buildings.

But *Sajudis* still had some resources. Its leaders got on the radio and appealed to the public to help guard the printing plants, both the main one on the edge of town, used for the republic's newspapers, and a smaller, older one in the center of town that printed magazines. Several thousand Lithuanians answered the call, ringing the larger building. One independent radio station organized an impromptu, all-night music festival outside the main plant. *Sajudis* volunteers entered the plant and formed a second "guard" that stood by the Soviet Interior Ministry guards. "Our guard was psychologically stronger, and controlled the situation," Vaisvila recalled. It helped that nearly all the workers in the plant supported *Sajudis.* The plant continued to turn out the same newspapers it had turned out before independence, most of them staunchly pro-Lithuanian and anti-Soviet.

"A week later," Vaisvila continued, referring to April 20, "the administration of the smaller, older printing house asked us to help because the internal troops had created an atmosphere very bad for work. The Supreme Council authorized volunteer guards for this factory as well and issued them special tickets. They started to guard it, as well.

"I went down there to see what the situation was. It's in the Old City, and it's grimy. It was built before the Second World War and the Soviet occupation. I spent about a half an hour there, and I heard from the soldiers that their leaders were coming, so I decided to wait a little bit in order to have a talk with Colonel Fyodorov, who is the commander of the operative regiment.

"We met in the guardhouse at the entrance to the plant and had a discussion, a very peaceful discussion. I said that our volunteers are acting in accordance with the decisions of our Supreme Council and the administration of the plant, and I hoped this double guard would be as peaceful as the one at the main printing plant. But Colonel Fyodorov said he would act in accordance with the decision of the Soviet Council of Ministers and that we had to leave this territory. I said that this question was too broad for us to decide on the spot and that it should be resolved at a higher level.

"So he called someone up on the telephone. After this, a group of soldiers started to appear in the guardhouse. When about twenty or thirty of them had entered, Colonel Fyodorov broke the telephone from the wall and gave the command to take us out. And the soldiers just started to beat our unarmed volunteers with rubber truncheons. I had shown Colonel Fyodorov my documents indicating I was a deputy in both the Lithuanian Supreme Council and the Congress of Peoples' Deputies in Moscow. He knew who I was. So I shouted, 'I am a deputy, I want to stop this cruel beating, I demand that you stop this!' But there was no reaction from the soldiers or their commander. They kept beating people, including me. I was hit on the arms and on the back. Some of the volunteers tried to surround me to protect me from them, and I remember someone shouting that the main thing is to cover our heads. So we stood in a circle and covered our heads with our hands. They beat us into the ground."

Vaisvila spent two weeks in the hospital and two months at home recovering from internal bleeding and wounds to his skull. He no longer had any illusions about whether the new government could hope to enforce its writ within the republic. It could not, unless Moscow wanted to allow it.

* * *

While Vaisvila lay in the hospital recovering, Moscow ratcheted up the pressure in another area, the Lithuanian economy. The squeeze came at the republic's most vulnerable point, its dependence on Soviet energy. Lithuania got 97 percent of its fuels from the Soviet Union, paying for them in rubles. On April 13, Landsbergis received a letter from Gorbachev and Prime Minister Nikolai Ryzhkov, informing him that the Supreme Council had two days to repeal the March 11 declaration of independence or begin paying hard currency (dollars, German marks, or any other currency freely convertible on world markets) for all the goods it received from the rest of the Soviet Union. Lithuania, of course, had precious little hard currency.

Landsbergis and the rest of the *Sajudis* leadership had long been expecting a blockade. Some of them had gone out the day after they voted for independence and bought extra gasoline for their cars. They refused to give in to a mere letter from Moscow. On April 17, the director of the Lithuanian Natural Gas Association received a telegram from Minsk, where the republic's natural gas supplier was headquartered, warning that there would be an abrupt, severe drop in gas deliveries, effective immediately; the drop, when it came, amounted to about 84 percent. The next evening, the flow of oil to the Lithuanian refinery at Mazeikiai was cut off.

The blockade immediately discouraged some of those who had been less committed to immediate independence. Algirdas Brazauskas, the Communist Party leader who had become an independence advocate only during the 1990 election campaign, was one of the first to waiver. Brazauskas, who was head of the Supreme Council's Blockade Commission, told the deputies on April 20 that the economy faced severe shortages of wood, metal, and energy supplies. He urged them to seek an immediate political solution with Moscow, even if it meant repealing some of the legislation passed since March

11. But most deputies, recalling the travails of their grandparents' generation, were ready to resist further.

The next blow to their morale came from Washington. Some *Sajudis* members had thought that if the blockade had a silver lining, it was the pressure it placed on President Bush to do something tangible in support of the Lithuanians. But Bush had a lot riding on good relations with Gorbachev. His negotiators were working on a bilateral trade agreement, a summit was planned for late May, and arms control negotiators were tantalizingly close to agreements to reduce conventional forces in Europe and strategic weapons. On April 24, Bush announced that he would impose no economic sanctions against the Soviet Union, lest he inflame an already tense situation. Landsbergis complained bitterly that the West was selling Lithuania out. Two days later, Landsbergis received a letter from Chancellor Helmut Kohl of Germany and President François Mitterrand of France. They suggested that a "temporary suspension of the effects" of the March 11 declaration could encourage Gorbachev to begin serious negotiations.

While this was going on, Landsbergis sent a delegation headed by Bronius Kuzmickas to Moscow. Kuzmickas, in effect, cooled his heels for four days. Ryzhkov met only with delegation members who were also members of the USSR legislature, and he made a point of saying that these were not negotiations, merely informal meetings. He insisted that there could be no negotiations until Lithuania returned to the status quo of March 10, the day before its declaration of independence. By the time April ended, the *Sajudis* government was facing the prospect of introducing food rationing, and it knew that if it wanted to stand firm on its declaration of independence, it would stand, essentially, alone.

The blockade hurt Lithuania, but no worse than the realists in *Sajudis* had expected. Idle factories laid off about thirteen thousand workers. Hospitals experienced shortages of supplies, from gauze to medicines. Staple foods were rationed in the government-owned stores. But in the free peasants' markets, people could buy honey, oranges, tomatoes, and radishes. Neither heat nor electricity was affected, thanks mainly to the fortuitous arrival of spring. People who could no longer drive cars told each other that walking and riding bicycles would make Lithuania a fitter nation, and give it cleaner air. Some people found their lives only marginally affected.

"I didn't have a car by that time, so I didn't see great changes in my personal life," said Zigmas Radzvilas, the deputy chairman of *Sajudis*. "People with cars or small children had problems, because all the trains and buses were overcrowded. It was practically impossible to get gasoline for personal cars, except on the black market."

Yet the *Sajudis* leadership rather quickly decided to abandon its insistence that the declaration of independence remain in force. Prunskiene was the first to shift her position. Landsbergis reluctantly followed. On June 29, the Supreme Council voted 69–35, with 2 abstentions, for a moratorium on independence. To be more precise, the council said its March 11 declaration, and all of its legal consequences, would be suspended for one hundred days, beginning with the commencement of formal negotiations between Lithuania and the Soviet Union.

I asked both Radzvilas and Romualdas Ozolas why *Sajudis* had decided to make this concession, despite all the talk I had heard in March about how long Lithuania could hold out against a Soviet blockade. Five months after the fact, they had different recollections, but two reasons stood out in what they said.

As Radzvilas saw it, most *Sajudis* deputies were prepared to suspend their March 11 declaration because they doubted the Soviets would formally negotiate. Therefore, the conditions would not be met and the independence act would remain in effect.

Ozolas had a different angle. According to his account, the *Sajudis* leaders, beginning with Prunskiene, became convinced that adopting the moratorium would lead to diplomatic recognition by the West and at least partial recognition by Moscow of Lithuanian independence. "It would have been on the level of prewar Finland," he said, referring, I assumed, to the special, autonomous status Finland had within the Russian Empire before 1917. Ozolas was very vague when I asked him to explain how the *Sajudis* leaders got this impression. He would not say who had given it to them. But he did feel that Prunskiene had been duped by Gorbachev and that Gorbachev had no intention of negotiating seriously about Lithuanian independence. "There was no deal, there was a game, which he [Gorbachev] won," Ozolas said.

That became evident, to Ozolas at least, on September 24, when he was part of a small Lithuanian delegation that sat down with Gorbachev in Moscow for what was supposed to be a preliminary meeting to arrange the start of the promised negotiations. Ozolas, sitting with me in his empty office at the Lithuanian Council of Ministers, pulled out some notes that he had written on white paper at the meeting.

"We met in one of his offices off the Supreme Soviet. He came with Ryzhkov and some others, and they said that we had about forty-five minutes to talk, because it was an intermission between sessions. The conversation was serious. First Gorbachev and then Prunskiene spoke. He started off by saying, 'Hello, prodigal sons and daughter.' We laughed, of course, when he said it. The whole time he spoke, he tried to persuade us that we needed to be together [in the Soviet Union]. He called what we had an unhappy marriage, but then said, 'What can you do? The marriage exists, there are children to be raised.' Then he threatened us. He reminded us how the Gagauz [a minority group within Moldavia] and the Abkhazi [a minority group within Georgia] were asking for autonomy and separation. Then he said, 'Well, look, your Poles are creating something.' It was a suggestion that if we broke away, they would not let us have the area where the Polish minority lives. But if we stayed in the new Soviet Union, everything would be fine.

"Prunskiene said that all this could be referred to the talks between the official delegations. She wanted to raise the question of a special status for Lithuania during the talks, a status not in the Soviet Union but with the Soviet Union. And Gorbachev laughed in our faces and said, 'That's a past epoch.' And Prunskiene said, 'Mikhail Sergeyevich, you *promised,*' " Ozolas recalled, emphasizing the last word with a querulous whine, like a child complaining to her parents. It was clear he felt Prunskiene had been foolish to trust anything Gorbachev had not put in writing.

There were a few more preliminary meetings in Moscow, but they degenerated into the sort of petty squabbles that occur between two sides who are compelled to sit down together for appearances' sake but truly cannot see enough common ground for an agreement. Ozolas remembered them mainly for the way Ryzhkov and other Kremlin apparatchiks had reacted to the little barbs that the Lithuanians inserted into their Soviet hides. "At first, Ryzhkov tried to address us as *Comrades,* but we referred to them in reply as *Gentlemen,*" Ozolas recalled. The difference, of course, carried a lot of ideological baggage. *Comrade* was the form of address introduced by the Bolsheviks. *Gentlemen* was the form of address in the old, bourgeois days. By using it, the Lithuanians were making a point, and Ryzhkov could hardly argue with them. If they did not want to call him a comrade, he could hardly call them comrades. So he called them gentlemen.

Then the Lithuanians insisted that English be accepted as a third official language for any texts that might emerge from the negotiations. Again, they were trying to make a point—that this was not a meeting between members of the Soviet Union, where Russian was the lingua franca, but an international negotiation that might, at some future point, involve third parties as guarantors. Ryzhkov did not have to ask which potential third parties spoke English. "He got very angry," Ozolas recalled. "Very angry." That issue was not resolved. Nor was the main Lithuanian precondition for the actual negotiations, which was the acceptance of a protocol stating from the outset that the goal of the negotiations was the independence of Lithuania.

As a result, the real negotiations did not get started. It became apparent that Moscow, if anything, was moving further away from a willingness to bargain seriously about Lithuanian independence. Gorbachev saw Lithuania as one of fifteen republics with which he had to deal, and he knew that any concessions he made to the Lithuanians would quickly be demanded, in turn, by Estonia, Latvia, Georgia, Armenia, Moldavia, and perhaps the Ukraine and even Russia. Therefore, as the summer of 1990 turned into autumn, Gorbachev began to speak more and more of a comprehensive solution, a union treaty. It would, he promised, be the charter of a new, just federation, in which each republic could live as a sovereign entity, but which would remain a unified whole.

So Lithuania's confrontation with Moscow congealed, temporarily, into a stalemate. Moscow could not persuade the Lithuanians to abandon their attempt to become independent. Lithuania could not persuade Moscow to let it go. Of course, it was not a stable deadlock, because one side, Moscow, had the power to break it, should it choose to use force.

As time passed and this stalemate continued, the euphoria most Lithuanians had felt in March faded into depression, a depression born of dashed expectations. They were like people who dream for years of being able to buy a piano and fill their house with music. Finally, their dream comes true and the piano arrives. Then they discover they have to learn to play it.

Their new government did not work as they had thought it would. They had dreamed that, once they had free elections, they would elect a government that would function like an idealized Athenian democracy. They found that the new government was no more immune than any other in the world from ambition, backbiting, and duplicity.

I dropped by the offices of *Respublika,* the newspaper that had been founded by *Sajudis* but split with it, and spoke there with one of its senior editors and reporters, a woman named Valentina Cepleviciute. She had been in the Supreme Council on the night of March 11, and, when she recalled her emotions at the moment the government declared its independence, her eyes filled with tears and she turned away for a moment. At first, she said, she had covered the Supreme Council. But, after a few months, her disillusionment had reached the point that she transferred to the economics beat.

For everyone at *Respublika,* the government's shortcomings were symbolized by the affair of their new printing press. Vitas Tomkus, the editor, had attended a journalists' conference in Copenhagen in April, a month after independence, when Soviet troops were occupying the republic's main printing plant. His Danish host, the newspaper *Naestved Tidende,* in a moment of generosity, had offered to donate a twenty-six-year-old press that they were about to replace. Tomkus assumed that, despite his problems with *Sajudis,* the government would be happy to help in ending a printing monopoly that gave the Soviets a dangerous point of vulnerability to exploit.

Respublika applied to the city government for a lease on an empty plot of land in the same block as the existing printing plant. The city approved. But then the labor collective at the printing plant raised an objection, stating that its enterprise had always intended to use that land for expansion. They appealed to Arturas Paulauskas, the *Sajudis*-appointed procurator. And Paulauskas, incredibly, supported them, citing an old Soviet law that was designed to prevent the breakup of collective farmland. After several months, the city government rejected Paulauskas's position, and the transfer of land seemed on the verge of approval. But the upshot was that, eight months after it was donated, the Danish press still sat in Copenhagen.

Just as in Romania, there was a tendency for the rulers of the postrevolutionary Lithuania to slide into the comfortable niches left by the old rulers. Just as in Romania, it was a temptation that not all the new rulers felt it necessary to resist. Under the old system, for instance, the Lithuanian Communist Party's ruling elite had its own community of weekend houses, in a woodsy village outside Vilnius called Turniskes. They were not luxurious, by Western standards, and they were furnished with blocky, polyester-covered Soviet furniture. But they were roomy, and Turniskes had its own commissary, a store that had always been stocked with things ordinary Lithuanians had to stand in line for, if they could get them at all.

The new Supreme Council, as it began its work, faced the problem of housing those members who did not live in Vilnius. It could have paid them a salary, or housing allowance, and let them find quarters on their own; it could have offered Vilnius residents with large families and small apartments the opportunity to move into Turniskes, creating vacancies for council members. But, of course, it did neither. It kept the Turniskes residences for itself, as housing for out-of-town members.

I went to Turniskes one evening to see Ina Navazelskis, a Lithuanian-American writer whom I had met in March. She was living with her fiancé, a Supreme Council member, in an apartment that had once been the weekend residence of the head of Lithuania's Communist Youth League. My taxi driver could not take me directly to their apartment; a uniformed policeman in a guardhouse stopped him. Only residents' cars were permitted past his turnpike. After he had called to make sure I was invited, I walked the rest of the way, through a light snow, along a road cut straight through a forest of towering evergreens. The lights of the houses, set well back from the road, were barely visible.

Living in such a privileged enclave mildly embarrassed Ina. The worst part, she said, was what the peasants who lived in the village had said after the *Sajudis* leaders had decided that they could not shop any longer in the special commissary: "The old masters let us shop there."

But I think that what depressed Lithuanians most of all was the knowledge that their leaders had no clear and feasible strategy for turning the March 11 declaration into real independence. Once the

West failed to come to their aid, they floundered, and grew bitter. Landsbergis expressed this in a speech to the British Parliament on November 14:

> Ladies and Gentlemen:
>
> Some political leaders and heads of state dream fine dreams. I, too, would like to tell you about one particular dream.
>
> I see a man trying to break out through the barbed wire encircling a concentration camp. He comes with empty hands, but bloodied by the wire. He is certainly not dressed in a dinner jacket for a Western reception, and it is clear that he has no cheese in his mouth, that is, no smile on his face.
>
> More actors appear on the scene. Some spit on the man breaking for freedom. Others threateningly hold back growling dogs on their leashes, who are ready to swiftly bolt for his throat. And yet another group is busy digging a ditch for the man to fall in.
>
> In the distance, a group of observers, dressed in their dinner jackets and Western gowns, occasionally wave at the man from beyond the barbed wire. They have old business contacts and other matters with the camp guards and don't want to quarrel with them.
>
> Some of the observers think the prisoner is still well off, because he is at least still alive, and believe that he is destabilizing the barbed wire much too quickly. They confer with one another about this and offer advice to the prisoner on good behavior.

When they were not venting this bitterness, the *Sajudis* leaders tended to fall into apocalyptic musings when I asked them how they intended to end the stalemate and gain real freedom.

Zigmas Radzvilas, the *Sajudis* deputy chairman, told me he thought that Gorbachev's efforts to force the republics to remain in the Soviet Union under Moscow's dominion would touch off a civil war, "a war of all against all. A total war, without any demarcation lines. The army will split up. And the Baltic countries will not be the focus of the fighting. In Lithuania, the principal task of the political leadership will be to persuade the Soviet Army located here at least to become more or less neutral."

That seemed an unlikely prospect to me, given the fact that army officers were in the forefront of those calling for Gorbachev to use force, if necessary, to keep the Baltic republics in the union. I asked Radzvilas how he expected it to be accomplished.

"The officers are not so primitive as it may appear from first sight," said Radzvilas, who was, not surprisingly, a philosophy professor. "They know that, according to our law, they can become citizens of Lithuania if they want to. So they will have to make their choice."

The major political grouping that advocated an alternative strategy for independence was the Lithuanian Communist Party's majority faction, which had broken with Moscow in December 1989. They constituted the only group of career politicians in the republic, and their strategy was to induce Moscow, over a period of years, to give Lithuania more and more of the attributes of an independent state until finally they agreed on an amicable separation.

I spoke one morning with Algirdas Kasperunas, a member of the Party's Central Committee and secretariat. I asked what his attitude toward the declaration of independence had been. "We figured that the key to our independence was in Moscow. But the leaders of the council thought that they wanted to have done with the East, and they thought the key to freedom was in the West. They had hopes that the West could immediately recognize us, and that Gorbachev, therefore, would have to recognize us," he said. He was not optimistic. Back in April and May, he thought, Gorbachev might have been amenable to serious negotiations, given the right approach from Lithuania. Since then the Soviet economy had deteriorated, internal Soviet politics was polarized, and, if Gorbachev were to agree to independence for Lithuania, "it would cost him his job, because the Russian public isn't ready for it now."

The Party was advocating a transitional strategy, he said, beginning with efforts to improve Lithuania's contacts on the international market, its ability to obtain credits, to export and import without going through Moscow. Then, he thought, the republic should concentrate on getting control of its borders—taking from Moscow the power to issue visas and conduct customs. After a while, he believed, it might be ready for independence. "It wouldn't be a short time," he said, when I asked how long this would take. "We're talking about years. Five, three, eight—it's very hard to say. It depends on how much goodwill there is on the two sides."

Kasperunas thought that people like Radzvilas, who were placing their bets on a civil war, were being reckless. "If the empire falls apart, some of the bricks might hit us," he said.

But the Party was in a poor position to advocate its views. Justifiably, given its long history of toadying to Moscow, most Lithuanians mistrusted it. Its membership had fallen from 200,000 to 56,000 in the previous two years. As Kasperunas and I spoke, the Party was in the process of changing its name, to the Democratic Social Labor Party, in an effort to put its communist past behind it.

A certain fatalism permeated the political atmosphere in Vilnius, a feeling that this generation of Lithuanians was destined to share the fate of the generation of 1940. They were determined, though, that the Russians would never again be able to say that the Lithuanians submitted peacefully and voluntarily.

In November, Romualdas Ozolas gave an interview to *Gimtasis Krastas,* one of the republic's major newspapers, in which he promised that "I'll act so that my children couldn't accuse me of never firing a shot, as happened in the 1940s."

As my interview with Ozolas, a couple of weeks later, drew to a close, I remarked that if the Kremlin decided to send tanks into

Vilnius that night to arrest the government, it would do so in vain, because so many of Lithuania's leaders were abroad.

Ozolas smiled, a little crookedly. He reached into the right-hand pocket of his trousers and pulled out a slim black pistol. Then he pulled out the clip to show me it was loaded.

"Not only that," he said. "We're ready to defend ourselves here."

MOSCOW

December 1990

Back in Moscow, a meeting with Roy Medvedev measured for me the hardening of Russian attitudes about the empire over the past twelve months.

In the years I had known him, Roy Medvedev had always embodied courage, dignity, integrity, and whatever remained of the idealism that had once been a major component of Russian Marxism. Roy's father, Aleksandr Medvedev, had been a pillar of the Bolsheviks, a political officer in the Civil War of 1918–1920 and later a teacher at the academy which trained officers for the Red Army. Then Stalin's terrible purges swept him away. The police came for him in 1938, when Roy and his twin brother, Zhores, were twelve years old. He died in a Siberian camp in 1941.

As the son of an "enemy of the people," Roy had no immediate access to a purely scholarly career in the social sciences, despite his excellent grades at the university. The best job he could get was teaching in a village in the Urals. As he taught history, he collected it, talking to people about what they had experienced under Stalin. He never gave up the belief his father had instilled in him in a humane socialism. In 1956, after Nikita Khrushchev denounced Stalin at the Twentieth Party Congress, Roy felt encouraged and joined the Communist Party. And he continued his research. In 1961 he began working on a book that would become *Let History Judge,* a monumental history of the Stalin period. In 1969 he was expelled from the Party for attacking the Stalinist revisionism that was becoming orthodox under Leonid Brezhnev. In 1970 Zhores Medvedev wrote an exposé of the farcical science of Trofim Lysenko, Stalin's top scientist, who claimed that genetic characteristics could be altered by changes in the environment. The authorities confined Zhores to a mental hospital, then allowed him to go into exile in England. Roy, in 1971, published *Let History Judge* abroad.

By the time I got to know him, Roy had lived for a dozen years in a small, gray area, the far margin of which was exile or jail. He had formally retired from teaching, and he devoted his time to research and writing. He published unauthorized books about Soviet history in the West; he maintained discreet contacts with some old friends in the Party. And he frequently gave interviews to Western correspondents who made their way out to his fifth-floor walk-up in a tired, gray building on Dibenko Street, on the northwest end of Moscow. He provided a unique voice in pre-Gorbachev Moscow: an independent, Marxist voice. He did not, like so many of the dissidents of that era, want to emigrate; nor did he wish to go back to a Russian monarchy or replace socialism with Western capitalism, as other dissidents did. Above all, he respected the truth, and he was willing to speak it at a time when the Soviet government still thought truth should be found only in the pages of *Pravda.* No doubt he had protectors somewhere in the Party, people who respected his Marxism and his scholarship. No doubt his prestige abroad helped protect him from repression. But his primary shield was his own courage.

He had demonstrated that to me in 1984, when Yuri Andropov died and the Politburo selected a doddering old Brezhnev aide, Konstantin Chernenko, to run the country. *Newsweek,* for which I then worked, wanted me to find a Soviet writer to comment on the change. Chernenko's election had profoundly discouraged the Moscow intelligentsia. They saw it, correctly, as an effort by the corrupt Brezhnev apparatus to reclaim its perquisites after a brief period of purges and discipline under Andropov. The sight of another feeble, dull, old apparatchik representing their nation to the world shamed many of them. Roy Medvedev was the only man I could find willing to put those views in print.

The article must have outraged Chernenko's men, because the consequences were immediate and frightening. The police set up a round-the-clock guard at the door to Roy's apartment and forbade foreigners to enter. Roy himself was interrogated and threatened. I feared expulsion for myself, and worse for Roy. In a telephone call, I volunteered to stop contacting him, on the assumption that this would mollify the unseen people whom the article had offended. Calmly, Roy said he would prefer to continue as he had, as much as possible. He had broken no laws that he knew of, and he would operate on the assumption that the authorities would break no laws either, dubious though that assumption was in light of the history of his family. We continued to meet, in a park near his home or at my office. And we both survived the year of Chernenko's interregnum.

It gave me great pleasure to watch as *glasnost* and *perestroika* brought first rehabilitation and then honor to Roy Medvedev. In 1988 Soviet publishers began asking for his works and preparing Russian editions. In 1989 voters in a Moscow district elected him to the Congress of Peoples' Deputies. The Party reinstated him. He served on a commission investigating allegations of corruption in the government; in a rather delicious turnabout, among those he interrogated was an apparatchik who had threatened him in 1984. In the Congress and its adjunct, the Supreme Soviet, he became a moderate who, as often as not, supported Gorbachev. In 1990 he became a member of the Communist Party's Central Committee.

The reversal of his fortunes was so startling that Roy became a bit defensive about it and was quick to point out that he had not changed; the Party and the system had. And, in fact, there was much about him that had not changed. We met in the same tiny, book-lined study, in the same fifth-floor walk-up. He was, as always, a bit rumpled; he wore a yellow shirt hanging over plaid pants; it made his complexion seem all the more pale. His hair, which had been white for many years, had become the light and wispy white hair of an older man, and his blue eyes were bloodshot from the stress of attending a constant stream of plenums and congresses and sessions, while still trying to write, among other things, an Andropov biography. And, as always, he was a pleasure to listen to. Somewhere, perhaps in his teaching days, he had picked up the ability to speak distinctly and clearly, even when his thoughts were complex. Listening to him, I had first realized what a melodic and elegant instrument the Russian language could be.

When I told him I wanted to talk about the separatist movements in the republics, Roy prefaced his opinion by reminding me of what I already knew, that people in the Baltics and the Trans-Caucasus respected his reputation for integrity and willingness to pursue the truth, regardless of whether that truth might embarrass the Party. Baltic deputies in the Supreme Soviet, he said, had asked him to chair a commission that was supposed to investigate the 1940 treaties by which the Baltic states had become Soviet republics. "They understand that if the commission were chaired by a Latvian or a Lithuanian or an Estonian, they'd be accused of being subjective," he said. "Therefore, they wanted to find a man in Moscow, who is known abroad, whose objectivity is generally believed. So, I agreed. The commission is supposed to start its work after the New Year."

That said, Roy went on, "I don't approve of everything they've done in the Baltics, of all their policies. I think they've been in too much of a hurry and they act unjustly."

I asked him whether he did not think that, regardless of tactical errors their leaders may have made, the Baltic republics had a right to secede. His answer surprised me.

"You see, I do think there has to be a constitutional right to secede, but to really carry it out is impossible. The fact that Lithuania wants to leave is an emotional, nationalist feeling. It's understandable. But you understand that, in reality, it's as hard to separate Lithuania as it would be for California to separate from America. Although California is also conquered, taken from Mexico. It was Mexican territory and maybe part of the population is Mexican now, or mixed, or black. And suppose they decided to secede from America?"

Apart from the historical flaws in his analogy (among them that the country of Mexico still exists), I said, the fact was that the Mexicans in California didn't want to secede.

"No, but imagine if they did. It would be difficult from many points of view. The economy—you can't cut it up. Moreover, it's necessary to solve the problem of the army. The Baltic military district will not be liquidated," he said, with a tone of flat finality. "That is already ruled out. The army will remain in its posts, in all districts, just as the U.S. Navy retained its base at Guantánamo in Cuba."

I asked why he felt this was necessary.

"For the defense of the Soviet Union, as the military calculate. It's a matter of twenty-five or thirty divisions, rocket troops, an enormous infrastructure that cost billions."

At this point, Roy's argument started to ramble and contradict itself.

"There's no place to take it [the military infrastructure]. We could take it away, but only if Lithuania did as Germany is doing and paid. Pay for everything, and we'll leave. Pay for homes for the officers, for rocket silos, relocate the rockets. Russia won't pay for that. Germany agreed, and is paying. But Lithuania can't do that. Because who will help Lithuania with hard currency? Who'll cover the expenses connected to the independence of Lithuania? It doesn't even want to leave the economic territory of Russia. It wants to be politically independent, but it demands the preservation of all economic ties, so that Russia delivers oil, gas, gasoline, animal feed, and so on, and not for dollars but for rubles. This is unrealistic. If the

Lithuanians declare their independence, they will stop getting oil and gas from us, cotton from Central Asia, because they won't be able to pay for it."

I pointed out that the Lithuanian leaders had said they would be prepared to pay market prices for Russian raw materials if Moscow paid market prices for Lithuanian products, such as the meat Lithuania shipped to Moscow each year at artificially low prices.

"That's because earlier they had received from Moscow agricultural equipment, feed, and so on," he replied. "And now, Moscow figures, why buy meat for dollars from Lithuania if we can get better meat from Holland, or France? Lithuania is falling into a tough position, just like Poland, Hungary, and Czechoslovakia. Those countries have jumped into economic ruin. They got their freedom, you see, but, starting on January 1, all accounts will be in hard currency. And now they're asking us to wait, not to switch to dollars. They say they can't because America isn't buying their products. They had an illusion that the West would give them everything, almost for free. Now they can't get more credit, they're not receiving aid, they're constantly raising prices, their standard of living is constantly going down. Now they feel that they're turning into second-class, poor countries. They have no resources, no minerals."

I asked whether, as a historian, Roy understood the strength and importance of the nationalist emotion in the republics.

"They're very strong," he agreed. "That's a reaction to what has been for seventy years [since the Russian Revolution]. But emotions pass and reality remains. Russia hasn't developed just over the past seventy years. That's an illusion. Russia has been developing for a thousand years, and the ties to these nations have been developing for centuries. The Baltic was joined to Russia in the time of Peter the Great. And all the economic ties, cultural ties, and demographic composition of the population developed since Peter's time. The independence of those [Baltic] republics lasted only twenty years. Before Peter they were Swedish provinces. After Peter they were Russian. The Lithuanians had an independent state in the Middle Ages, but Latvia and Estonia were never independent. Therefore, they have no experience in independent life, in foreign policy. They don't have government officials capable of doing state work.

"So, of course, that emotional side is understandable to me, and I think what we need is patience, to calmly, peacefully change the form of the union, to make entry into the union voluntary and attractive, so that those states themselves won't want to leave. They're trying to leave the old union, the dictatorship, the old ties, which still exist today. But they can't walk away with everything. They'll be left without electricity, oil, gasoline. So it's not so simple."

I said that I thought the Balts were prepared to shiver in the dark for five or ten years, if they had to, because they believed that if they could free themselves from the Soviet Union, they would eventually emerge on the economic level of neighboring countries like Finland.

"No," Roy said. "That's not possible because, you see, Finland has figured out how to create a self-sufficient economic structure during these past fifty years. Whereas these republics have lived for fifty years in the Soviet Union, and their economic character has completely changed. Their economies are based on supplies from the Soviet Union. They can't quickly become Finlands. Of course, they're good workers, and they could become like Finland over several decades. But for that they have to have good relations with the Soviet Union. And there won't be good relations, because they're carrying out a policy that puts their Russian populations in an unequal position. Therefore, Russia won't help them. Would America help countries where Americans lived but didn't have citizenship rights?"

Roy's argument had moved to a new and more personal, emotional level. He told me a little about his personal history.

"I'm a Russian, but I was born in Georgia," he said. "My family includes many nationalities. My wife is a Ukrainian. My sister is married to a Georgian. Among my relatives, there are Armenians and Georgians. I'm very glad I live in Moscow and not in Lithuania. It would be tough there, psychologically tough. I know this because when I visit Georgia now, I feel different than in Moscow. I sense that they look at me unpleasantly. I go into the store and I want to buy something, but I don't understand the Georgian language, so they don't sell to me. The sales clerk knows Russian but pretends that she doesn't. In Georgian, she asks me what I want. I say I want to buy milk, bread, cheese. She shrugs her shoulders. You see? They make it clear that I'm not wanted. This creates a bad psychological climate for the Russians. A lot of obstacles are being created to induce people to leave. We always had an unfair nationalities policy, but today that unfairness has been turned."

Against the Russians?

"Against the Russians." He nodded.

The multinational character of his own family was far from unique, Roy went on. "Our national formation has become mixed. We have 60 million people in the Soviet Union living on the territory of other nations [i.e., Armenians living in Azerbaijan, Russians in Latvia, and so on]. Sixty million! Plus we have an undetermined number of mixed families, probably no fewer than 50 million, where the husband is Russian, say, and the wife is a Tatar or a Latvian or a Ukrainian. Or the husband is Armenian and the wife is Russian. There's been a mixing of populations, and you can't reverse it. In Tataria [the Volga region that Ivan the Terrible had taken back from the Tatars in the sixteenth century] there are half Russians and half Tatars. What can you do there? Expel the Russians? So if in Latvia they declare that Latvians have an advantage and the Russians and Jews who live there don't have these rights—"

I interrupted, pointing out that only the most radical of the Baltic groups favored disenfranchising any Russians, and then only those Russians who had moved in after 1940. The mainstream groups, like *Sajudis,* proposed only that people wait through a residency period before acquiring citizenship. Great Britain, I pointed out, had required the same of his brother Zhores.

"Yes, yes," he said, almost annoyed. "But these people don't want that, these Russians. They consider themselves citizens of the Soviet Union. They are accustomed to considering themselves people who belong to a great power. And they don't want to be citizens of little Latvia."

But it was not only that, he said. Russians living in the Baltic republics feared that regardless of what the separatist movements might say, Russians would inevitably become second-class citizens if the republics gained their independence. "I get a lot of mail from them," Roy said. "I know a lot of facts. In Estonia, in Latvia, in Lithuania, they want to create an advantage for the indigenous nation, just as, for instance, white Americans have an advantage over black. In Tataria, in Bashkiria, in Yakutia [autonomous regions within the Russian republic] even, they are beginning to say, 'Don't give Russians jobs, don't vote for them.' There's discrimination in education, difficulties for children. This poses a lot of problems, emotional and economic and psychological. We need time." He paused. "We need time."

I said that as a historian, he must agree that all empires, eventually, disintegrate.

"The Russian Empire cannot be an exception," he agreed. But without concluding his sentence, he immediately began to argue that it might be. "But the Russian Empire is a peculiar empire, unlike others. The empires that fall apart are those with a metropolitan power and colonies that are territorially separate. India, America, Australia, all separated from Great Britain. That empire fell apart. But the Russian Empire was created on a single territory, and therefore it has a unified economic system, a common market. And what's more, you have the mixing of populations. Siberia wasn't part of Russia. In Siberia there is also a population that previously owned it. The northern Caucasus wasn't part of Russia. There was a war there for fifty years to conquer it. Crimea also wasn't part of Russia. But to return it now is already almost impossible, because changes have occurred. Could America become Indian again, for example?

How can you separate the Ukraine when in the Ukraine live 15 million Russians? How can you separate Latvia when half the population is Russian?"

A year or two previously, I might have asked Roy whether the process of reform and decentralization would not produce prosperous, democratic societies in Latvia and the Ukraine, societies in which Russians could be satisfied to live. But, by the end of 1990, that question would have sounded wildly optimistic and naive.

As we spoke, Moscow was suffering another dreary and difficult December, even worse than the previous one. Temperatures dropped just far enough to chill but not enough to maintain a clean cover of snow. Instead the snow and sleet melted, then mixed with the dirt in the streets to form a perpetual roux of dark gray slop that spattered everyone's clothing, shoes, and mood. Gloomy portents abounded. Moscow had rapidly become one of those unfortunate cities where foreign cigarettes are an alternate currency, and, from September to December, the ruble fell against the pack of Marlboros by about 100 percent, from about fourteen rubles to nearly thirty per pack.

When, a year previously, I had first heard Russians express a fear of famine, I had considered them alarmist. Now there were signs that hunger was, if not at hand, much closer. Only ration coupons and a Moscow identity card could buy staple items in the state stores; long lines, which a few years previously had been reserved for items such as women's boots imported from Czechoslovakia, now signaled the availability of things such as lard. The spectacle of Gorbachev soliciting aid from the West evoked more shame than consolation, as did the fact that the Germans, whom the Soviets had proudly vanquished in 1945, were the biggest donors.

Nearly everyone with whom I spoke in Moscow by this time regarded *perestroika* as profoundly flawed, if not an absolute failure. They all expected that a period of reaction and retrenchment was approaching. It was not a propitious climate for imaginative or benevolent thinking about the future of the empire.

The economic failure of *perestroika* undermined all else. To learn a little more about it, I dropped in one afternoon on one of the few Soviets who had prospered under Gorbachev, Vakhtang Makharadze. He turned out to be a young, aggressive Georgian who ran an enterprise called Interferma, in a suite that occupied much of the second floor of Moscow's old Peking Hotel. The furnishings immediately distinguished Interferma from the normal Soviet enterprise. A brightly colored sign in the lobby said "welcome" in half a dozen languages. Chairs upholstered in soft gray leather actually blended with the gray carpet on the floors.

Makharadze possessed in abundance precisely the kind of entrepreneurial imagination that *perestroika* was supposed to unleash. He was a partner in the venture that had created a fad for Soviet bread in Bloomingdale's in New York in 1989. His firm had made itself a success by such stratagems as going out into the Russian countryside, where apples were being fed to the pigs because there was no one to collect them and transport them, buying those apples for two rubles a kilo, shipping them to Vietnam, where there were no apples, and trading them for bananas, which it brought back to Moscow and sold for six dollars a kilo to the city's foreign community in a special store that accepted only hard currency.

But Makharadze had had no luck in putting food on Russian tables, primarily because Gorbachev had consistently tried to avoid the fact that, if he wanted a market system, many of the prices the old system had long controlled and subsidized would have to rise sharply.

"In 1987, when the law on cooperatives was passed, I knew I had to work on something of my own," Makharadze said. "I was tired of the bureaucracy where I was working. So I started a cooperative with my sister and her husband and fifteen thousand rubles we had from the sale of a family house in Georgia. It was still unthinkable that they'd give me land, but they rented me a feed lot on a farm outside Moscow to raise steers and pigs. I found that you could raise some food, but there was nothing after that to do with it. The state meat-processing factory paid only two rubles and fifty kopecks per kilo, live weight. And it cost five rubles just for the feed required to produce that kilo of meat, not to mention the electricity and so on. It was a 100 percent loss on each kilo! I lost 28,000 rubles. There was no place else to sell it, unless I wanted to sell it in the peasants' market or make shish kebabs, and I didn't want to do that. I just wanted a farm business. But our structure, then and now, didn't permit it."

Makharadze would have gone under had he not started a joint venture with a German partner who provided fresh capital and launched him in the business of selling food to foreigners. When I spoke to him, he was still trying to find a way to sell food to Soviets. He had plans to create a network of small farms, food-processing factories, and grocery stores, bypassing the state apparatus entirely. But as we spoke he took a phone call and for a few moments shouted angrily into the receiver. Local officials in the district where his farm network was to be established were balking, it appeared, at breaking up state farms and turning the land over to individuals. That was not surprising. At its December session, the Russian federation Parliament had passed a law permitting private land ownership. But, at the December Party plenum, Gorbachev had rejected the same idea. No one knew whose writ extended where. Five years of *perestroika* had brought only disorganization to the countryside.

"We had a huge harvest in the country this year," Makharadze went on. "Even so, we're buying grain all over. So much of it perished, particularly the vegetables. It used to be the Party would order students into the fields for a couple of weeks to pick potatoes. It would order enterprises to lend workers and trucks to help get the crops in. This year no one paid attention to those orders. It all rotted in the fields. It's because of a structure that doesn't have a full chain from farm to market, with incentives. I'm a supporter of Gorbachev. All of my success is due to his beginning *perestroika*.

Otherwise, I'd get fifteen years in jail for what I'm doing. But as long as the system pays only trifles for produce, the situation will get worse."

Even in those markets where the state apparatus had not stifled production, reform had not worked as Gorbachev intended. All too often, cartels had emerged to replace the state. The Moscow taxi market served as an example. For a year or so, taxi drivers had been able to ask for hard currency from foreigners staying in Moscow hotels, and a rough fare structure had emerged: three to five dollars for trips within the center of town, ten or fifteen dollars to the airports. By Soviet standards, those were enormous sums. On the black market, ten dollars would bring about two hundred rubles, which was near the average factory worker's monthly salary. In a free market, the high fares would have attracted more drivers, and the price would have come down. But in Moscow, a small group of drivers seized control of the market at each hotel and airport. When I asked a driver one day how he and his friends would react if a new driver tried to work at "their" hotel, he replied, simply: "We'd beat him up."

The state, however, did not respond to the emergence of cartels, or mafias, as the Russians called them, by enforcing the right of newcomers to enter the market and compete. Instead it attacked the high profits that the cartels earned. In many cases, conservative apparatchiks simply ordered them out of business, even when they had earned their profits by finding a way to import and distribute goods, such as personal computers, that the state itself had failed to provide.

In Gorbachev's original conception, *perestroika* was supposed to have compensated for the technological backwardness of Soviet industry by abandoning Stalinist autarchy and attracting Western partners into joint ventures with Soviet enterprises. The Westerners would supply the modern technology and management skills, such as marketing, that the Soviets lacked. The Soviets would bring raw materials and cheap labor to the effort, and the result would be new, better goods for Soviet consumers and for export. But the joint ventures, too, had largely failed to deliver.

A firm called Combustion Engineering, from Stamford, Connecticut, had signed the first Soviet-American joint venture, late in 1987, in partnership with a Soviet ministry in charge of petrochemicals. The joint venture, called PRIS (the Russian initials for "applied engineering systems"), was supposed to assemble and sell Combustion Engineering's production control systems, devices that enabled petrochemical factories and other plants to monitor their operations more accurately and therefore produce more efficiently. The Americans, who owned a 49 percent share of the venture, sent a Russian-speaking engineer named Andy Pechkovsky, a soft-spoken, unassuming Canadian, to be deputy director of the enterprise. When I met him in early 1989, he had bubbled with optimism about the joint venture. Customers were lining up, he said, and they had placed $30 million worth of orders in the first year of operation.

A little less than two years later, when I tried to contact Pechkovsky, I found that he had left Moscow in disgust, and PRIS was in trouble. "We've had a very difficult time," he said when I reached him at his home in Toronto. "They're not interested in expanding the business." He reeled off a list of complaints about his Soviet partners. They wouldn't hire a sales staff. They could not delegate responsibility, and they were too bureaucratic to make decisions quickly. They were happy with their share of a million-dollar annual profit and did not want to do the work required to expand it. By trying to stand still, they had fallen back. Orders had dropped from $50 million in the second year to $20 million in the third. The Western partners had, finally, offered to buy up a controlling interest in the joint venture. The Soviets had refused. And Pechkovsky had left. "If we ran the organization, I might have stayed," he said.

I heard similar complaints from other Western businessmen in Moscow who had entered joint ventures as minority partners. Virtually all of them were trying to gain a controlling interest in their ventures, to free themselves from the dead hands of Soviet partners who were too used to the old ways of doing things to change.

Worse, from the Soviet standpoint, many other companies had held back from completing deals and making investments. Gorbachev had made little or no progress toward a convertible ruble. This meant that a joint venture might earn millions of rubles by manufacturing and selling goods to Soviet consumers. But the rubles were worthless outside the Soviet Union, and nearly worthless inside. The quarrels between the center and the republics only made Western investors more reluctant and negotiations more complex. Chevron, for instance, was trying to start an oil production joint venture under the umbrella of the American Trade Consortium. In the midst of this negotiation, the republics began to declare that the oil and other minerals under their soil belonged to them, not to the central government, and were not the central government's to dispose of. With whom was Chevron to negotiate?

In an effort to assure that they earned hard currency, many joint ventures wound up, like Vakhtang Makharadze's, selling the promised bounty of *perestroika* only to people who had foreign currency. This suited the taxi mafiosi and other Russians who had a way to earn dollars. But in many people it only instilled a frightening suspicion that in the new economy they would be the new underclass. I walked up Gorky Street one night to Pepsico's new joint venture restaurant, a Pizza Hut with two sections. In the gleaming hard currency section, pretty young Russian waitresses greeted customers with broad, carefully trained smiles, seated them, and quickly brought them their choice of pizzas, salads, and beer. For ruble customers, the restaurant had a carry-out window on the sidewalk, and a long line of Russians was standing, somberly, in a cold, driving rain, waiting for a chance to buy something. Inside the warm restaurant, sipping a beer, I felt like an English colonial having tea at his club in Delhi, gazing at the wogs pressed up against the fence. I wondered, if I had asked, how many of them would have endorsed *perestroika*.

* * *

The spectacle of revolt in the various republics had only fueled this fear that things were spinning out of control, to the detriment of the average Russian. Even though the separatist movements had been scrupulously nonviolent and democratic in the Baltic republics, the violence in Central Asia and the Trans-Caucasus, particularly the *izgnaniya* in Armenia and Azerbaijan, created a fear that if the center loosened its grip the old, feral competition for space and survival would break out, adding new miseries to those the Russians were already suffering. I spoke one morning with Aleksandr Tsipko, the scholar-politician who had participated in the formulation of Gorbachev's Eastern European policy on the Central Committee staff from 1986 to 1989. Regretfully, he told me how he perceived the change in Russian attitudes.

"Three or four months ago, in a practical sense, the public was a lot more prepared to afford the republics the right to leave than it is now. Right now there has been a sharp shift in the direction of imperial attitudes. It's caused by the threat. Everybody understands that if the union dissolves, it would lead to the triumph of nationalist regimes, and Russia will have to take in millions of refugees. So there has appeared an instant desire to preserve everything as it was, and it's permeated the Russian population very strongly—the army as well. It's become a major political factor. At the Congress of Peoples' Deputies of the Russian republic, every other deputy was talking about it."

Russian liberals, Tsipko said, could make all the rational arguments they liked about the rule of law and the necessity of allowing the minorities their democratic right to secede. They would be spitting into the wind of an aroused, irrational public opinion. "Our democrats," Tsipko said, using the term that in Russia describes the most liberal, Western-oriented politicians, "have no idea what Russia is. They grew up in the cities. They're people of the city, of the ivory tower. To have an idea, they'd have had to grow up in a village, or at least to have relatives there, roots. And they have no idea of the movement of the psychology of the simple, average people."

Tsipko's assessment was all the weightier because he himself was one of the democrats. "From my point of view," he said, "it would be very good for the country if the Baltic republics left—good from the point of view of history, of justice. If we're doomed to torture ourselves on this land, why torture other people? But they have lost the best time."

I said that a year previously I had drawn the impression that a strong consensus prevailed in Moscow against using force in the republics. Did it still?

"I don't know," Tsipko said. His sadness was almost palpable. "But I don't have any faith that there won't be tanks."

Since the beginning of *perestroika,* Mikhail Gorbachev had shown himself brilliantly capable of managing the periodic surges of reactionary opinion of the sort that Tsipko had observed gathering strength. Sometimes he would offer the conservatives a sop: a hard-line speech, a compromise, a pause in the momentum of re-form. But he was like a halfback who knows how to fake right and run up the middle. After every brief period of retrenchment, Gorbachev emerged again, pushing the country in a Western, liberal direction. As often as not, his conservative opponents would wind up, a few months later, squeezed out of office.

But that was in the days when the only political arena that mattered was the Communist Party and its Politburo, an arena in which Gorbachev had maneuvered for all his adult life. By the end of 1990, politics had shifted, at least partially, to new arenas. And even though he was the one who had shifted them there, Gorbachev showed himself much less adroit in these settings.

Whether he had anticipated it or not, democratization in the republics deprived him of a critical base of support. In the Baltic republics, particularly, movements of intellectuals that began as supporters of *perestroika* quickly transmogrified into separatist movements. Gorbachev had to choose between granting their de-mands or forfeiting their support. In Russia itself the democratic process resurrected Boris Yeltsin, and Yeltsin cannily preempted much of the progressive support that had once been Gorbachev's.

By the end of the year, Gorbachev either no longer could or no longer wanted to finesse the conservatives. He moved into their camp. In October he rejected the five-hundred-day plan for transition to a market economy that had been devised by a team of progressive economists headed by Stanislav Shatalin. In December he replaced his interior minister, Vadim Bakatin, with Boris Pugo, a Latvian apparatchik who had made his career in the KGB. A few days later the chief of the KGB, Vladimir Kryuchkov, spoke on central television. Kryuchkov's speech proved that five years of *glasnost* had not extirpated the old thinking. He told his audience that "the threat of collapse of the Soviet Union has emerged. National chauvinism is being whipped up. Mass disturbances and violence are being provoked. . . . Exaggerations in people's notions of national sovereignty have led to a real war between union and republic laws and to disregard for human rights. . . . The emergence of some extremely radical political tendencies is far from spontaneous, but is single-minded and well thought out. Some of them are enjoying lavish moral and material support from abroad." It amounted to a declaration of war on the separatist movements, justified on the grounds that they jeopardized human rights and acted as the surrogates of forces "from abroad" that wanted to hasten the collapse of the Soviet Union.

Lest any doubts remain about the new course, nine days later, as the Congress of Peoples' Deputies convened in Moscow, Foreign Minister Eduard Shevardnadze abruptly and publicly resigned, warning of a "coming dictatorship." I asked a friend, Dr. Nodari Simonia of the Institute of World Economy and International Relations, what Shevardnadze's resignation meant. "All Georgians are emotional people, without exception," Simonia said. "I can say this because I am Georgian. I think he realized that the center would be tightening its grip in the republics, including Georgia, and that, since he is Georgian, people would blame him for it. [By tradition, members of the Soviet central government who come from a particular region retain some control over that region, even if its affairs do not formally fall into their portfolios.] So he just suddenly decided to resign."

The Communist Party's conservatives, so recently on the road to extinction, had come back. Moreover, they had begun to join forces with the intellectuals from the Russian Writers' Union, giving them one of the key attributes of a political movement. The previous autumn, I had wondered if the Party conservatives would unite with the nationalist writers. Now it appeared that they had.

Long before *perestroika,* the conservative Russian writers had offered a carefully circumscribed critique of Soviet society, following a tradition that had flourished in the nineteenth century, when Russian intellectuals had divided into Slavophiles, who felt that the salvation of the country lay in respect for its roots and traditions, and Westernizers, who wanted Russia to adopt the technology and values of Europe. The roots of the division were even deeper, stretching back at least to the time when Peter the Great visited Holland, adopted Western dress, and insisted that all the nobles shave their beards. When they resisted, Peter took to snipping off the whiskers himself.

The conservative Russian writers of the Brezhnev era had objected not so much to authoritarianism, or socialism, as to aspects of Soviet modernization. Some of them deplored the movement of population to the cities and the impoverishment of Russian villages. Some objected to the tendency of the central authorities to confuse the rape of Russian land with progress and development. Conservative Russian writers, for instance, had been in the forefront of the movement opposing a 1984 Party plan to divert the northward-flowing waters of some rivers in the Russian heartland to the Volga, and thence to the cotton-growing area of Central Asia. The longer *perestroika* continued, the more they found to criticize, and gradually they developed alliances with Party leaders who felt the same way.

I went to see one of them, writer Anatoly Salutsky, at his

apartment in central Moscow, a few blocks from the Stalin Gothic
tower of the Foreign Ministry. He lived there when he was not at his
village dacha outside Moscow. Salutsky is a stocky man with hair
turning iron gray and a bristly, closely cropped mustache. He likes to
write about military and agricultural affairs, and his writings reflect a
preference for the days when the Soviet Army's virtue and power
were unquestioned, just as was the collectivization of agriculture.

He could be almost nostalgic about Stalinism. Once, when he
had picked me up driving a new car, we had gotten into a discussion
of economics, sparked by his observation that, more and more, new
cars were reserved for the speculators and cooperative entrepre-
neurs who had taken advantage of such reforms as had occurred at
that time. (He himself did quite well on the royalties from his books.)
He said he preferred the wartime distribution of goods under Stalin.
Everyone got the same rations, via coupon, except people who did
manual labor, who got a little extra.

Like most Russians, he was generous and hospitable. When I
was in Moscow, he invariably invited me for dinner, and his wife,
Lucia, would lay out whatever sausage, cheese, salad, and roast
meat could be found in Moscow. He loved to expound, loudly and
heatedly, on whichever of *perestroika*'s atrocities had engaged his
attention at the moment. One night it might be that speculators and
their foreign partners were sucking the wealth out of Russia via joint
ventures. Another night it might be the cabal that he insisted was
waging "propaganda terror" on conservatives through its control of
the media.

When I asked him what he meant, he might leave the dinner
table, rummage through the piles of papers on the shelves and floor
of his study, and emerge with a tiny clipping from a Moscow newspaper stating that the limousine of Gorbachev's liberal adviser, Aleksandr Yakovlev, driven by a chauffeur, had struck and killed a
pedestrian. Then he would demand that I explain why the press had
not made this accident a cause célèbre. If I pointed out that before
glasnost information of this sort would never have been published,

he would dismiss my argument as the deluded statement of someone whose knowledge of Russia had come mainly from liberals in
Western-oriented institutes that were in collusion with Yakovlev
and the newspaper editors. The only reason more had not been
made of Yakovlev's accident, he insisted, was "propaganda terror"
against conservatives. He would speak a little louder to make sure
I understood.

In the year since I had seen him last, complaints about the
dissolution of the empire had moved to the forefront of Salutsky's
agenda. Gorbachev, Shevardnadze, and the Americans, he told me,
had erred in allowing the swift reunification of Germany. The Americans had thought a united Germany would strengthen NATO. They
would eventually realize that Germany was a threat to both the
United States and the Soviet Union. Gorbachev and Shevardnadze
had acted out of weakness. Now they were compounding the weakness by flirting with the possibility of independence for the Baltic
republics. Peter the Great had realized that Russia needed that
territory, and its ports, to stand up to Germany. If those states
became independent, they would inevitably fall under German domination, posing a threat to Russia. Therefore, they simply could not
become independent.

Salutsky had begun a new project since we had last spoken,
helping former Politburo member Yegor Ligachev with his memoirs.
Ligachev interested me, particularly in a time of conservative revival. Like Gorbachev, he had moved up in the Party hierarchy with
the patronage of Yuri Andropov, who wanted to bring in fresh and
uncorrupted personnel to replace the decidedly tired and corrupt
cohort that had surrounded Leonid Brezhnev in his final years.
Ligachev came from Tomsk, a city in Siberia, with a reputation for
both toughness and integrity, and he had become the informal second secretary in Gorbachev's Politburo during the early years of
perestroika. But by 1988, as the pace of reform picked up, a division
between the two became apparent, and, by the Party conference in
the summer of 1989, Ligachev had become the public spokesman for

the branch of the Party that believed *glasnost* and *perestroika* had gone too far in repudiating the past. Gradually, the reformers within the Party had squeezed him out. First they relegated him to supervising agriculture. Then, at the Party Congress in 1990, they squeezed him off the Central Committee. But as Boris Yeltsin had demonstrated, losing positions within the Party no longer meant the end of a political career. So when Salutsky suggested that Ligachev might be available for an interview, I told him I was interested.

Ligachev, it turned out, was quite particular about where he would be interviewed. It would not be seemly, I was told, for him to come to my hotel room. Nor could I go to his apartment, because Gorbachev had an apartment in the same building (although Gorbachev presumably actually lived in the general secretary's dacha outside Moscow), and it would be awkward to clear my visit with the security bureaucracy. I rented a business conference room at the *Mezhdunarodnaya* hotel and office complex, Moscow's most modern, but Ligachev did not go there either. Finally Salutsky called to tell me that Ligachev had arranged to receive me inside the Kremlin on the following day, a Saturday.

Salutsky picked me up, and we parked just off Red Square, between St. Basil's Cathedral and the Kremlin's high brick walls. A uniformed *militioner* walked over and told him only officials could park there. Salutsky argued. We had an appointment with Ligachev, and we certainly could park there. To my surprise, the cop shrugged and relented. We walked through the Spassky Gate, with a bright red star atop its tower. A closely shorn young soldier, with the blue epaulets of the KGB on the shoulders of his greatcoat, checked our identification.

Just inside the Spassky Gate, the Kremlin has the look of a crowded, old European city, with yellow government buildings pushed up close to the exterior wall, creating narrow, shaded little streets. We were early, so Salutsky suggested that we walk a bit before going into the Council of Ministers' building. As we walked, Salutsky told me his perception of the conservatives' political strategy. They did not, he said, aspire to replace Gorbachev. They wanted to influence him, to get him to adopt their policies. Ligachev, he predicted, would play a role similar to that of Deng Xiaoping in China, the gray eminence who provides policy direction without holding formal office. The idea would not have surprised any veteran of court politics in old St. Petersburg, where the conservatives had always aspired to influence the czar by surrounding him with conservative advisers. These were not, of course, czarist times, and I did not doubt that the conservatives' goal might change if Gorbachev resisted their influence. But, for the moment, it seemed to explain what was happening in Moscow's sessions and congresses and plenums.

We entered the ocher-colored building. In contrast to the polished ceremonial rooms in the Kremlin, which still look as if the czar were entertaining, it was surprisingly shabby. The parquet floors were scuffed, and the red floral runner down the hallways was faded and frayed. These were literally the corridors of power. We walked past one set of doors with Gorbachev's name on them and entered a conference room with a splendid view of the sixteenth-century bell tower erected (in one of his repentant periods) by Ivan the Terrible.

Ligachev walked in a moment later, wearing clothing that corroborated his reputation as a personally ascetic man—a gray checked suit that might have come off the rack at GUM, a plain white shirt, and a Soviet-made wristwatch with a leather band. He has an elliptical face with eyebrows that tent his blue eyes and a thatch of snowy white hair. When I had seen him before, at public appearances, he had always seemed a dour man, but in this setting he smiled and affably agreed when I asked whether I could tape the conversation.

Ligachev quickly made it clear that the conservatives, insofar as he reflected their thinking, were not picking a quarrel with the ideas and policies that had led to the dissolution of the outer ring of the empire, the countries of Eastern Europe.

He had joined, he said, in the decision to get out of Afghanistan, reached a year or a year and a half after Gorbachev's accession. "We understood that it was hopeless, and, besides that, public opinion was asking what were we doing this for. The loss of our soldiers began to grow, to about fifteen thousand, plus tens of thousands wounded. We realized that exporting revolution, especially without consideration for the social and economic development of the country, was adventurist. So we decided to get out."

I asked if there were lessons from Afghanistan, just as there were lessons for the United States from Vietnam. He nodded emphatically.

"We would be very bad politicians if we didn't learn some lessons from such a bitter experience. I'm confident that, in deciding questions about regional hot spots like Eastern Europe, Angola, and so on, we have Afghanistan always in mind, just as the Americans have Vietnam. I think that's sensible, correct, natural. We have such a big Afghan syndrome now that if we were to try to send soldiers to the Persian Gulf, neither Gorbachev nor the Supreme Soviet would survive."

He also agreed with the assessments that had led Gorbachev to make a series of concessions to the United States in arms control negotiations.

"I used to work in an oblast [Tomsk] that was closed [to foreigners] because it had a big concentration of military industry. Naturally, I visited these factories often. And, I'll tell you, when I would return, I'd have an ambivalent feeling. On the one hand, I saw that we had what was required to rebuff an aggressor. On the other hand, I saw such colossal material resources being used for weapons of mass destruction, while the people suffered huge deficits of food, consumer goods, and other things. I became convinced that without reductions of military expenditures, there could be no *perestroika*, no renewal of socialism. And that's the hot stove we started to dance on, so to speak. It was what persuaded us that we had to accept the zero option [for intermediate-range nuclear weapons] and other things, preserving, at a sufficient level, the military capability of the country. The concessions we made were of course unbalanced, if you look only at a given type of rocket. But if you look at the whole supply of weapons you have and we have, then they were balanced enough."

In that post-Afghanistan atmosphere, informed by an urgent desire to reduce military expenditures, the Politburo had, by the end of 1988, come to the decision that the principle of noninterference in the internal affairs of other nations must be observed. The breakup of the empire in Eastern Europe awaited only the realization by the people of those countries that the Soviets would no longer prop up their rulers. "We'd been proclaiming that policy before, but, at this point, we decided to observe it," Ligachev said, confirming what I had heard from Aleksandr Tsipko. "I must say that we weren't farsighted enough to see that the communist governments were doomed to perish. But we understood that, in the modern world, military intervention brings more losses than gains."

Ligachev, like Tsipko, insisted that there had been no quarrels within the Politburo during the turbulent summer and fall of 1989, when, one by one, the Eastern European countries had spun out of the Soviet orbit. No one had argued that the outer empire was worth preserving. He quarreled only with what Gorbachev and Shevardnadze had done in 1990 on the issue of Germany. He thought that the presence of Soviet troops in the country should have enabled them to extract better terms on German membership in NATO and the deployment of German troops on what had once been East German soil. But, even on these questions, he professed a kind of equanimity, a belief that the last chapters of that story had not been written. He suggested that the unified Germany which the West had intended as a bulwark against Russia might someday become a threat to the West. And he predicted that the Eastern European countries, after a taste of poverty and unemployment, might turn back to socialism.

*   *   *

But the Politburo had divided, deeply and bitterly, over the internal empire, the republics on the periphery of the Soviet Union. When he spoke of the republics, Ligachev seemed to be speaking of a different country than the one I had traveled in. I had come to believe that most of the republics, certainly those in the Baltic, had deeply and bitterly resented their incorporation into the Soviet Union and that *glasnost* and democratization had inevitably led them into a struggle to be free from it. That seemed so self-evident that it was hard to believe anyone could not see it. But Ligachev did not, as I learned when I asked him whether, back in the Brezhnev days, he had truly believed in the propaganda line that the Soviet Union, through the genius of Lenin's nationalities policy, had solved the problem of a multinational state.

"I believed it fully, and I still believe it," he said, very assertively. "I can name a whole series of regions where, even today, when inter-nationalities hatred is being stirred up, people live in harmony. Take Daghestan [a region in the Caucasus, north of Armenia and Azerbaijan], for instance. Dozens of different nationalities live there. The papers come out in five languages. And there's not one case of national hatred, even in this time. If we want to understand what is happening in the republics, then we have to keep in mind that there is one opinion among the elite element that has now come to power and is trying, on a wave of nationalism and chauvinism, to strengthen its grip. The people are another matter. I'd like to ask you. Why haven't they moved to a referendum in any of these republics? They, who all proclaim democracy and *glasnost*? I am deeply convinced that there is just one reason. The people will not vote to leave the Soviet Union."

There were a lot of answers I might have given him. I might have told him of the Lithuanian philosophers' obsession with their legal position. I might have asked whether it would be just to let the status of Ventspils depend on a referendum, after half a century of immigration from outside Latvia. I might have asked when his Communist Party had submitted to a free referendum. But it seemed like a waste of time, so much did Ligachev's understanding of the republics differ from mine. So I asked him whether the separatist crisis had provoked quarrels within the leadership over the past two years.

The question made Ligachev uneasy. The notion of quarrels within the Politburo implied the existence of factions, and, in the Communist Party that had raised Yegor Ligachev, factionalism was very close to treason. Trotsky and Bukharin had been guilty of factionalism. In their turn, so had the old Stalinists whom Khrushchev had vanquished in 1957. "I never was involved in any factions or groups," he told me. "Ligachev never did that," he emphasized, referring to himself in the third person for the only time in our conversation.

There had never, he went on, been a particular point when the Politburo members had it out over the question of separatism. But there were, he recalled, a couple of key moments when one group, with himself in the forefront, insisted that the Politburo take a stand against the separatists. It had done so, but only rhetorically. A second group, which seemed to be headed by Aleksandr Yakovlev, Gorbachev's most liberal adviser, had managed to blunt those sharp stands.

"There was a single fundamental decision," he said. "There could be no changes in the territorial state arrangement. That was a decision of principle, taken in 1988, when the events in Mountainous Karabakh began it all. It was clearly stated in a decision of the Politburo. Despite that, the Armenian nationalists—then we called them extremists, now they're called nationalists—demanded the unification of Mountainous Karabakh with Armenia. [This was the decision that Silva Kaputikyan had cited as the one that ruptured Armenia's faith in Moscow.] I think if we had stood on our principles, then the course of events would have been different. I went to Baku as a member of the Politburo, and Comrade Yakovlev was sent to Armenia. I made a speech there on the basis of the decision of the Politburo. Comrade Yakovlev never mentioned it."

Ligachev recalled another pivotal moment, late in 1989, when the Kremlin had confronted the possibility that the Lithuanian Communist Party would separate from the Soviet Communist Party. The Lithuanian communists, it was clear, had decided to do so because they knew they stood no chance in an election against *Sajudis* if they were part of a Moscow-based organization. But, within the Soviet Communist Party, the Lithuanians' intentions caused great alarm. "If we had at the right time taken a clear and precise position, an international position, on the situation in the Lithuanian Communist Party, then I don't think there would have been a split. I'm deeply convinced of it," Ligachev said. "There were forces, including Yakovlev, in favor of not condemning the actions of [Lithuanian Communist Party leader Algirdas] Brazgausas [he mangled Brazauskas's name]. There were people who were in favor of national separatism. I think Yakovlev took an absolutely incorrect position on this question. This is shown by his trip to Lithuania. After it, events in Lithuania, rather than coming under control, accelerated. A personnel shuffle began, and people who took the correct position were, unfortunately, required to leave. All the time Yakovlev and others kept telling us, 'Don't get nervous.'"

Obviously there had never been a faction within the Soviet leadership that openly favored permitting dissolution of the union. The only debate had been over whether the time had come to crack down. Some of the progressives, like Yakovlev, had tried to forestall violence, knowing it could be fatal to reform. They hoped that they could buy enough time to revive the economy, after which, they calculated, most republics would probably opt to stay in the union, and the government would be popular enough to withstand the reaction if a few chose to leave. Gorbachev had straddled the two groups for a long time. But, by the end of 1990, he could straddle no longer. Shevardnadze had left the government. Yakovlev was in eclipse. The conservatives were Gorbachev's only potential base of support. And this gave Ligachev great satisfaction.

"From my point of view," he said, "the leadership of the country underestimated the danger from separatism. It threw all its forces into the battle with so-called conservatism. But the main evil forces, as I've been saying for a year now, are those which are trying to break up the Soviet Union, the national chauvinist forces. And Comrade Gorbachev finally, finally has agreed."

I asked Ligachev how he proposed to put the union back together again. He replied that the Communist Party would do this. "The whole Party has to work hard now to persuade the people of the advantage of the union. We have no other weapon, no other means except political methods. We want it all to be voluntary."

Thinking of the dispirited and demoralized skeletons I had found in the Communist Party buildings in Armenia and Lithuania, it was again hard to believe we were talking about the same country. Ligachev's prescription sounded, to me, like Stalin getting ready to send the Party out into the countryside to "persuade" the people to give up their land and join collective farms. If Moscow seriously tried it, it could not help but be a bloody process.

As I left the Kremlin that day, I thought again of Romualdas Ozolas, sitting in Vilnius, with his pistol. Obviously, he was going to need it.

EPILOGUE

To anyone familiar with the histories of Hungary in 1956 and Czechoslovakia in 1968, the news from Vilnius in the first half of January 1991 seemed both predictable and distressing.

The first hint of what was to come appeared in *Pravda* in the last days of 1990, in the form of a long interview with Vladislav Schved, second secretary of the Lithuanian Communist Party faction that had remained loyal to Moscow—the group that Lithuanians had derisively nicknamed the "Night Party," because it could only find places to meet at night. Schved said nothing remarkable in the interview, beyond an assertion that Lithuania ought to remain in the Soviet Union. But the attention paid to him by the Party journal suggested that someone in Moscow had decided to raise his profile. Schved, it would become clear, was being groomed for the role once played by Janos Kadar in Hungary, Gustav Husak in Czechoslovakia, and Babrak Karmal in Afghanistan, the role of the faithful communist installed in power to restore orthodoxy.

The beginning of 1991 found Vilnius tense and nervous. In the early hours of New Year's Day, Romualdas Ozolas's son, a university student, was beaten to death on the streets after leaving a party.

Eventually, two people were arrested, and most Lithuanians came to the conclusion that the boy had simply gotten into a fight with the wrong people. But at the time, the death added to the sense of foreboding all Lithuanians felt as they watched the political maneuvering in Moscow.

A few hours into the New Year, the Lithuanian government raised prices on many consumer goods and issued ration cards for the few remaining food staples that had previously been freely sold. For the first time in most Lithuanians' memories, milk and meat were both rationed. The decision to raise prices was Kazimiera Prunskiene's. As an economist, she realized that the government could not continue indefinitely with the irrational system of subsidies bequeathed to it by Moscow. Her timing, however, could have been better.

On January 1, troops identified as belonging to the Soviet Ministry of Internal Affairs took control of the Communist Party's Institute of History in Vilnius, repository of the archives and records of the Soviet era. A day later, they took control of the Party's huge office complex and headquarters in the heart of Vilnius, on the boulevard now named for Gediminas, the founder of medieval Lithuania. At almost the same time, troops took over the main printing plant in Riga, Latvia. The timing of these seizures suggested a coordinated effort. But Boris Pugo, Gorbachev's Minister of the Interior, insisted that Moscow had not given the order. In Vilnius, spokesmen for the Night Party insisted that they, the faithful faction of the Lithuanian Communist Party, were the rightful owners of the buildings, and that they had made an agreement with the local unit of the internal troops to protect their property.

A few days later, on January 7, Minister of Defense Dmitri Yazov announced a further escalation in the campaign of intimidation. The army would deploy an additional division to the Baltic area to enforce the conscription law, which young men in the three republics had been flouting in ever greater numbers.

The next day, some one hundred troop trucks rolled noisily

295

through Vilnius in the predawn hours, just as they had in the days following the March 11 declaration of independence. This time, the Lithuanian government was far less united. Prunskiene, in trouble over the price increases, flew to Moscow to try to talk to Gorbachev about the troop deployments. Gorbachev met with her, but refused to negotiate. If she had a problem with troops, he said, she could take it up with Yazov. Rebuffed, she returned to Lithuania, where her support in the Supreme Council had evaporated. That night, she and her government resigned, leaving in command Vytautas Landsbergis and the other *Sajudis* leaders, who had never quite gotten over their suspicion of her because of her former membership in the Communist Party.

But it was quickly becoming unclear how far outside the Supreme Council building their writ would run. The Night Party organized a rally outside the building to protest price increases. Some of the demonstrators tried to storm the building and seize it. They were driven back by fire hoses. The government began broadcasting appeals for loyal Lithuanians to come down to the building to protect it. It was obvious, Landsbergis said, that "events are unfolding according to someone's advance plan."

The next two days brought more evidence that he was right. Gorbachev ordered two Supreme Soviet officials to receive a group of Lithuanian residents loyal to Moscow. It was never made clear who belonged to this group, or whom they represented. But the discussion was ominous. The Lithuanians, according to Soviet reports, complained that the *Sajudis* government was abusing their human rights and asked that President Gorbachev use his power to suspend the Lithuanian government and take control directly—a form of martial law.

On January 10, Gorbachev issued the equivalent of an ultimatum to the Lithuanians. It was addressed in such a way as to amount to a calculated insult: "To the Supreme Soviet of the Lithuanian Soviet Socialist Republic." In other words, he was saying, nothing that the Lithuanians had done since March 11, 1990, had any legal validity.

The message was terse. The crisis in Lithuania, he charged, was rooted in the "crude violations and deviations from the Constitution of the USSR and the Constitution of the Lithuanian SSR, in the trampling of the political and social rights of the citizens, in the effort, under the slogans of democracy, to bring about a policy directed at restoration of a bourgeois order, contrary to the interests of the people." Those people, he went on, were demanding presidential rule. "I propose to the Supreme Soviet of the republic to immediately restore in full measure the validity of the Constitution of the USSR and the Constitution of the Lithuanian SSR and to cancel the anticonstitutional acts adopted earlier.

"The Supreme Soviet of the Lithuanian S.S.R. must understand the full measure of its responsibility before the people of the republic and of the Soviet Union," he concluded.

Coming when it did, this statement removed any doubt as to Gorbachev's involvement in a coordinated effort to squelch the Lithuanian independence movement. Other elements of the plan quickly became apparent. As Gorbachev's statement was circulated, a group called the National Salvation Committee formed in Vilnius and issued an immediate demand that Landsbergis either accept Gorbachev's demands or yield power. The precise membership of this committee was never revealed. From what did become known of it, it appeared to be a front organized and led by the Night Party, in collusion with the army. Its spokesman, Juozas Jurmalavicius, was also a Night Party spokesman. The committee's intended role would be to serve as a fig leaf for the violent coup d'état the army, the Ministry of the Interior, and the KGB were planning if, as could be expected, the Lithuanian government refused to capitulate to Gorbachev's ultimatum. In the evident scenario, the committee would declare itself the legitimate government of Lithuania and appeal to Gorbachev for help in restoring order. The plan seems, in retrospect, rather bald. But it was no more so than the plans that had led to the incorporation of the Baltic states in 1940.

On January 11, the National Salvation Committee organized protesters to march on the Supreme Council. Paratroops seized the building occupied by Lithuania's embryonic defense ministry, on the grounds that it properly belonged to DOSAAF, a Soviet organization that supports the armed forces and trains youngsters in paramilitary activities like parachuting. Troops loyal to the center occupied the main printing plant, evicting the Lithuanian police guards who had been there for months. Shots were fired, and the Lithuanians reported two wounded.

Most Lithuanians replied to this massive, intimidating pressure with a quiet courage that should be long remembered and celebrated by them and their progeny. In response to calls for help broadcast on the republic's television and radio, thousands of them gathered at the printing plant, the Supreme Council, and the broadcast center itself. For the most part, they carried only their flag; they faced tanks and armored personnel carriers. At one rallying point a priest exhorted them to prayer and nonviolent resistance.

The plan was clearly reaching its climactic moments. In Moscow, in fact, *Pravda* reported as much. "The drama which began on March 11 is nearing its culmination," the Party organ predicted. TASS, the Moscow news agency, reported that the National Salvation Committee "considers it its duty to take all power and avert the economic crisis and a fratricidal civil war." Early on the evening of January 12, a group of about thirty men who purported to be workers mobilized by the National Salvation Committee approached the Supreme Council. According to the Lithuanians, they tried to storm the building, and were repulsed. According to later Soviet accounts, they wanted to complain about the "anti-Soviet" broadcasting by Lithuanian television and radio, and were beaten up.

In fact, transcripts of the broadcasts on the days in question show that the Lithuanian journalists called on their compatriots to defend certain buildings, transmitted live the proceedings of the Supreme Council, and otherwise tried to report objectively on the progress of the coup. There was one false alarm, broadcast late in the evening on January 12, reporting that troops were trying to seize the Council of Ministers building. But in later days, Soviet leaders like the hard-line Interior Minister, Boris Pugo, would insist that the Lithuanians were guilty of "broadcasts of a blatantly provocative nature, amounting to incitement."

Shortly after midnight on January 13, tanks and armored personnel carriers rolled toward the broadcast center, intent on taking control away from the Lithuanians inside. Sound trucks accompanied them, blaring the assertion that "all power" had fallen to the National Salvation Committee. The attacking forces ran over civilians and fired on crowds that stood in the way. A twenty-five-year-old woman named Loreta Trucillauskalte recorded this account of what happened to her:

> "[A friend and] I went to the [television] tower, although during the confusion we lost one another because there was panic, people screaming, tanks were firing, small tanks, automatic weapons. Someone from the crowd started to scream that everyone should pull away and everyone started to pull back from the tower. I pulled back with them, but I slipped and fell. A few more people fell on top of me. While lying on the ground I saw the cannon of a tank above me and suddenly I felt a huge weight on my leg and felt much pain. I did not lose consciousness and was able to pull one leg out from under the tank treads, but not the other."

One Soviet officer, a member of a uniformed KGB detachment, died during the shooting, along with thirteen Lithuanians. The officer's death was later used by the Moscow authorities to justify the killing; the soldiers, they said, had responded to a plea for help and protection from the National Salvation Committee and were firing in self-defense.

The critical moment was at hand. With the broadcasting facilities under control, the commander of the Vilnius garrison gave the Supreme Council until noon on January 13 to vacate the premises and, presumably, turn power over to the National Salvation Committee. The Lithuanians, with one notable exception, refused to budge. (The exception was the new Prime Minister, Albertas Simenas, who fled the city in a private car, apparently hoping to escape arrest. He was quickly replaced.) They called on their supporters to form a human wall around the Supreme Council, and thousands did.

And Moscow backed off.

No tanks rolled over the human barricades and shot through the doors of the Supreme Council. Gorbachev did not declare presidential rule. The plan, in effect, aborted.

Very gradually, over the ensuing weeks and months, a precarious semblance of normalcy returned to Vilnius. The Soviet troops did not give up the buildings they had occupied, and there were occasional incidents of harassment and violence. But the Supreme Council continued to function. Within a few days, Lithuanian radio and television got back on the air, broadcasting from the city of Kaunas. On January 25, the National Salvation Committee, anonymous to the end, announced that it was suspending its activity. On February 1, Gorbachev named a team of negotiators to sit down with each of the Baltic republics.

The *Sajudis* government, suddenly more sympathetic to the idea of a referendum than it had been a year ago, hastily organized a February 9 vote on the question, "Do you favor the Lithuanian state being an independent, democratic republic?" Of the 2.24 million people who voted, 90.47 percent said yes. Gorbachev, in advance, refused to recognize the validity of this poll. On March 17, the Soviet government held its own referendum, in which the Lithuanian government refused to participate. Not surprisingly, 86 percent of the 500,000 Lithuanian residents who voted in the Soviet poll, including soldiers stationed in the republic, voted for preserving the Soviet Union. If the votes in both polls are lumped together, about 82 percent of all ballots cast favored independence, which was, perhaps, a fair reflection of Lithuanian popular opinion.

A month or so later, on April 23, Gorbachev met with the leaders of the only republics still willing to act as members of the Soviet Union: the Russian republic, the Ukraine, Byelorussia, Azerbaijan, Uzbekistan, Kazakhstan, Tadzhikistan, Kirghizia, and Turkmenia. This represented, essentially, the Slavic and Turkic components of the inner empire. The leaders of Armenia, Georgia, Moldavia, Lithuania, Latvia, and Estonia refused to attend.

The leaders present agreed to go forward with the work on a new union treaty, and a new constitution, which would, presumably, emphasize the rights of the republics over the center. In their postmeeting statement, the leaders of the union republics (but not Gorbachev) said they recognized the right of the six absent republics to make their own decisions regarding accession to the treaty. If the republics chose not to participate, they warned, the sanctions would be economic. Those choosing independence would not have access to the same trade terms, presumably meaning subsidized, ruble prices for oil and other commodities, that republics inside the union would get. The door seemed open for the six absent republics to make an exit, albeit a costly one, from the empire.

No outsider could tell whether this meeting amounted to more than another tactical shift by Gorbachev. But the events in Vilnius in January, in a perverse way, suggested that it might. The aborted coup demonstrated that the Soviet leaders, like the British elite of the nineteenth and twentieth centuries, were rapidly losing the capacity for cruelty that would be required to sustain their empire.

Nothing made this more apparent than the way that Gorbachev, Interior Minister Pugo, and Defense Minister Yazov evaded responsibility for the January 13 killings. Yazov, on January 14, maintained that the garrison commander decided on his own to protect the National Salvation Committee. In the ensuing months he maintained that no one in Moscow gave the army the order to fire and insisted that it was not even proven that the dead had been killed by army bullets. Pugo pointed the finger the other way, insisting that the military forces, not his, "fired to hit" the demonstrators after being provoked. Gorbachev, asked by reporters at the Supreme Soviet, danced around his own responsibility. "As for the protection [of the

National Salvation Committee], I er, no, it was already morning when I found out," he was recorded as saying.

The evidence overwhelmingly indicates that these statements were, at best, clumsy evasions. Everything that happened in Vilnius in the first two weeks of 1991 points to an orchestrated plan to either topple the Lithuanian government or force it to capitulate: the dispatch of extra troops to the Baltic; the round-up of draft evaders; the occupation of buildings; and Gorbachev's January 10 ultimatum. The fact that a KGB officer (the one slain) was leading the troops marching on the television tower on January 13 belies the contention that the local army commander made an independent decision to use force. Probably the most accurate dissection of the event came from Viktor Alksnis, a conservative army colonel who, from his seat in the Supreme Soviet, was one of the most vociferous supporters of the old order. Alksnis, in an interview, said he had spoken with members of the National Salvation Committee, who told him, "We did everything that Gorbachev asked us to. After this action, he should have imposed presidential rule. However, he betrayed us."

Why was Gorbachev unable to finish a job that had not fazed Lenin, Stalin, Khrushchev, or Brezhnev?

In part, because he faced complications they had not faced, complications of his own inadvertent making.

None of his predecessors had to cope with significant internal opposition when they expanded or defended the empire; they had allowed none. Gorbachev, thanks to *glasnost,* did.

On the afternoon of January 13, thousands of Russians gathered spontaneously in Manezh Square, outside the Kremlin, to protest what was happening in Vilnius. They marched, peacefully, to Old Square, in front of the Central Committee building. Their message was delivered by Sergei Stankevich, the young deputy mayor of the city, a former communist who had been elected on an insurgent slate that drove out the old apparatchiks. The demonstration, Stankevich said, "means that the conscience of Russia has not gone to sleep. It means that democracy has not perished, as far as we are concerned, and we are prepared to defend it."

Boris Yeltsin, like Stankevich a former Party member turned insurgent, reacted quickly and powerfully. In Tallinn, Yeltsin signed a statement of solidarity with the Baltic republics. (Landsbergis, holed up in Vilnius, signed the document and transmitted his signature by fax, another element Stalin had not had to cope with.) The statement held that committees like the National Salvation Committee were illegal, and that the use of force was unacceptable. It was transmitted to the United Nations.

Yeltsin went even further, addressing the Russians among the troops in Vilnius with advice not to shoot, even if ordered. "Before you undertake the storming of urban installations in the Baltic lands, remember your own homes, and the future of your own republic."

While some elements of the Soviet media, particularly central television, obediently carried the official line about the events in Vilnius, others did not. *Moscow News,* a vanguard publication of *perestroika,* printed an issue with black borders, calling the events in Vilnius a "last-ditch stand by a regime in its death throes." It published a formal statement of protest signed by its editorial board. Among the signers were Aleksandr Bovin, the *Izvestiya* columnist who had told me a year earlier how much the rule of law meant to him, and Aleksandr Tsipko, the scholar who had suffered for trying to point out, in 1980, that the foundation of the empire was rotten.

Not even the Soviet government seemed united behind the coup. The Foreign Ministry, the agency that controls the movement of foreign correspondents within the Soviet Union, allowed virtually the entire Moscow press corps to decamp to Vilnius, where it saw and recorded what happened. The correspondents' accounts immediately belied the version disseminated on Soviet television.

The reaction from abroad also played a role. President Bush issued a statement condemning the violence. More important, the European Community reacted; there was no chance for the Soviets to play the Europeans off against the Americans. On January 20, the European Community voted to withhold $1 billion in food credits. There is some evidence that the Kremlin misjudged the scale of the Western reaction. Axel Lebahn, the director of Soviet affairs for

Deutsche Bank, said Soviet officials whom he visited in Moscow after January told him as much and asked him, "Why didn't you tell us this in time?" Gorbachev's management of the economy had placed him in a position where he could not afford to ignore the opinion of Western investors.

Faced with all these complications, the Kremlin could not move ahead with a plan that, thanks to the courage being demonstrated by the Lithuanians, clearly would have required the slaughter of hundreds, perhaps thousands of people.

As this is written, the situation in the Soviet Union seems to grow more volatile every day. There is no predicting what will happen in the next few months, or even years. But it is not hard to predict what will happen to the Soviet Empire.

History shows that an empire inevitably declines. The Soviet Empire will be no exception. The fierce desire of at least some of its peoples to establish their independence supplies the necessary centrifugal energy. Military power, which built and maintained the empire from the time of Ivan the Terrible through the era of Stalin and Brezhnev, has become a degraded asset in a world of nuclear weapons. Most important is the Russians' diminishing capacity for imperial brutality. For earlier generations, faith in Marxism, in the bright communist future, gave that brutality a veneer of morality, just as "the white man's burden" rationalized British colonialism and Manifest Destiny justified to American settlers the slaughter of the North American Indians. That faith no longer exists. As an earlier generation of Russian Marxists might have said, objective historical forces have doomed the Soviet Empire to the ash heap of history.

But, to paraphrase Tolstoy, that chronicler of the grandeur of the Russian Empire, every declining empire declines in its own way. The decline of the Soviet Empire will not follow strictly the scenario set by any of the other great European empires. In earlier eras, the neighbors of declining empires tended to prey on them and accelerate their fall, much as Russia, Austria, England, and France tore at the declining Ottoman Empire until only Turkey remained. As long as the Soviet Union possesses nuclear weapons and the means to deliver them, none of its neighbors will attack it.

The disintegration of the Soviet Empire will proceed exactly as rapidly as the Russians decide that they either cannot or will not expend the blood and money required to hold it together. As far as Eastern Europe was concerned, they made that decision in 1988. The revolutions of 1989 inevitably followed. There were, at the time, ideas that the inner empire, the non-Russian republics, would quickly spin off as well. That did not happen. For one thing, the Eastern European countries already had the attributes of sovereign nations, particularly armies, currencies, and membership in the United Nations. They needed only to take independent control of them. The Soviet republics, obviously, lacked all three of those attributes and could not become independent without them.

More important, the consensus within the Russian leadership against using force to retain the Eastern European countries did not necessarily apply to the republics of the inner empire. That is not surprising. The British found it much easier to give up India than Northern Ireland, partly because of contiguity and partly because of the migration of British settlers into Northern Ireland over the years. Russia is surrounded by Northern Irelands, and the future of the inner empire will be as painful for the Russians to resolve as the fate of Northern Ireland has been for Britain. As the events in Vilnius in January 1991 show, the Russian attitude toward force in the republics remains ambiguous and subject to change.

The future of the Soviet Empire is really a matter of how quickly Russian leaders absorb a new paradigm of power, how soon they understand that they live in an era when the attributes of a great power have changed. Vast territories, colonies, and ownership of raw materials no longer determine power; the intelligence and industry of a nation's people do. No ruling elite learns this lesson easily. The Germans and the Japanese had it forced upon them by the victors of World War II. The Americans, whom the Soviets simultaneously see as their rivals and their models, have yet to learn it. The Soviets, understandably, will find it difficult.

Their difficulty will be all the greater because there is no evident fairness, from the Russian point of view, in the proposition that they must divest themselves of their inner empire. Why must Russia give up Lithuania if no one contests French rule over Brittany, or (outside of Wales, at least) English sovereignty over Wales, or (outside of Mexico) American sovereignty over Texas?

The answer lies in the fact that the concept of a nation's right to self-determination is a relatively recent effort to impose law, order, and justice on an inherently cruel, disorderly, and unjust process of conquest and assimilation that has been going on for centuries throughout the world. In this process, there are degrees of absorption. A nation may be conquered but retain its boundaries, its language, and its culture. The Lithuanians are one such nation. Another nation may be conquered and, over as long a time, lose its boundaries, its language, and its culture, becoming assimilated by the conquering power. That has been the fate of many nations in the area now controlled by the Soviet Union. The Russians have wiped out any traces of the non-Russian tribes that once lived in the Moscow area. A people called the Albanians once lived in what is now the border region between Armenia and Azerbaijan. They have disappeared. This is a messy process that defies attempts to impose a single fair solution; in fact, there is no just or fair solution. There is only a harsh reality. Where the Russians have more or less completely digested a particular nation, much as France has digested Brittany, that nation will likely remain part of Russia. Where the process of digestion has not been complete, the Russians will likely have to let nations go.

In one of two ways, the Russians will reach the point of releasing parts of the inner empire. It could happen after a prolonged and bloody conflict. If, for instance, the Soviet government tries to impose its will on one of the well-armed Trans-Caucasian nations, the Armenians or the Georgians, it could meet violent resistance.

Russian mothers would not tolerate indefinitely the sight of their sons coming home in zinc boxes for the sake of keeping unwilling Armenians or Georgians in the Soviet Union.

Alternatively, the Russian leaders could learn the new paradigm of power and conclude that their own interests require them to offer each republic a legitimate opportunity to leave and face its own uncertain future. The generation of Mikhail Gorbachev may not be capable of this; it may be that as long as Gorbachev or one of his more conservative peers is in power, the Soviet leadership will cling to the notion that a great power must be able to maintain an empire. Gorbachev displayed his own deep attachment to this view in his televised speeches before the March 17 referendum. The Soviet Union had painfully made itself a superpower, he warned on February 6. "Huge efforts were made to make [the Soviet Union] so powerful, and we could lose it very quickly." On March 16, he returned to that theme. "Our yes vote will preserve the integrity of a state which is a thousand years old, which was created by work and common sense, by the countless sacrifices of many generations."

But the generation that follows Gorbachev's will likely differ as much from its predecessor as Gorbachev's generation differs from Brezhnev's. Thanks to *glasnost* and the freedom to travel, it has seen more of the world; communist ideology exerts almost no influence on it. The next generation of Russian leaders will realize that, for all its flaws, the Western model of a liberal, democratic state offers the only alternative to Stalinism. It will realize that in liberal, democratic atmospheres, nations have a tendency first to assert their independence, and only after that independence is secured, to begin considering federations with other independent nations. This is the way the European Community has developed. It is the way that the small Soviet republics might choose if they have the freedom to choose, and if the Russian economy can stabilize itself and claim its naturally prominent role in the region. It is the only way that the nations now forming the Soviet Union will ever form a stable and productive partnership.

Given a free choice, the various republics might not all bolt for independence. The Baltic republics certainly would. Moldavia, or at least that part which does not have a Russian-speaking majority, would probably opt for union with Romania. Armenia and Georgia would want independence, but perhaps within the framework of a Soviet military protectorate. The Turkic-speaking republics, from Azerbaijan east to Kirghizia, would likely want to reshape their relations with Russia and perhaps to form a very loose Turkic confederation. But they have no recent history of independent nationhood and might prefer to remain in the Soviet Union. The Ukrainians and Byelorussians are Slavs, like the Russians; they might opt to remain in a Slavic federation.

But the choice must be theirs. As long as nationalists in any Soviet republic can credibly charge that the Russians are holding the empire together by force, the centrifugal energy will remain and any union will be unstable. In the long run, the Russians can hope to salvage a part of the old empire only by first showing a genuine willingness to let it fall apart.

The nations of the West cannot control the choices that the Russians and the other nations of the empire make. But they can enhance the likelihood that the empire evolves peacefully into something looser and more democratic.

Nearly all the Soviet republics, including Russia, harbor substantial minority populations. In Azerbaijan and Armenia, the presence of minorities and the intolerance of the majority populations have already led to horrible pogroms and *izgnaniya*. In republics like Latvia, the potential for violence is even greater, should the minority Russian populations become convinced that independence will bring them the same fate that befell the Armenians of Baku.

Similar problems plague the former satellite countries in Eastern Europe. Romania, with its Hungarian minority, is but one example. The Soviet subjugation of these countries after World War II arrested their development. The Soviet retreat of 1989 leaves them in some ways as they were fifty years ago. And fifty years ago, no Eastern European nation could be described as a beacon of toleration, democracy, or prosperity. Romania, and parts of what is now the inner Soviet Empire, could dissolve into violence and chaos if their minorities have no confidence that their rights will be protected.

The nations of Europe and North America, at a meeting of the Conference on Security and Cooperation in Europe held in Copenhagen in the summer of 1990, unanimously adopted what amounts to a bill of rights for European minorities. It provides a detailed list of guarantees of religious, educational, and linguistic autonomy. The CSCE countries ought to work assiduously to ensure that these rights are protected in fact, as well as on paper. The human rights enforcement mechanism within the CSCE is embryonic. If members suspect a violation in another country, the most they are presently entitled to do is demand an explanation. They should work to develop that mechanism to include on-site inspection of compliance with minority rights guarantees.

The retreat of Soviet power leaves both Eastern Europe and the Soviet republics with government structures and factories installed in accordance with Soviet plans. The new local leaders and factory managers—if in fact the old elite has been replaced—may be all too willing to slip into the privileged roles that Moscow's servants once played. The West must recognize that simply replacing the old communist governments only begins the process of transforming these countries or republics into what their populations want them to be: modern, European states.

They will need a lot of help, and they should get it. To begin with, Western governments can encourage investment by Western businesses in the Soviet and Eastern European markets by reducing tariffs, extending investment protection guarantees, and eliminating outdated controls on high-technology exports, such as telecommunications systems. They should be wary, however, of the path of least political resistance, which is helping the Eastern Europeans and the

Soviets borrow money. They cannot, in most cases, productively invest it until they have reformed their economic systems. Adding more debt to their present burdens will not help them.

The situation within the Soviet Union demands imaginative Western responses, more subtle than the suggestions that are sometimes heard to try to channel aid directly to the republics, bypassing Moscow. That would do very little to improve the Soviet attitude toward the loss of the inner empire. On the other hand, if, through the World Bank, or the new European Development Bank, the West helped build housing in Russia for Russians who wish to leave the republics but presently cannot, it might measurably ease the way out for the Baltic republics. There is a precedent for this. Germany, as part of its unification deal with Moscow, agreed to build housing for all the military personnel who will be transferred back to the Soviet Union.

All of this would serve Western interests, as well as the interests of the Eastern Europeans, the Soviet republics, and Russia itself. If Eastern Europe and the republics prosper as they pull away from the empire, they will blaze an attractive trail for the Russians to follow. But if they fall into poverty, strife, and new forms of authoritarianism, that will only strengthen the hand of those Russians who would prefer to retreat to an imaginary vision of an ideal socialist empire that never in fact existed.